FIRST BRICK COURTHOUSE.

THE NACOGDOCHES STORY

AN INFORMAL HISTORY

Joe E. Ericson

HERITAGE BOOKS
2008

HERITAGE BOOKS
AN IMPRINT OF HERITAGE BOOKS, INC.

Books, CDs, and more—Worldwide

For our listing of thousands of titles see our website
at
www.HeritageBooks.com

Published 2008 by
HERITAGE BOOKS, INC.
Publishing Division
100 Railroad Ave. #104
Westminster, Maryland 21157

Copyright © 2000 Joe E. Ericson

Other Heritage Books by Joe Ellis Ericson:

Early East Texas: A History from Indian Settlements to Statehood

They Came to East Texas, 500-1850, Immigrants and Immigration Patterns
Joe E. Ericson and Carolyn R. Ericson

All rights reserved. No part of this book may be reproduced or transmitted in any form or by any means, electronic or mechanical, including photocopying, recording or by any information storage and retrieval system without written permission from the author, except for the inclusion of brief quotations in a review.

International Standard Book Number: 978-0-7884-1657-6

**OLDEST KNOWN PHOTO OF MAIN STREET
1850S**

THE NACOGDOCHES STORY

TABLE OF CONTENTS

PREFACE i

CHAPTER ONE   THE BEGINNINGS 1

CHAPTER TWO   THE OUTPOST 17

CHAPTER THREE   EL ESTADO 33

CHAPTER FOUR   THE REPUBLIC 53

CHAPTER FIVE   THE STATE 69

CHAPTER SIX   THE PROGRESSIVE ERA 91

CHAPTER SEVEN   THE TRANSITION ERA 119

CHAPTER EIGHT   THE IMPACT OF GLOBAL WAR 145

CHAPTER NINE   POST-WAR TRANSFORMATIONS 165

CHAPTER TEN   THE ECONOMY RECOVERING 197

CHAPTER ELEVEN   EXPANSION OF PUBLIC AFFAIRS 213

CHAPTER TWELVE   THE GROWTH CONTINUES 241

CHAPTER THIRTEEN   TRENDS AND DEVELOPMENTS 275

ANNOTATED BIBLIOGRAPHY 287

INDEX 291

THE STORY OF NACOGDOCHES

PREFACE

The underlying purpose of this volume is to set forth the "story of Nacogdoches," one of the oldest towns in Texas, in a non-technical yet informative fashion. As the story unfolds, an effort has been made to fit the history of Nacogdoches into the context of American history as a whole. Footnotes have not been provided, but instead, an annotated bibliography indicates the principal sources from which the information presented has been drawn. Those interested in some portion of the story and wanting additional information should consult one of the sources indicated in the bibliography. In this account of the evolution of Nacogdoches from an Indian village to a modern American town, an attempt has been made to locate and make use of the most reliable sources available.

Since not every detail in the centuries-long history could be related in this telling of the story, this account emphasizes some of those considered most significant or interesting. They include: developments in the community's social and political life, structure and operation of its local governments, the inception and growth of education and health care centers, and developments in its economic life — including those in agriculture, business and industry. It attempts to pinpoint trends, identify important personages, and provide descriptions of the community at various times in its history.

Carolyn R. Ericson and Linda Ericson Devereaux have assisted in gathering materials and provided valuable editing assistance. Carolyn is also responsible for the selection of illustrations and other graphic material. To them this story owes much, and their contributions are gratefully acknowledged.

The author alone, it must be emphasized, is entirely responsible for any and all errors.

THE NACOGDOCHES STORY
CHAPTER ONE
THE BEGINNINGS

Before it became a European settlement the area in and around present-day Nacogdoches had been the site of an Indian village for many years. A band of Hasinai Caddo Indians established a small community there sometime after 1000 A. D, but it is likely that others preceded them.

The Village

A Caddoan village of that era consisted of a number of small units of varying size frequently strung out for perhaps twenty miles along a valley. Such a community would contain a ceremonial center with earthen platform mounds that were utilized for temples and special political events. A center of this type was almost certainly located in East Texas at the confluence of two flowing streams (later acquiring the Spanish names of La Nana and Banita Creeks) between two low hills, a site chosen many years later for the Spanish settlement of Nacogdoches. The word Nacogdoches in the Caddoan dialect can be translated "the place of the Hickory trees." The early Spanish settlers named Banita Creek, meaning "a little place to bathe," and La Nana Creek, meaning "mother creek."

Evidences remain along Mound Street in present-day Nacogdoches that Caddoan ceremonial earthworks were once located around that locale. Time and European style construction have long since obliterated virtually all traces of them. How many mounds were ultimately situated in that area and whether a sizeable number of persons lived around them cannot now be determined.

The Hasinai Caddos lived in sedentary villages and maintained a peaceful horticultural society. They cultivated and harvested corn, beans, squash, pumpkins, tobacco, and sunflowers in small garden plots in the fertile valleys along rivers and streams. They also tended orchards of peaches, plums, figs, and chestnut trees. Both men and women worked the gardens and orchards, and, in addition, men hunted deer, fish, and small animals. Occasionally bison were slain for food and for hides used for bedding and clothing.

Caddo tribes were nominally governed by two equally powerful men: the *caddi*, a political leader who handled all matters dealing with war and peace, and the *chenesi* or *xinesi*, a high priest who directed all ceremonial affairs. Co-operative effort was expended in erecting houses and in planting crops. The principal unit, the ceremonial center, of the extended village contained the temple and the houses of the principal political and religious leaders. The present-day City of Nacogdoches, at least for a time, almost certainly was one such center.

Caddoan houses were large and substantial up to fifty feet in diameter. Posts were set in the ground vertically in a circle forming a wall some five feet in height. A high conical roof consisting of a framework of rafters and cross-beams lashed together and covered over with overlapping bundles of grass forming shingles was erected over the wall. The finished product was a house some twenty to thirty feet high with a spacious interior.

Along with other tribes, the Caddos venerated fire and erected temples to keep a perpetual fire burning. The mounds they laboriously shaped served as platforms for their temples. One of their more unusual customs involved welcoming travelers and all strangers who entered their villages with loud and prolonged wailing by all members of the community. Early French and Spanish explorers who first came in contact with these Native Americans during the last decades of the Seventeenth Century reported that they were universally greeted with greatest friendliness and were treated with elaborate feasts, entertainments, and a variety of gifts.

The Mission

Europeans began to explore the forests of East Texas as early as the summer of 1542 when the remnants of the Hernando De Soto expedition under the leadership of Luis de Moscoso de Alvarado crossed the Sabine River in search of an overland route back to New Spain (Mexico). Most modern attempts to reconstruct the route followed by this small party of Spaniards agree that they entered the region from northwestern Louisiana, turned south until they reached the vicinity of present-day San Augustine where they turned west following along well established Indian trails that passed near the site of Nacogdoches. From that point they traveled westward toward New Spain along what became the Old San Antonio Road (El Camino Real).

Later Seventeenth Century Spanish explorations of Texas that originated in New Spain failed to extend their efforts further east than the Trinity River. During that time period, however, reports began to filter down to Mexico City and Spanish authorities there that French explorers were finding their way into Eastern Texas and making an attempt at settlement. In fact, René Robert Cavalier de La Salle from his base at Fort St. Louis in 1685 or 1686 made two forays to the villages of the Hasinai Indians. Some evidence suggests the likely possibility that on at least one of them the French passed through or quite near the location of the Indian village site of modern Nacogdoches.

Faced with the possibility that France or some other European power might enter and take possession of the region now known as Texas, concerned Spanish officials belatedly realized that the nation's claims to the area would never be recognized until the Spanish took actual possession of it. In addition, Catholic Church leaders in New Spain were eager to enter Texas, especially when they learned that the Tejas and other tribes there were asking for missionaries. They also learned that "the woman in blue," Maria de Jesús de Agreda a Spanish nun, had experienced miraculous bilocations between 1631 and 1670 that took her to Northern Mexico and Western Texas. In her nun's cloak of coarse blue cloth she appeared to Indians in those regions and told them of the teachings of Christ and her church. This, in turn, caused those Indians to request missionaries to further instruct them. Moreover, in the 1840s a mysterious woman in blue reportedly traveled the Sabine River valley aiding victims of malaria.

In May 1690, a missionary expedition consisting of four priests and a military escort marched into East Texas and established a mission near Weches in present-day Houston County. Named San Francisco de los Tejas, it ultimately consisted of a few buildings and number of resident Indians. The enterprise was abandoned in 1693, however, after an epidemic caused the death of many of the mission's Indians; one of the missionary priests died; and a severe drought destroyed the crops on which the mission depended. Moreover, a sizeable number of the Tejas became insolent and hostile adding to the problems faced by the missionaries.

Lack of adequate support and overall neglect were the causes of the failure of this first Spanish effort to occupy Eastern Texas. Despite the failure of this effort, the attempt provided the Spanish authorities with valuable knowledge of the region's geography and of the nature of its Indian inhabitants. It also demonstrated conclusively that occupation efforts could not succeed without presidios (forts) and civilian settlements to sustain them.

For a decade following the failure of La Salle's enterprise in Texas and the lower Mississippi River region the French monarch was embroiled in the military actions of King William's War (1689-1697) and was not interested in authorizing any further exploration and occupation of the lower Mississippi Valley. This respite ended, however, when information reached Paris that the English were threatening to occupy the lands along the coast of the Gulf of Mexico and that the feeble-minded Spanish king was not taking decisive steps to protect his nation's interests. Acting on this knowledge, the French monarch determined upon a course of renewed French activity. In 1699, he dispatched an expedition to the Gulf to establish a post at Biloxi and in 1702 another to create a second at Mobile.

Coming down the Mississippi River from their bases in Canada and the Great Lakes, the French also established forts and trading posts as they came. In Louisiana on the very rim of Spanish Texas, in 1714, they established a trading post at Natchitoches on the Red River, and in 1718 a second at New Orleans.

Spurred by this renewed French activity which concerned officials in Mexico City viewed as a serious threat to Spanish claims to the area now known as Texas, they determined upon countermeasures. Initially, a series of missions would be founded in Eastern Texas to act as a buffer against possible French encroachment from the east. At the Natchitoches post the French were less than fifty miles east of the Sabine River. By 1716, the Spanish had planted six missions, five of them extending on a line from the Neches River on the west to Los Adaes near the Red River on the east only a few miles west of Natchitoches. A garrison of troops was also quartered at a new presidio erected on the Neches River.

One of six new missions was planted just east of the Angelina River in 1716 at the site of an important Hasinai village. Named Nuestra Señora de la Purísima Concepción, it represents the first formal occupation by Europeans of present-day

Nacogdoches County. Nearby the Presidio Nuestra Señora de los Dolores de los Tejas, was erected on a hill just west of the mission to provide protection.

A second mission, Nuestra Señora de Guadalupe de los Nacogdoches, was located some nine leagues (about 22 miles) east-southeast. It probably stood on a slight rise overlooking Banita Creek, but its exact location has never been established beyond question. The founding of a Catholic mission at that site marked the beginning of European occupation of the location of the modern city of Nacogdoches. By July 9, 1716, a temporary log church and dwellings for the missionaries had been erected and placed in charge of Father Antonio Margil de Jesús representing the College of Nuestra Señora de Guadalupe de Zacatecas.

Known to many as "the Apostle of Texas," Father Margil spent some thirty years in apostolic work in Mexico and Central America, after which, late in life, in 1716 he came to Texas. Margil had been born in Valencia, Spain in 1657, entered the Franciscan order there in 1673, and volunteered for missionary service among the Indians of America in 1683. He arrived in New Spain in 1683 and almost immediately engaged in preaching missions in Yucatan, Costa Rica, and Guatemala. In 1706 he was placed in charge of the new missionary college (that is, a body of clergy living in a foundation) in Zacatecas.

By the time Father Margil arrived in East Texas, he had already become a legendary figure. He was frequently called upon to arbitrate disputes by the Spanish settlers and by members of his own Franciscan order. He was a man who walked everywhere he went, and thus on foot he had come from Piedras Negras to Nacogdoches. During his first visit to the mission at Nacogdoches, according to a widely held legend, he preformed a miracle that has become a part of the history of the community.

Drouth and famine visited East Texas in 1717 and 1718,

and the residents of Nacogdoches suffered greatly from a shortage of water. Learning of their plight on a return visit from missions further east, Father Margil knelt in prayer on the banks of La Nana Creek. He asked God for relief for his people, rose, and struck the bank with his staff. Whereupon, cool and life-saving water flowed forth from two small springs. Thereafter, those springs were known as "The Eyes of Father Margil."

Despite near heroic measures adopted by their missionary priests, the new East Texas missions did not prosper. Priests and soldiers alike were plagued by sickness, some soldiers deserted, and the Indians, preoccupied with their traditional tasks of hunting and harvesting their crops, refused to congregate around the missions. A severe winter in 1716-1717, a series of epidemics among the Indians, and scarcity of supplies further handicapped the mission priests in their efforts to Christianize the local Native Americans.

By 1719 Spain and France were again at war. Spanish forces were defeated at Pensacola that year encouraging the French in Louisiana to launch an attack on Spanish forces in East Texas. Following orders given him by Governor Bienville, Commander of French forces at Natchitoches, M. Blondel, moved against Mission San Miguel de los Adaes and captured the undermanned garrison there. Rumors soon reached San Antonio that the French planned to invade Texas with a sizeable military force. Although the invasion never materialized, Spanish authorities believed the possibility created a serious crisis.

When the news of possible French invasion spread to the missions in Eastern Texas, the soldiers manning the nearby garrisons were panic stricken and refused to remain at their posts. Father Margil and the other priests had no choice but to accompany the soldiers as they retreated westward. By the autumn of 1719, soldiers, priests, and others associated with missions had retired to San Antonio.

Later, in 1721, a military force of some 500 men entered Texas from New Spain bent on reestablishing Spanish authority there. As this body of troops reached East Texas, French commander Louis de St. Denis at Natchitoches met them and relayed the news that a truce and peace had been agreed upon by their nations. Whereupon, the Spanish commander Miguel de Aguayo reestablished all the abandoned missions and returned them to the authority of their assigned priests.

As a precaution, he reconstituted the presidio at Los Adaes and left there a garrison of 100 men and a quantity of military supplies. The mission, presidio, and small civil settlement was designated the capital of Texas. There within a few miles of each other, the French established at Natchitoches and the Spanish at Los Adaes, two great European empires in America touched. There the Spanish penetration toward the northeast came to an end, and French expansion westward from the Mississippi reached its limits.

For thirty-five years (1727-1762) relations between France and Spain on the Louisiana-Texas boundary were relatively quiet and uneventful. Although they continued to squabble over the exact line of separation, they generally accepted a small stream running between Natchitoches and Los Adaes, the Arroyo Hondo, as a practical compromise.

In any event, the Governor General of Texas, Marqués de San Miguel de Aguayo, sent a detachment of troops to accompany Father Margil on his way to rebuild the mission at Nacogdoches. When the Governor reached there, August 16, 1721, on his return journey to San Antonio and Mexico, he gave Father Margil formal possession of the reestablished Mission Nuestra Señora de Guadalupe de los Nacogdoches as the representative of the College of Zacatecas. Whereupon, Father Margil placed Father Joseph Rodríguez in charge of the reconstructed mission.

THE STORY OF NACOGDOCHES

Just over five years later, however, a survey of military posts in Texas conducted by Pedro de Rivera resulted in the reduction of the number of soldiers in the eastern region of the province by more than half. The border garrison at Los Adaes was reduced from 100 to 60 troops, and the presidio on the Angelina River abolished altogether. Two missions in the vicinity were removed first to the Colorado River in 1730 and the next year to San Antonio. Those retrenchment actions substantially weakened Spain's position in the region and laid the groundwork for future problems.

Although the mission at Nacogdoches was not one of the three forced to move, it never really prospered, few Indians came forward for baptism, and maintenance continued as a drain upon the royal treasury. Gradually a community of Europeans, mostly settlers from New Orleans and San Antonio, grew up in the area near the mission. In these early years, no Spanish municipality (local government) was created for these residents, though their numbers slowly increased, and many of them prospered. Among the most successful was the family of Antonio Gil Y'Barbo, soon to play a vital role in the evolution of Spanish Nacogdoches.

By 1731, Spain's claims to Texas had been recognized, its capital firmly fixed at Los Adaes, and three East Texas missions remained in operation: at Los Adaes, at Nacogdoches, and at Ayish Bayou near present-day San Augustine, although no one of the three fared well. Trade with the French in Louisiana was forbidden by royal decree, but settlements on the eastern rim of the king's possessions in North America, hundreds of miles from San Antonio and still further from Spanish settlements in Northern Mexico, of necessity depended heavily upon Natchitoches for ever-increasing quantities of day-to-day supplies, especially food. Conditions at Los Adaes deteriorated steadily. By 1734, the presidio was a virtual ruin; soldiers were without uniforms or any decent clothing; military supplies were almost nonexistent; and women and children lacked adequate wearing apparel. At the same time, chronic sickness, lack of soap to maintain cleanliness, and poor food made living conditions almost unbearable. The missions fared little better, if as well. From 1730 to 1767, circumstances under which they labored were almost unendurable. Epidemics among the Indians, lack of essential military support, insufficient stores of supplies of all kinds, and Indian resentment of any use of force to coerce them combined to seriously handicap them in their efforts.

In 1768, an inspector from the College of Zacatecas visited the mission at Nacogdoches and described it to his superiors. He reported that it was located on a small plain overlooking Banita Creek with its shingle-roofed adobe church and the missionary's wooden house set down in a shady wood. The buildings, the visiting priest remarked, were clean but demonstrated signs of decay. A wooden stockade surrounded the mission and contained within it a kitchen, a granary, soldiers' quarters, and other buildings.

He recorded that the mission's orchard contained peaches, blackberries, persimmons, pomegranates, and other fruits; but the fields on which the mission depended were poorly cultivated, the corn and other crops almost overgrown by weeds. The mission's livestock included eighty head of sheep and goats, thirty oxen, and fifty head of cattle. In addition, he found twenty-five gentle horses, twenty gentle mules, and two herds of mares, each with a stallion. Plows, hoes, and other farm implements were in evidence.

The Nacogdoches mission demonstrated what little success had crowned its more than forty years of effort. Father José de Calahorra y Saénz had labored there for forty-three years but such were the almost insurmountable conditions under which he toiled that he had managed only twelve baptisms, eight burials, and five marriages. No Indians lived at the mission, although, from time to time, some would come in on feast days or when compelled by sickness or death to seek aid. The priest had only two soldiers, their families, and a few half-breed servants to aid him in his task.

The future of this frontier mission at Nacogdoches appeared uncertain, at best. Circumstances were conspiring to bring its existence to an end. The cession of Louisiana to Spain in 1763 following the French and Indian War had eased the threat of French encroachment which earlier had prompted the establishment of missions and presidios on the frontier. Colonial officials saw an opportunity to eliminate the expense of maintaining outposts in East Texas.

Those conditions and numerous complaints of mismanagement led to a second inspection of the frontier in 1765-1768. This inspection was conducted by the Marquís de Rubí who in 1768 submitted his report to his superiors in Mexico City. For the Province of Texas, its East Texas missions and presidios, he recommended their complete abandonment. In September 1772, the Spanish monarch issued a decree commanding that the presidio at Los Adaes be dismantled and the settlers in the vicinity relocated in San Antonio. The missions at Nacogdoches, Ayish Bayou, and Los Adaes, he ordered abandoned, and their settlers also removed to San Antonio.

Although this royal command was promulgated earlier, its content did not reach Baron de Rippera, Governor of Texas, until May, 1773. The Governor's order, in its turn, did not reach Los Adaes until the following month. Despite his sympathy for the settlers in the East Texas region and his reluctance to enforce the King's orders, on June 26 Rippera directed the residents of Los Adaes to abandon the presidio, the mission, and their homes and withdraw westward down the Royal Road to San Antonio.

Many of the people of the first capital of Texas, rather

than abandon their homes, fled to the forests surrounding them or to the villages of their nearby Indian friends where they remained until it was prudent to return to their homes and resume their customary way of life. As many as thirty persons may have remained in and around Los Adaes, while others abandoned the trek along the way from Los Adaes and Nacogdoches.

Because it was mid-summer when they were forced to leave, and they were given only five days notice, settlers were unable to gather their crops, herd their scattered livestock, or make other necessary preparations for the long overland journey. Their long trek toward the west began June 25, 1773 with the Los Adaes military commander Lieutenant José Gonzales leading the expedition. Gonzales was an elderly man who had lived at Los Adaes for thirty-seven years and who, on reaching Nacogdoches just thirty leagues west of his starting point, succumbed to the rigors of the hot summer without sufficient food and other necessities. Following his death on July 30, 1773, he was interred in the Spanish cemetery at Nacogdoches.

Along the way, the journey took the little caravan to El Lobanillo, the rancho founded by Antonio Gil Y'Barbo about 1749 or 1750, located on Lobanillo Creek not far from the site of the Spanish Mission at Los Ais and modern San Augustine. At that time, fourteen families with sixty-five members were living at Y'Barbo's rancho. Although all of them were technically required to join their neighbors from Los Adaes, twenty-four were left behind including Y'Barbo's mother, sister, and sister-in-law. Somehow, Gil Y'Barbo had obtained formal permission for these persons to remain, along with one of his sons to take care of them.

At this juncture, Y'Barbo emerges to play a vital even preeminent role in the Nacogdoches story for the next two decades. Following the death of Lieutenant Gonzales, the trekers chose him to lead them on to San Antonio. Overcoming exposure, famine, and fatigue, Y'Barbo, then about age forty-five, led 167 disheartened travelers, worn-out and broken in health, into San Antonio de Bexar. Ten of the sick, the weak, the elderly, and the very young died during the march and were buried along the trail. Thirty or more of those who straggled into San Antonio were so broken in health and spirit that within three months they also died.

In many ways, Y'Barbo was typical of the sturdy early Spanish settlers who for a variety of reasons found themselves living on the frontier between France and Spain in the Eighteenth Century. He had been born about 1729 at Los Adaes where his father Matheo Antonio Y'Barbo was a soldier stationed at the presidio and his mother, Juana Luzgarda Hernandez, was a daughter of a prominent San Antonio family. As a child Gil was given the advantage of all available opportunities for an education at the frontier post. His superior education combined with a remarkably sound judgment prepared him to become a community leader.

Gil Y'Barbo grew to manhood in Los Adaes when it was a thriving frontier settlement. There he learned much about trading among the French settlers of nearby Louisiana, the Spanish settlers of East Texas, and the Caddo and other Indians of the area. By 1772, now more than forty years of age, he had become one of the most influential and affluent men among the Spanish settlers on the frontier. For many years he had engaged in traffic in horses and furs which were collected throughout Central Texas, brought through the Nacogdoches area, smuggled into French Louisiana to Natchitoches, and shipped from there to New Orleans. For most of those years, he maintained commercial connections with French merchants in Louisiana.

When the dispossessed East Texas settlers reached San Antonio they were allowed to select parcels of land from designated areas; but they were required to bear the cost of building irrigation ditches, flumes, and other aids to cultivation. Since most of them were without the necessary funds, they could not possibly meet these requirements; there was no practical way whereby they could hope to support themselves and their families. The result was that they refused to choose lands or to accept any offered them. Instead, the steadfastly indicated their only wish was to return to their homes on the eastern frontier.

Eight days after their arrival in San Antonio, Y'Barbo called a meeting of the heads of families, and a petition was drafted addressed to authorities in Mexico City seeking permission to retrace their steps and regain their homesteads. The petition was signed by seventy-six of the leading men of the group, representing some 127 of the other exiles.

On Governor Ripperdá's suggestion, Gil Y'Barbo and Gil Flores were chosen to deliver their petition to Mexico City. The Viceroy heard them but refused to allow them to return to their old homes, but he did permit them to locate eastward from San Antonio in a "suitable place." Taking advantage of the Viceroy's permission, Governor Ripperdá designated a site on the right bank of the Trinity River at Paso Tomas where the Camino Real (Royal Road) and the La Bahia Road intersected, that is, at a point above the mouth of Bidais Creek in present-day Madison County.

Preparations for the removal were completed in August 1774, and Gil Y'Barbo was designated captain of the company and *justicia mayor* (chief judge) of the new settlement which was designated Nuestra Señora del Pilar de Bucareli. Gil Flores was named his lieutenant and Juan de la Mora his alferez or sub-lieutenant.

The group left San Antonio in August 1774 and reached the new location in February 1775. Within four months more than fifty wooden houses along with corrals, fields, roads, and an improved river crossing had been created at Bucareli. The official

THE STORY OF NACOGDOCHES

1775 census reported 347 inhabitants there.

All went reasonably well until 1779 when the combination of a series of Comanche Indian raids and a Trinity River flood caused most of the families, including that of Captain Y'Barbo, to abandon their new homes. While this exodus was going on, a fire destroyed half of the houses at Bucareli.

With its future residents poised precariously near Bucareli, Nacogdoches was about to be reborn, not as a Spanish mission site but as a permanent settlement for Europeans. Taking advantage of the opportunity offered by exodus from the Trinity River site, Captain Gil Y'Barbo reasserted leadership and the displaced colonials set out for their former East Texas homes. They were accompanied by Father José Francisco Mariano de la Garza, who served as their chaplain. A native of Guadalajara, Mexico, the chaplain was a Franciscan who might well be regarded as the co-founder of modern Nacogdoches.

On the way to Nacogdoches other stragglers from earlier parties joined the march. By April 30, 1779, the expedition had arrived at the site of the old mission. Y'Barbo then sent a full report of conditions at Nacogdoches and implied that virtually all in his party wished to settle at that place. He explained to the Spanish authorities that he had chosen Nacogdoches because there was a small chapel located there where their chaplain could preform holy sacraments, a house for him to serve as his residence, plenty of water, good land, and a ready supply of materials for houses.

A new governor and a new viceroy readily allowed the settlers to remain at Nacogdoches. In October the settlement was given legal status when Gil Y'Barbo was appointed Captain of Militia and Lieutenant Governor of Nacogdoches with an annual salary of 500 pesos. With this reoccupation a new epoch in the Spanish settlement of Texas began with Nacogdoches as its focus rather than the earlier capital at Los Adaes.

OLD STONE FORT
BUILT ABOUT 1779
CORNER OF MAIN AND FREDONIA

CHAPTER TWO
THE OUTPOST

The reborn East Texas settlement was legally designated the Pueblo of Nacogdoches, acquiring for the first time the status of a European town. Thereafter, it underwent a twenty-year period of growth marked by steadily increasing numbers of residents. Spanish colonial regulations mandated an annual census of each colony. The 1783 count revealed a population of 349 in what was at that point referred to as the Nacogdoches District. Ten years later the total had reached 539, and in another ten years climbed to 770, reaching almost 900 by 1808 when unsettled conditions returned to plague the frontier outpost.

The Pueblo

Soon after Captain Gil Y'Barbo had settled his little band of displaced persons in the Nacogdoches area he sought to create a measure of stability in the new community. He ordered that corn be sown and that beans, squash, and peas be planted to support the people and thereby insure their survival. At the same time, he issued a criminal code aimed at guaranteeing order in the settlement. This set of laws contained fifty-four offenses, twenty-two of which were punishable by death. Typical offenses and their punishments included: burglary, forfeiture of property; theft of twelve or more sheep or goats, death; theft of five or more horses or hogs, death; theft of beef cattle, death; murder, death; arson, death; rape, death; and speaking evil of the king, death and forfeiture of all property. There is no evidence to indicate that these laws were strictly enforced nor their harsh punishments imposed. Perhaps their mere existence was enough to deter most thoughts of criminal activity.

In addition, legend has it that horse-and-rider traffic caused a serious problem in downtown Nacogdoches. Thus, so the story goes, town leaders resorted to the use of traffic lights. Lanterns were suspended from poles to mark intersections and to prohibit left-hand turns. At the same time another regulation gave pedestrians the right-of-way at all crossings.

Thereafter, the Lieutenant Governor directed the settlers to construct homes for their shelter. Using available materials, they placed sharpened tree trunks in the ground to form palisades in a square or rectangular pattern, strengthening them with interlaced vines, and covered all over with red mud for insulation. Hipped roofs of shingles extending well beyond the walls protected them from rain and other elements. A stick and mud chimney at one end provided warmth, illumination, and a place to cook the family's food. None of these early dwellings possessed windows or other than dirt floors.

Almost as soon as he had settled his charges, Y'Barbo requested and received permission to establish a commissary or trading post at Nacogdoches for trade with the Indians. Almost certainly, he constructed the Stone House (now known as the Old Stone Fort, although it was used as a fortification only once for a short time) to accommodate his trading venture, and it served as his headquarters and his residence was a half block east on what is now Main Street.

In these early weeks and months, Y'Barbo seem to be everywhere. He furnished the colonials encouragement, tools, servants, and his personal supervision in planting their crops and building their houses. He provided for the sick and aged in his own Stone House and supplied medicine and clothing to the needy among them.

Y'Barbo's Stone House was built of native stone and hewn timbers with walls two and one-half feet thick. It was rectangular in shape and was two-storied with stone fireplaces. By 1800, a frontier village had grown up around the house which faced the Plaza Principal (town square) on its northeast corner. Spanish towns were traditionally laid out around a series of plazas or squares: a military and government plaza (plaza principal), a church plaza, and a number of residential plazas. Frequently included, as was the case in early Nacogdoches, space was provided for a ring for staging bull fights.

Settlers wanted and needed land on which to erect their dwellings and on which to plant their crops, but no authority to grant legal title to land had been given Lieutenant Governor Y'Barbo. No provision, in fact, had been made for creating titles to their land. Confronted with the settlers demands and the absence of any legal authority to act, Y'Barbo adopted the tactic of making simple verbal grants to many settlers in the area, several of whom received eleven square leagues (some 48,000 acres).

The Lieutenant Governor began making his verbal grants in 1780, but twelve years later officials in Mexico City learned of the practice and launched an investigation. This resulted in a proclamation that all persons not having written grants to their lands should petition the government for legal titles. Many settlers complied but few written titles were ever issued.

The San Antonio Road (El Camino Real) ran through the Plaza Principal connecting Natchitoches in nearby Louisiana with San Antonio and the settlements along the Rio Bravo (Rio Grande). On special occasions residents walking about the Plaza observed people wearing clothing native to a variety of ethnic backgrounds and overheard an assortment of languages being spoken. In fact, Nacogdoches had become the second largest Spanish settlement in Texas, second only to San Antonio.

Law and order, land grants, houses, crops, and morale were not the only problems faced by the infant settlement.

Indians in the area quickly began complaining to Lieutenant Governor Y'Barbo that Spanish officials were not providing them with trade goods as they had been promised. The Indians were able to secure the goods they wanted from French traders located in Natchitoches. Spanish officials were, as usual, slow to take action, causing Y'Barbo to take matters in his own hands, as he had in the past.

In 1780, he sent five men with trade goods to the Indians. But the natives, not satisfied, seized the traders and threatened to hold them until their demand for gifts as well as goods were met. No one was given legal permission to trade among the Indians until June 1782, but by that time, at least nine agents were already in the field. As late as 1789, Y'Barbo reported that the Indians were still dissatisfied with the government's distribution of gifts and that he had been forced to purchase presents from his own funds to pacify them.

In 1791, persons who had been tried and punished for illegal trading (smuggling) by Y'Barbo who served as Judge Commissioner of Seizures and Contraband had made repeated complaints against him alleging that the judge himself engaged in illicit trading. The Viceroy dispatched Don Manuel Gaspar de Verazadi to conduct an official investigation. Not satisfied with the results of this inquiry, the Commandant General of the Eastern Interior Provinces, Ramón de Castro, was ordered to conduct his own investigation. Anticipating this second inquiry, Gil Y'Barbo tendered his resignation as civil governor and militia commander. Nevertheless, he was ordered to San Antonio where he was arrested and retained until 1796 when authorities decided there was not sufficient evidence to prove the alleged infractions.

Although Y'Barbo was released from custody and his commission as a captain of militia restored, he was forbidden to return to Nacogdoches. An order issued in 1802 permitted him to take up residence in Louisiana. After a few years with the tacit consent of Spanish authorities, he was allowed to return to Nacogdoches. Then, near the end of a long and eventful life, he established a rancho known as La Lucana on the east bank of the Attoyac River, south of the King's Highway. There at age eighty he died in 1809 and was buried in then Old Spanish Cemetery in Nacogdoches.

The success of Y'Barbo and his small band of countrymen, acting on their own initiative, in establishing the Pueblo of Nacogdoches demonstrated what several thousand permanent Spanish settlers might have accomplished toward a successful colonization of the province had they been allowed, even encouraged, to move into the fertile forests areas of East Texas.

From 1779 to 1791, Y'Barbo had been a strong and able governor, and replacing him proved a difficult task. Finally, in January 1795, Don Cristoval Cordova, who had been in temporary command since 1774, was replaced by Lieutenant Bernardo Fernandez, a cavalry officer, who served until September 1796 when he was replaced by Don José Mariá Guadiana. The new commander's behavior soon prompted an investigation. Reports reached San Antonio that he accepted bribes, was drunk on duty, and improperly collected duties on horse trading. In 1799, Guadiana was removed and command temporarily turned over to Don José Miguel de Moral from La Bahia.

Commandants at Nacogdoches were plagued continually by two difficult tasks assigned them: the near impossibility of enforcing the prohibition against trade with Louisiana and the equally impossible responsibility of preventing foreigners from entering the province. Smugglers and foreigners without passports evaded the small garrison stationed at Nacogdoches by the simple expedient of bypassing the post. The garrison was constantly below effective strength, never above twenty-five men to guard and patrol the entire eastern border.

By 1780 a "Smugglers Trail" (Trace) had been established as an alternative to the Camino Real in traveling from Natchitoches to San Antonio. During the Spanish and Mexican colonial period and during the days of the Republic of Texas this route was used by traders, illegal immigrants, and any others who wished to avoid customs duties and official inspection. It continued to be used for decades because it had become a well-beaten track. Users almost invariably went one way and returned another to avoid easy detection. In addition, many other trails led to and from the Trace. One went through Crockett in present-day Houston County west to the Trinity River landing, another to nearby Indian villages and scattered Spanish and French settlements, most of them crossing and recrossing the San Antonio Road.

At the turn of the century, the Pueblo of Nacogdoches was described by its commandant, José Miguel de Moral, as containing two public squares, the Plaza Principal and the Church Plaza. Just south of the King's Highway west of the Plaza Principal was the Old Spanish Cemetery. The businesses of the town were located around the Church Plaza and eastward on Main Street (El Camino Real) to the Plaza Principal. Residences extended northward along La Calle Real del Norte (North Street).

The Gateway

By 1800, the Pueblo of Nacogdoches had become one of the three principal entry points (Gateways) of the Province of Texas. On the northern frontier one of them, Pecan Point and Jonesboro, was situated near the crossing of the Red River from Arkansas; a second, Nacogdoches, was located on El Camino Real near the crossing of the Sabine River in eastern Texas; and the third, the Port of Galveston, was situated on the Gulf of

Mexico on the southern boundary. Through those gateways a trickle of migrants, both legal and illegal, began making their way into Spanish Texas from French Louisiana, from the United States, and from a number of European nations. In 1796, the Spanish commandant José Mariá Guadiana, reported a number of Anglo-Americans in Nacogdoches, but he and others reporting to authorities in San Antonio and Mexico City did not attempt to estimate the number of foreigners who had entered illegally, who had slipped by officials at Nacogdoches, and who then made their way unhindered to the interior.

As early as 1789 Americans gradually began to enter the Eastern Interior Province of Texas. Two of the earliest to settle in Nacogdoches were William Barr and Peter Samuel Davenport. Davenport was destined to become the most enterprising and successful merchant and trader in East Texas during the Spanish colonial period. Samuel Davenport (early in life he abandoned the name Peter) had been born in Pennsylvania, but at age sixteen (about 1785) he migrated to Louisiana. Left an orphan by 1794, he determined to immigrate to Texas and that year entered the province through the Sabine gateway to Nacogdoches.

While living in Louisiana, he was employed by a number of trading firms and in time entered business ventures of his own. After residing in Nacogdoches some four years, in 1798 Davenport entered into partnership with William Barr, Luther Smith, and Edward Murphy to operate a trading post under the name "Barr and Davenport." In 1800, Barr secured from the Spanish authorities a monopoly over trade with all Texas Indians for the firm. Davenport was designated the local agent for the firm. He quickly established its headquarters in the Stone House on the Plaza Principal.

Nacogdoches County land records disclose that on June 20, 1806 William Barr paid José de la Vega $350 for the Stone House and the land on which it was located. Four years later, Barr obtained from the Governor of Texas, Manuel de Salcedo, a decree perfecting his title to the property.

Senior partner William Barr was a native of Ireland who had immigrated to Pennsylvania in 1774, resided for a time in Philadelphia, but soon moved westward to settle in Pittsburgh. After serving in the United States army, in 1786 he moved on to Louisiana, then a Spanish possession. There the next year he became a subject (citizen) of the king of Spain and continued to engage in the mercantile business in Natchitoches. Still later, in 1793, he immigrated to Nacogdoches where he also conducted a mercantile business.

In his will filed in 1810 Barr left some three-fourths of his considerable estate to Samuel Davenport. The size of the estate can be gleaned from an inventory Barr had prepared in 1810. In it he declared that he owned two houses and lots in Nacogdoches, two ranches with one house and one farm, 700 head of cattle, over 100 hogs, about 150 horses and mules, six droves of breeding mares with stallions. and two breeding burros. His Natchitoches property alone was valued at more than $156,000, a remarkable sum for the time.

Another of the partners, Edward Murphy, was also a native of Ireland. Sometime before 1780, he also immigrated to Pennsylvania, and he too immigrated to Spanish Louisiana, settling there by 1786. Murphy presumably remained in Louisiana residing in and around Natchitoches, where he managed the firm's Louisiana business interests.

Luther Smith, the remaining partner, is a shadowy figure. Although at some point in his earlier life he had lived for a time in New York, but by 1800 or so he was living in Spanish Louisiana. By 1810, three of the original partners: Barr, Murphy, and Smith were dead, but for two years thereafter Davenport continued to operate the business.

For more than a decade the House of Barr and Davenport

was the principal trading enterprise in East Texas and in the Neutral Ground--a long and narrow strip of land lying between Louisiana and Texas, whose ownership was disputed by Spain and the United States for approximately fifteen years. During those years, settlers, most without official sanction, moved into the area; and traders, filibusterers, and fugitive slaves used it as a staging area before illegal entry into Spanish Texas.

Spanish colonial regulations at this time restricted or prohibited commercial intercourse between Louisiana and Texas, but urgent need for supplies frequently compelled frontier authorities on both sides of the disputed area to amend or ignore any restrictions whenever necessity dictated. The partnership of Barr and Davenport, therefore, was allowed to freight merchandise across the Neutral Ground from Louisiana to Texas and transport furs and livestock back to Louisiana.

The firm was allowed to engage in this forbidden trade because Spanish officials recognized the necessity of supplying Spanish troops in East Texas and securing presents to distribute to the Indians to ensure their loyalty to Spain. In addition to their normal business of supplying the friendly Indians with articles of merchandise, the partners also furnished the quartermaster's department of Nacogdoches with flour, beef, salt, soap, and chili as supplements to supplies furnished from San Antonio.

Although by 1810 the partnership had been dissolved by the death of three of the partners, Davenport emerged as an independently wealthy man and one of the most influential men in the Pueblo of Nacogdoches. He had been commended as a loyal and obedient subject of the Spanish crown by the Governor of Texas, the Spanish commandant in Nacogdoches, and by both Catholic priests in Nacogdoches.

Not everyone who crossed the Sabine River into East Texas in the early years of the Eighteenth Century contributed to the steady growth and prosperity of the Nacogdoches

Community. Some, in fact, posed a serious threat to its continued existence. Beginning around the turn of the century, a series of filibustering expeditions brought near chaos to the region. At that time traders from Louisiana contested successfully for trade with the East Texas Indians and offered a market for horses stolen from the Spanish outposts. The most famous of these was Philip Nolan, a confederate of American General James Wilkinson. Nolan entered Texas as early as 1790-1791 when he became a resident of the Nacogdoches post. In 1794, the commandant in Nacogdoches gave Nolan permission to capture horses with the aid of local citizens. Thereafter he proceeded into the interior acquiring horses on several different occasions and quite probably with the tacit approval of the Spanish and French local governors engaged in contraband trading. Spanish officials ultimately became suspicious of Nolan's motives in visiting Texas, and by 1800 had forbidden him to enter the province again.

Nolan ignored the Spanish order, and in 1800, entered Texas with a party of twenty-one men, reached the Brazos River, and proceeded to gather a herd of several hundred horses. The following year a superior Spanish military force engaged the Nolan band in a skirmish in which Nolan was killed. Nevertheless, Nolan's fate did not deter other American adventurers. They continued to pass quietly into the province to acquire horses for which there was a ready market and to participate in the lucrative Indian trade.

Affairs were further complicated in 1803 when Emperor Napoleon Bonaparte sold the Louisiana Territory to the United States. The emperor had persuaded the Spanish monarch to return this vast territory to France. Although the Spanish government formally protested the sale and threatened war with the United States over the purchase, hostilities did not develop. Thenceforth, the eastern neighbors of the Spanish in Texas would be the more aggressive land-hungry Anglo-Americans in the United States. Faced with this situation, Spanish authorities determined to employ a three-part strategy concerning their eastern frontier. They determined to maintain their boundaries with the United States unchanged, to increase their garrisons in the province and colonize it with loyal Spanish subjects, and to prohibit immigration by Anglo-Americans.

In keeping with those objectives, in 1806 an agreement was reached that for the time being the boundary between Louisiana and Texas would not be determined but the Americans would remain east of Arroyo Hondo and the Spanish west of the Sabine. This agreement thus retained the concept of the Neutral Ground or Neutral Strip as it was sometimes known.

Spanish efforts to implement their colonization policy were not particularly fruitful. Spanish authorities found it very difficult to entice settlers on whose loyalty they could depend. In 1809, the annual colonial census estimated the total non-Indian population of Texas at 4,155 persons, most of them clustered around San Antonio and Goliad in the west and southwest and Nacogdoches in the east.

Following the Neutral Ground agreement, tensions along the Texas-Louisiana frontier eased noticeably for the next few years. However, the commandant at Nacogdoches, charged with the duty of maintaining order and preventing smuggling with only small garrison, continued to be harassed by both smugglers and illegal immigrants.

The Nolan excursions had little adverse effect on the growing European community around Nacogdoches, but with the advent of filibustering expeditions in the years between 1800 and 1820 that would no longer be true. Population for the community stood at approximately 900 in 1810 but by 1823 it had decreased to approximately 200.

In 1811, Bernardo Gutiérrez de Lara, a Mexican

revolutionary, journeyed to the United States in an effort to secure assistance in the overthrow of Spanish authority in Texas. Gutiérrez was a wealthy merchant, blacksmith, and property owner from Tamaulipas in Mexico. He had participated in the unsuccessful 1810 revolution in Northern Mexico. Some Texans in Nacogdoches and San Antonio, interested in separation from Spain, assured Gutiérrez that Texas would revolt in support of an invading army.

He was joined by Lieutenant Augustus W. Magee, a disgruntled former U.S. Army officer and West Point graduate, who recruited a group of Anglo-American adventurers, Mexican revolutionists, French soldiers-of-fortune, and a band of Indian allies that constituted the invading army of the Magee-Gutiérrez Expedition. In January 1812, this military force left Louisiana and set out to conquer Texas.

When the invaders arrived at Nacogdoches in August 1812, the Spanish garrison deserted or fled, the civilians drove away the officers, and a procession marched out to greet the liberators. La Bahia (Goliad) fell to the invading force in November. Although Magee died soon thereafter, in April 1813, the army went on to capture San Antonio. In August, a Spanish military force of some 2,000 troops later met and routed the invading force on the Medina River, west of San Antonio, and the expedition collapsed.

Following his victory at Medina, Joaquin de Arrendondo, Commandant General of the Eastern interior Provinces, ordered a purge of Texas aimed at ridding the province of all Anglo-Americans and liberal Mexicans. He directed Lieutenant Colonel Ygnacio Elisondo to pursue the invaders to and beyond San Antonio and Nacogdoches. As the Mexican colonel marched eastward, the residents of Nacogdoches heard rumors of a brutal and unrelenting punishment to be meted out to those who had supported the uprising. Fearing reprisals most of the settlers in

Nacogdoches fled across the Sabine River to safety in Louisiana. Only a few, most notably Edmund Norris who later played a major role in the history of the community, remained behind.

The experiences of Samuel Davenport as a participant in the Magee-Gutiérrez affair serves to illustrate the plight of many of the Nacogdoches residents who willingly joined forces with the invaders. The wealthy trader had become acquainted with Guitérrez as an outgrowth of his business transactions in Louisiana. For reasons that are not at all clear, in 1812 Davenport underwent a radical change of attitude toward the Spanish government, and learning of the projected filibustering expedition he elected to become a major contributor.

In June 1812, while in Natchitoches and New Orleans, Davenport assembled supplies for the liberating army, doing so as a result of his commission as quartermaster-general of the expedition. Returning to Nacogdoches that summer, he was able to convince the greater part of the inhabitants support the revolutionaries. In addition, he attempted to enlist the active participation of the Indians along the Texas Gulf Coast.

Serving as captain of a force of some 150 Nacogdoches volunteers as well as quartermaster-general, he remained with the invading forces until after they captured La Bahia (Goliad). Shortly thereafter, perhaps because he anticipated the collapse of the invasion, he left the Army and made his across the Sabine River to Natchitoches. Ultimately, Davenport was outlawed, forbidden to return to Texas, and a reward of 250 pesos offered for his capture, 500 pesos if a Catholic killed him.

As political tensions eased, some of those who fled the wrath of Spanish authorities drifted back to their homes in Nacogdoches, although for some months the province of Texas remained virtually depopulated, except for the settlement at San Antonio de Bexar. Having learned nothing from their attempt to enforce the frontier policies introduced after American acquisition of Louisiana in 1803, Spanish officials continued their ineffective efforts to lure loyal subjects to settle in Texas. But the rich lands, opportunities for profitable trade, and other inducements continued to attract Anglo-Americans. Moreover, in 1819 the United States and Spain entered into a treaty whereby Spain ceded Florida to the United States and the United States acknowledged the Spanish claim to Texas. Many Anglo-Americans, especially in the southern states, resented this "surrender" of Texas. One of them, Dr. James Long, acting on plans formulated at Natchez, Mississippi in 1819, organized an expedition aimed at freeing Texas of Spanish troops, organizing an Anglo-American government there, and attracting immigrants by offering them generous land grants. Long arrived in Nacogdoches in June 1819 with a force of some 300 men. There the invaders established a civil government, adopted a declaration of independence, and invited immigrants to come and share the blessings of liberty.

Having learned of the invasion, Governor Antonio Martínez dispatched Lieutenant Colonel Ygnacio Pérez with a force of 650 men to drive Long's invaders out of Texas. By mid-October 1819, Pérez had completed his task. In this attempt to overthrow Spanish rule in Texas, Samuel Davenport eagerly joined. He furnished much needed supplies to the little army and served as a member of the governing council of Long's Republic.

For a second time in less than a decade residents of Nacogdoches abandoned their homes in the face of political confusion and fled to safety in the United States. In 1820 an American visitor described the frontier settlement as a desolate place of no more than 100 persons. While a year later Stephen F. Austin was able to assemble only 35 persons for an important public meeting. Austin recorded in his diary that "Nacogdoches lay in ruins with only five houses and a church still standing." Thus, on the eve of the Mexican Revolution, Nacogdoches was little more than a deserted village, no longer a growing prosperous frontier settlement. But in the coming decade it would experience another of its rebirths.

BANITA HOTEL

CHAPTER THREE
EL ESTADO

When Mexico gained its independence from Spain in 1821, the once flourishing Spanish frontier outpost at Nacogdoches lay virtually in ruins. As a consequence of its decline during the years the Mexicans were struggling to rid themselves of Spanish control, Nacogdoches played no significant role is this independence movement.

Upon gaining independence, the Mexican people chose to follow the example of the United States, creating a federal government composed of a number of states. One of the new estados (states) was Coahuila y Tejas which was formed by uniting those two frontier provinces. The new state was divided for purposes of government into several departments, one of which, the Department of Bexar with its headquarters at San Antonio, had jurisdiction over all of Texas.

The Municipality

Following the traditional pattern for Spanish-style local governments, the territory of the State of Coahuila y Tejas was subdivided into a number of municipalities. These local units had jurisdiction over more area than that within its corporate limits. They regularly included a substantial portion of the surrounding rural area. The Municipality of Nacogdoches, for example, was given authority over a wide area of East Texas. Its boundaries ranged from the Trinity River to the Sabine River and from near the Gulf Coast to the Red River. Its government, therefore, exercised most of the functions customarily associated with three separate units of local government in the United States: the township, the county, and the municipality. In 1833, moreover, the town itself was granted four sitios (some 17,700 acres) of land.

Municipalities such as Nacogdoches were ordinarily governed by an alcalde, four regidores, an alguacil, two escribanos, and a mayor domo. Traditionally, these officers were elected annually and were ineligible for immediate reelection. They were also required to be literate and loyal subjects. In this era, these requirements could not be strictly enforced in frontier areas such as East Texas. The literacy requirement was totally unrealistic as few of its settlers could read or write.

Despite its designation as a municipality in 1821, an regular government was not immediately instituted. From that time to 1826, an alcalde who was also referred to as the commandant, served as the sole officer of government. Elections for alcaldes were held at irregular intervals. James Dill was initially appointed as temporary alcalde, serving from 1821 to 1823.

Dill, a native of Pennsylvania, as a young orphan immigrated first to Louisiana and later to Arkansas. He, his wife, and their three older children, settled in Nacogdoches in 1793 where he became a licensed Indian trader. His lack of educational and other legal qualifications led to considerable opposition and finally to his forcible removal from office.

Juan Seguin then served for a year, followed by Patricio de Torres for four months, and thereafter by Pedro Procella and his son Luis Procella. Seguin was a native of Bexar, Torres of northern Mexico, and Pedro Procella of Los Adaes. All had been a part of the Nacogdoches community for some years.

Regular elections began to be held about 1825 and an organized ayuntamiento (municipal council) established at the same time. Elections were scheduled for December each year. In December 1825, Samuel Norris was chosen in a contested election, but he proved unable to fulfill the duties of the office. In any event, alcaldes were regularly elected until after the Fredonian Rebellion.

From 1820 onwards events occurred that involved Nacogdoches in considerable turmoil. One cause of increasing disturbance was the steadily increasing number of Anglo-Americans who kept crossing the Sabine River and settling between Attoyac Bayou and the river. Many, perhaps most, entered the area illegally. In an effort to stem the tide, in 1824 Alcalde Juan Seguin ordered all inhabitants of the district who wished to remain as residents and become Mexican citizens to come to Nacogdoches and take the oath of allegiance. Few complied and the tide continued.

The Fredonian Rebellion was an outgrowth of a new immigration policy initiated by the Mexican government. In order to strengthen their control over Texas, in 1824, the Federal Congress in Mexico City undertook the bold and ultimately fatal experiment of permitting foreign immigration. Mexican authorities believed it was absolutely necessary to populate the province, and, in that belief, they determined that the easiest and least expensive way to do so was to entice foreigners in considerable numbers as rapidly as possible.

To encourage that immigration, the Mexican Congress passed a colonization law which set forth a few general principals for guidance leaving the details to the state legislatures. Among the most important of those general guidelines were guarantees of the security of immigrants' persons and property, preferences to immigrants who were Mexican citizens, limits on the amount of land granted to any one person, and restrictions on absentee land-ownership. In accordance with this directive from Mexico City, on March 24, 1825, the legislature of the State of Coahuila y Tejas enacted a general colonization law.

This state statute invited immigrants that could furnish satisfactory evidence of their Catholic beliefs, their morality, and good habits. The were allowed to settle as individual families or in groups of families through an empresario. Each family would be allotted, upon payment of some nominal fees, a square league (4,428 acres) of land. They were required to cultivate or occupy the land within a period of six years. Native-born Mexican citizens might purchase for nominal fees as much eleven square leagues (48,708 acres). Empresarios could be granted as much as five leagues and five labors of land for each hundred families they settled up to a maximum of 800 families. Single men might receive only one-fourth as much land as heads of families until they married; whereupon they would be given a full one-league grant. Those who married Mexican citizens could be given one-fourth more land.

Among those who were awarded empresario contracts in 1825 was Haden Edwards, whose East Texas grant included Nacogdoches but extended on the east to the Neutral Ground with its quota of undesirable residents, on the southwest to the boundary of Stephen F. Austin's colony, and on the north and west to the clusters of Indians tribes recently driven from the United States. The town of Nacogdoches itself was the home of many dissidents who had taken part in the Magee and Long expeditions.

A native of Virginia, Haden Edwards also lived for a time in Kentucky before immigrating to Mississippi in 1815 with his wife, twelve children, and several slaves. He established a large plantation there on the Pearl River. Lured by the attraction of large land grants in Louisiana and Texas, he left Mississippi about 1822 and settled temporarily in St. Tammany Parish, Louisiana. As early as 1799 he had begun engaging in western land speculation and by 1815 had become a man with considerable financial assets.

Leaving his wife and children in Louisiana, Edwards made his way to Mexico City to petition for an empresario contract. While there he became acquainted with Stephen F. Austin and other aspiring empresarios. Austin later characterized Edwards as impetuous and quick tempered and correctly predicted that he would not get along well with Mexican officials. Others who knew him well maintained that he was stern, aggressive, outspoken, over confident, and highly opinionated. Still others felt he lacked common sense and adaptability. All these characteristics contributed to his troubles in dealing with the Mexican government and the settlers already living in the limits of his grant.

Three important conditions were attached the Edwards' grant: he was required to honor all preexisting Spanish and Mexican land titles granted to individuals; he was to organize a militia to protect the area and its inhabitants; and he was to request the formation of a land commission to award land titles after at least 100 families had been formally settled within the grant.

The Municipality of Nacogdoches was charged with the duty of maintaining tranquility between the Sabine and Trinity Rivers. The limits of Edwards' grant, on the other hand, ranged from twenty leagues north of the Gulf of Mexico on the south, to twenty leagues west of the Sabine River on the east, to fifteen leagues north of Nacogdoches, to the Navasota River on the west. The boundaries of the grant and of the municipality did not coincide, causing a conflict of authority and creating legal problems.

When Edwards arrived in Nacogdoches in August 1825 comparatively few persons were located within the limits of his grant. Most of the inhabitants of East Texas where settled in a band sixty miles in width between the eastern extremity of his grant and the Sabine River.

The most pressing problem confronting Edwards when he arrived in Nacogdoches was the inhabitants already living on the land he had been granted. Many of them had settled there illegally, and still others could produce no valid proof of ownership. A significant number of them had old Spanish grants, many of which had not been recorded since 1821, and still others occupied lands without any sort of grant but who had been allowed to live on them for generations by a sort of tacit agreement.

Edwards mistakenly believed that his empresario contract authorized him to determine the validity of all land claims within his grant. Acting on that belief, on September 25, 1825, at the principal street corners in Nacogdoches, he posted notices bidding all who claimed previous land titles from the Spanish or Mexican governments come forward immediately and validate their claims with firm legal evidence or their lands would be seized and sold to the highest bidder. A month later he posted a second preemptive notice.

Although he evidently exercised considerable political prudence in dealing with important persons in Mexico City, after taking charge of his grant Edwards apparently abandoned this practice. Instead, he displayed to high-ranking aristocratic Mexican political figures the code of behavior and social graces of a well-bred southern gentleman, but toward the Spanish residents of East Texas he exhibited neither consideration nor patience. He rapidly began the practice of attempting to remove from the limits of his grant the less prosperous older settlers and replace them with wealthy planters from the Old South. As in the case of many of his Anglo-American contemporaries, he was convinced of the superiority of his type of Southern gentlemen and determined to people his colony with as many of them as he could attract.

Anticipating that the new empresario might question the land titles of the old settlers, before Edwards arrived in Nacogdoches Luis Procela, alcalde by proxy, and José Antonio

Sepulveda, the local *sindico* (clerk), hurried to validate old Spanish and Mexican land titles which had lain dormant for many years. When Edwards learned of this practice, he immediately accused the two men of manufacturing fake deeds and forging land titles for those older settlers.

Haden Edwards should have left the task of validating land claims to a land commissioner who would be appointed by officials of the State of Coahuila y Tejas. In any event, shortly after provoking considerable antagonism over land titles, the empresario ordered an election of militia officers. José Antonio Sepulveda was elected Captain of Militia. Edwards ignored the results of that election and assumed command of the militia in accordance with the terms of his contract.

He ordered a second election to be held January 1, 1826 to chose an alcalde for Nacogdoches, an action that was not allowed within the terms of his contract. A hotly contested campaign ensued with two candidates contending for the office: Chichester Chaplin, a young lawyer and son-in-law of Edwards, and Samuel Norris, an Anglo-American who had married a Spanish colonial and sided with the old settlers.

Chaplin was declared then victor, but supporters of Norris appealed to the Political Chief of the Department on the grounds that most of Chaplin's vote came from unqualified electors. The Chief upheld their appeal and ordered Chaplin to turn over the archives and other accouterments of the office to Norris. Therefore, by April 1826, the empresario found both the major offices in his grant held by men who supported his opponents.

After returning to Louisiana from Mexico in 1825, Haden invited his brother Benjamin then living in Mississippi to come to Texas for a visit. Benjamin accepted the invitation and reached Nacogdoches before Haden and family had arrived from Louisiana. Finding that the Edwards family had not yet in town, Benjamin went on to Austin's Colony where he remained for several months. When Benjamin returned to Nacogdoches, Haden persuaded his brother to remain in Texas while he went to the American South to recruit colonists and obtain additional financial support.

Haden then made perhaps his most serious mistake as an empresario. He placed Benjamin in charge of affairs in his absence. The younger brother quickly demonstrated that he was even less able to deal with the problems facing the colony than his brother had been. Those who knew Benjamin before he went to Texas proclaimed that he had many admirable qualities. He was described as modest with unobtrusive manners, well educated, and a graceful and dignified public speaker.

Acting as his brother's deputy, he revealed very quickly that he did not sympathize with the Spanish-speaking settlers around Nacogdoches, could not understand their language, and would not treat them with patience nor tact. Quite likely, he preferred Anglo-Americans settlers and wished to alienate and drive off as many non-Anglos as he could.

Between April and October, 1826 conditions deteriorated markedly within the Edwards grant. Disputes over land titles multiplied and became more acute. Ownership was regularly resolved in favor of old settlers, and a band of "regulators" began harassing newcomers. Letters written by Benjamin to high-ranking Mexican officials at San Antonio and Saltillo were misunderstood, and their tone angered Victor Blanco, the state governor. Blanco informed Benjamin in October 1826 that the Edwards contract had been canceled by order of the president of the republic, and that the Edwards brothers should depart Texas immediately leaving any unfinished business unfinished.

When Haden learned of the Governor's order, he determined to retain his lands by detaching East Texas from Mexico. As a result, he initiated an armed revolt that became known as the Fredonian Rebellion. The initial step in the uprising was taken by a band of thirty-six men from the Ayish Bayou area east of Nacogdoches led by Colonel Martin Parmer, Major John S. Roberts, and Captain Burrell J. Thompson. They rode into town on November 22, 1826, arrested Alcalde Samuel Norris and Sindico José Antonio Sepulveda, and captured and released Benjamin Edwards on parole.

Parmer was a colorful late arrival from Missouri, who had gained a wide reputation there as an Indian fighter and spinner of yarns. He had styled himself as "The Ringed Tailed Panther" while living in Missouri where, for a time, he commanded a local militia force. Roberts was a dashing former deputy sheriff from Natchitoches who came to East Texas to protect and later marry the widow of Robert Callier. A veteran of the War of 1812, Roberts had participated in the Battle of New Orleans, while Thompson was a native of South Carolina newly arrived in East Texas.

A court martial was soon convened for the Alcalde and the Sindico. Found guilty of oppression, corruption, and other high crimes, the court consisting of Presiding Judge Colonel Parmer, Major Roberts, Captain Thompson, John W. Mayo, and William Jones removed the two men from office and declared them ineligible to hold another office the remainder of their lives. The court appointed Joseph Durst acting alcalde until an election could be held to fill the vacancy.

When news of the capture of Nacogdoches by rebel forces reached San Antonio, a detachment of Mexican troops composed of 110 infantry commanded the military commander of Texas, Lieutenant Colonel Matéo Ahumada, left December 11 to restore order in the Nacogdoches area. Reinforced by 250 militiamen from Austin's colony, the Mexican commander marched from San Felipe on January 22 and arrived in Nacogdoches February 8 where he was joined by an additional 150 men from the Anglo-American settlements in the Ayish Bayou district.

Before Ahumada's forces could reach Nacogdoches, on December 16, 1826, the rebel forces, under a flag inscribed " Independence, Liberty and Justice," took possession of the Stone House (Old Stone Fort) and proclaimed the Republic of Fredonia. A formal Declaration of Independence was signed Christmas Day. Around the first of the new year a delegation of Cherokee Indians led by Chiefs Richard Fields and John Dunn Hunter joined forces and subscribed to the declaration. Although upwards of 200 men assembled in Nacogdoches in support of the rebellion, many were only lukewarm revolutionaries having joined the uprising in an attempt to protect their property from possible confiscation by Mexican authorities.

A portion of the rebel forces was captured east of the Attoyac River in January, 1827, but some insurgents such as Parmer and Roberts had already abandoned the effort when they determined the movement would not succeed. The rapid approach of the Mexican colonel and his forces caused many such as the Edwards brothers to flee eastward across the Sabine River, and into Louisiana and safety.

Some of the rebels ultimately returned to Texas, notably Haden Edwards, Martin Parmer, and John S. Roberts. Edwards returned in 1835, obtained a Mexican land grant, established a homestead in Nacogdoches, and resumed his career as a land speculator. Parmer may have returned to East Texas as early as 1833, for in 1834 he also received a Mexican land grant, and settled temporarily in Tenaha. In late 1826, Roberts moved his family to Nacogdoches, where he established a home and a store at the northwest corner of the Plaza Principal.

For the most part, however, colonists in East Texas were law-abiding persons engaged in the task of establishing homes for themselves and furthering their personal fortunes. In the town of Nacogdoches and in the "Redlands" east of the town circumstances were not quite the same as elsewhere in the eastern portion of the state. Visitors to the old outpost in the years between 1825 and 1830 described it as a "gamblers' heaven" and a home for crooks of various kinds who constantly made their way across the Sabine River from the United States.

Situated only forty-seven miles west of the river and already one of the principal "gateways" for Anglo-Americans coming to Texas, by 1826 Nacogdoches had become a staging point for adventurers. Some of them stayed through raids and rebellions to become substantial citizens, while others became gamblers and land grabbers.

After order had been restored following the aborted revolution, Colonel José de las Piedras and the Twelfth Permanent Battalion of Mexican troops were stationed in Nacogdoches, Norris was reinstated as alcalde, and a general amnesty was proclaimed for the participants in the rebellion with the exception of the Edwards brothers, Martin Parmer, and Adolphus Sterne. Sterne, a native of Germany had visited Nacogdoches in 1824 and returned in 1826 to operate a mercantile business. With his commercial contacts it was an easy matter for him to obtain supplies for the Fredonian forces. Mexican authorities soon learned of his support for the rebels, tried and convicted him of treason, and sentenced him to death. He was incarcerated in the Stone House while his conviction was reviewed in Saltillo.

Ultimately he received a parole on condition that he renew his oath of allegiance to the Mexican Republic and swear that he would never again take up arms against its government. He faithfully adhered to those conditions and refrained from participation in the disturbances of 1832-1836, although in 1836 he gave substantial aid to the Texas Revolutionary forces in other ways.

After the Fredonian uprising collapsed, a measure of relative quiet and prosperity descended upon Nacogdoches. As a consequence, its 1823 population of approximately 200 had grown by 1828 to about 1,000 and was still steadily increasing. Its municipal government composed of Spanish and Anglo-American elements turned its attention to local matters, and Colonel Piedras' garrison assured the community of stability. Samuel Norris continued as alcalde until 1827 when he was replaced by Encarnation Chireno who as early as 1828 had come to Nacogdoches from Natchitoches.

Chireno was followed by José Maria Mora (1828-1829), José Ignacio Y'Barbo (1829-1830), Vicente Cordova (1830-1831), Manuel de los Santos Coy (1831-1832), with Chireno again serving until his death in the 1832 uprising. In 1827, the town's ayuntamiento began an effort to straighten its irregular streets and lay off the public square and town lots in accordance with government regulations. The Main Plaza was to be formed in a perfect square and called the Plaza of the Constitution. From it streets were to run north, south, east, and west in straight lines and widened. Nacogdoches residents complained that the new streets crossed some lots and left others without access to a street.

Between 1828 and 1832, the ayuntamiento enacted ordinances requiring property owners to clean their lots and enclose them with a fence. Home owners were also required to clean the streets in front of their houses, cover their wells, and pen their livestock at night. In addition, Mexican officials had a community water well dug in the center of the Main Plaza, established a school for the town's children, and inaugurated a postal system. An immigrant from Alabama who visited Nacogdoches in 1830 wrote friends and relatives there that 300 Mexican troops occupied the local garrison. He commented on their peculiar uniforms and still more peculiar personal appearance. He was amazed at the masses celebrated in the streets on Sunday, and the fandangos (dances) in which the priests and all participated. The number of Indians he observed on the town's streets also impressed him.

The religious life of the community also underwent some alterations during this time. The buildings of Mission Guadalupe were abandoned in 1801 after having been used for many years as a chapel by the Spanish garrison and the local settlers. Father José Maria de Jesús constructed a parish church on Church Plaza just east of the site of the present-day courthouse on North Street. The building was abandoned by Spanish officials during the Mexican War of Independence but was again in use for two years when Father José Francisco Maynes was sent to serve as chaplin and pastor.

After the failure of the Fredonian Rebellion this building was used as a barracks for the Twelfth Battalion. Church services were conducted by Father José Antonio Valdez, chaplin of the garrison, in the former residence of Nathaniel Norris located at the corner of Hospital and North Streets. By 1832 the "ancient" building was in ruins and was demolished in 1835. Thereafter no regular Catholic religious services were held in Nacogdoches until 1847 when a new church was built on the east side of North Pecan Street, a half block from the public square. This temporary demise of the Catholic Church allowed Protestant denominations, especially the Methodists and Baptists, over time to gain the ascendence.

A Twentieth Century history of Catholicism in Texas reports that in 1836 there were "about 600 Catholics" in the Nacogdoches parish and that "the abandonment in which local Catholics found themselves enabled the Methodists to begin erecting a meeting house on the "site of the ancient church."

Perhaps the most serious problem facing the officials at Nacogdoches after 1826 was the illegal entry of foreigners into Texas. The onus of enforcing the laws against illegal entry fell on Colonel Piedras and his Twelfth Battalion. The colonel received repeated complains from alcaldes throughout the district concerning the steady influx of foreigners and their refusal to present themselves for permission to settle. In characteristic Anglo-American fashion, they questioned the government's authority requiring the request and maintained that they had every right to settle wherever they pleased.

Moreover, illegal immigrants initiated a practice of bypassing Nacogdoches utilizing a Smugglers Trail that ran parallel to the San Antonio Road about one mile north of town to a point several miles northwest where it joined the San Antonio Road a few miles west of the town. Another trail ran in the southern part the county, crossing the Angelina River at Spanish Bluff Crossing. Piedras openly declared that he did not possess the necessary manpower to prevent people from going around him and his garrison and on into the interior.

In 1830, confronting an ever increasing volume of immigrants that were streaming into Texas from the United States that appeared to Mexican officials as a threat to the nations's continued domination over Texas, the national congress decreed on April 6, 1830, that citizens of foreign countries adjacent to Mexican territory would no longer be permitted to settle in the adjoining Mexican territories. In short, immigrants from the United States could no longer legally settle in Texas.

To the Mexican government this was an emergency measure deemed the best way for saving Texas as a part of the Republic of Mexico. To the Anglo-Americans already in Texas it was viewed as a disaster. It undermined their faith in the integrity of the Mexican government and clouded their future and indeed the future of Texas as well.

The Department

The Department of Bexar had exercised authority over the municipality of Nacogdoches since 1821, but its territory began to be divided in 1831 when the Department of Nacogdoches was created. From that time until the Texas Revolution in 1836 the Department of Nacogdoches included all of Texas east of the Trinity River.

The Mexican government's order banning further Anglo-American immigration fanned the already smoldering unrest in East Texas. It increased to the point of open rebellion in 1832 when Antonio Lopez de Santa Anna launched a full-scale revolution throughout all of Mexico.

Fearing the East Texans would join the revolt, in July 1832, Colonel Piedras issued an order requiring all Anglo-Americans in the Nacogdoches area to surrender their weapons to him. He hinted that failure to do so might result in a war of extermination waged against the Anglos by Mexican troops and Indians living in the area. The people of East Texas reacted promptly by organizing a militia force with which to defend themselves.

Another circumstance creating antagonism on the part of residents of the Nacogdoches area involved the Mexican garrison stationed in the town. These Mexican soldiers were primarily discharged convicts and vagabonds. They were required by army regulations to buy their own food and clothing, but many of them habitually stole those items rather than pay for them. They could have been restrained from engaging in these and other offensive practices, but their commander, Colonel Piedras, apparently enjoyed alienating the local citizenry. In any event, he failed to control his troops and allowed them to be insolent and overbearing.

Soon after the militia began organizing in Nacogdoches, many local residents again chose to move to the east as many had done at times in the past. In a short while they were joined by members of the ayuntamiento and other town leaders. The Nacogdoches militia was then consolidated with the militias organized in Ayish Bayou, Tenaha, Sabine District, and the Bevel

Settlement to form a "National Militia." Colonel James Whitis Bullock, a native of Georgia and veteran of the War of 1812, a member of the Ayish Bayou militia was chosen its commander.

In August the National Militia issued an ultimatum directed to Colonel Piedras giving him a last chance to join with them in assisting General Santa Anna in the revolution then progressing in Mexico. Piedras replied by asserting that he and his men would remain loyal to the Constitution and Laws of the legal government of his country.

Upon receiving the Mexican colonel's reply, the National Militia forces began advancing toward the town square in Nacogdoches. When they reached the edge of the town, the soldiers of the Twelfth Battalion opened fire and the Mexican cavalry was deployed. Some 100 of Colonel Whitis' men remained on the eastern side of town and engaged the Mexicans in hand to hand combat from house to house. This force ultimately captured the Stone House and other buildings on the square. Meanwhile a battle line formed on the north approach to the town and the remainder of the National Militia marched into town down North Street. Still later, on the advice of Adolphus Sterne, a portion of the militia forces circled the downtown area and approached from the west.

The Mexican forces were routed by the attacking forces, fleeing in the evening and night toward San Antonio on the Lower Douglas Road, camped at the Angelina River crossing. On the morning of August 3, 1832, the East Texans were surprised to learn that the town was theirs. Piedras was ultimately captured, agreed to all the conditions imposed on him, and was escorted to San Antonio.

The Battle of Nacogdoches is often referred to as the "Opening Gun of the Texas Revolution" because it cleared the eastern portion of Texas of all Mexican military forces which remained clear of them throughout the time of the Revolution permitting important meetings to be held from 1833 to 1836 in San Felipe and Washington-on-the-Brazos.

One of most enduring legends of Nacogdoches history is concerned with activities that grew out of the Battle of Nacogdoches. As the story is usually told, Colonel Piedras enlisted the services of blacksmith William Goyens, a "free man of color" as they were legally designated. Goyens, a native of North Carolina, immigrated to Texas in 1820 and soon became the principal craftsman in the Nacogdoches area. He was commissioned by the Mexican colonel to forge two large cans out of two large copper pots furnished by Piedras. When Goyens had finished the task, he was dismissed but told to return the following day. At that time, the colonel ordered him to seal the cans without looking inside to determine their contents.

Although Goyens did not examine the contents, he was convinced that one of them contained gold coins and the other jewels and valuables from the town's Catholic Church. When the lids had been soldered, Piedras ordered them buried west of town somewhere along the banks of Ysletta Creek. After the defeat of his forces and their subsequent withdrawal, he did not have an opportunity to retrieve the treasure. Treasure hunters have searched since that time, but have failed to locate the legendary treasure trove.

The Battle of Nacogdoches marked the end of Mexican rule in the town. Thereafter Nacogdoches grew steadily more Anglo-Texan in character. Two more Mexican alcaldes, José Ignacio Y'Barbo (1833-1834) and Vital Flores (1834-1835), were elected, but membership of the ayuntamiento was made up overwhelmingly of Anglo-American members.

A brief period of tranquility followed the Battle of Nacogdoches and the population of the Department quietly increased to the point that in 1835 there were more than 3,500 inhabitants. Nacogdoches remained, however, a frontier outpost populated, in some measure, by the rough and ready people usually found on the American frontier. Immigrants from the United States, especially the American South, continued to pass through Nacogdoches on their way to the interior. Many liked what they saw in the town or the surrounding rural areas and decided to stay. Among those deciding to remain, at least for a time, were Sam Houston and Thomas J. Rusk.

Turmoil in Anahuac over collection of customs duties and at Nacogdoches over a variety of issues in 1832 created tension throughout Texas. As a result, on August 22, 1832, the ayuntamiento of San Felipe issued a call for a convention to meet there in October. Fifty-eight delegates from sixteen districts attended, including Charles S. Taylor and Thomas Hastings representing the Nacogdoches district.

Taylor was a native of England who arrived in Nacogdoches in 1828 having made his way from New York to New Orleans before coming to Texas. He soon entered the mercantile business, first as a one-man enterprise but later in partnership with Charles H. Simms and later Adolphus Sterne. Hastings, a native of New York, came to Nacogdoches in the early 1820s and by 1826 was also engaged in the mercantile business in the town.

Convention delegates requested the federal government in Mexico City to repeal the ban on further Anglo-American immigration and separate Texas from Coahuila. Inexplicably these requests were never submitted to either the state or federal government.

In January of the following year a second convention was called to meet at San Felipe on April 1, 1833. Although Alcalde Y'Barbo attempted to prevent delegates being selected in Nacogdoches, at least three were chosen: Adolphus Sterne, Thomas Hastings, and Sam Houston.

A native of Virginia, Houston was a former governor of

Tennessee and veteran of General Andrew Jackson's campaign against Indians in the Old Southwest Territory where he distinguished himself as a young officer in the Battle of Horseshoe Bend (1814). Settling in Nacogdoches in 1832, he later became the dominant figure in Texas history in the years leading up to the Civil War.

The 1833 Convention delegates again requested repeal of the anti-immigration rule and separate statehood for Texas, but they also framed and approved a proposed state constitution for Texas. Houston was chairman of the committee that drafted this constitution for the projected Mexican state of Texas.

Relative calm settled over Texas following the Convention of 1833, but questionable land laws enacted by the state legislature, oppressive actions by Mexican President Santa Anna, Mexican determination to punish the men who had seized Anahuac in 1835 combined to revive sentiment for revolution. Responding to widespread demand for yet another meeting prompted the call for a Consultation to meet at San Felipe on October 15, 1835. Again over the opposition of the ayuntamiento, William Whitaker, Sam Houston, Daniel Parker, James W. Robinson, and Nathaniel Robins were chosen to represent Nacogdoches.

Whitaker came to Nacogdoches from Louisiana in 1820 and soon established himself as a prosperous area farmer. Parker, a native of Virginia, came to Texas in 1832 with the intention of organizing a Baptist church. Robinson, a lawyer by profession, was a native of Indiana who came to Texas from Arkansas in 1833 and served as lieutenant governor after the creation of the 1835 provisional government of Texas. Robins also came to Texas from Arkansas about 1826 and established a ferry across the Trinity River.

The 1835 Consultation stopped short of a declaration of independence, but it did establish a provisional government for

Texas, provided for the creation of an army, elected Sam Houston its commander in chief, and dispatched Stephen F. Austin to the United States to secure support for the Texian's cause. The Consultation adjourned November 14, 1835, to reassemble March 1, 1836 at Washington-on-the Brazos.

Meanwhile, by October 1835 a contingent of troops under the command of George M. Collingsworth had captured Goliad, S. F. Austin's forces had driven the Mexican contingent into San Antonio de Bexar and placed the old provincial capital under siege. The siege continued for some six weeks, during which time an engagement between a contingent of Mexican cavalry and members of the Texian Army ended in a Mexican defeat. After Austin was dispatched to the United States to secure aid for the revolutionary forces, Colonel Edward Burleson was chosen as the Texian commander.

At last, in early December the Texian volunteers stormed the city which was then defended by more than 1,500 Mexican troops. Following some four or five days of battle, General Martín P. Cos surrendered and agreed to take his soldiers beyond the Rio Grande. Thus, Texas, for a time at least, was free of Mexican military forces.

Throughout these troubled times Anglo-Americans continued to enter Texas through the Nacogdoches "gateway." One of these immigrants, who passed through in 1834, recorded his impressions of the frontier outpost. He observed that the original Spanish settlers had built homes known as *jacales*. These log and mud shacks, he recalled, looked old and woe begone. The Americans who arrived later, he reported, had built a number of elegant framed houses, well furnished and painted white. These he observed were scattered along and among the ancient log and mud "hovels."

CHAPTER FOUR
THE REPUBLIC

In early 1836, on the eve of the Texas Revolution, two European visitors penned descriptions of Nacogdoches. A German immigrant related that the town lay in a basin-shaped valley formed by surrounding low hills. It was bounded on its west, south, and east sides by two running streams and surrounded by beautiful woods. Prior to the Revolution, he reported, many Mexicans had lived there, but most of them had moved westward. Those that stayed behind were looked upon with distrust by the dominant majority of Anglo-Texans who regarded them as thinly disguised enemies.

About the same time, a distinguished visitor from Virginia recorded similar impressions. He observed that the town was situated on a sandy plain between two fine clear streams, each of them of sufficient fall for mills or machinery and with sufficient depth for a large canal. He was impressed as well by the several mounds on the north side of the town, where the Roman Catholic (or Mexican) burial ground was located, but noted that the cemetery for Protestants (or Anglo-Americans) was located several hundred yards from it on the east side of the town.

He described the buildings of the town with a few exceptions as miserable, shabby, old Mexican jacales, constructed by inserting pickets in the ground, fastening them at the top with a plate, and daubing the interstices with red mud. Some others were built of logs covered with clap-boards with chimneys of red mud. As for the residents of the town, he noted that there were a good number of Anglo-American families intermixed with the Spanish-surnamed families; but that much "ill blood" existed between them and among the Anglo-Americans as well.

As unrest escalated during the winter of 1835-1836, San

Antonio was besieged by a Texian force. This Siege of Bexar in October 1835 resulted in the capture of the city and the surrender of its garrison. Thereafter in early 1836, the Battle of the Alamo, the Goliad massacre, and the Matamoros Expedition, each ending in tragedy for the Texians, were accompanied by a proclamation by President Santa Anna announcing a full-scale invasion of Texas.

In this environment, the Convention of 1836 met in March at Washington-on-the-Brazos. A Declaration of Independence from Mexico was drafted and adopted March 2 with the four delegates from Nacogdoches: Thomas J. Rusk, Charles S. Taylor, John S. Roberts, and Robert Potter, voting for it and affixing their signatures. Thereafter, the delegates proceeded to draft a proposed constitution for the newly-proclaimed Republic of Texas.

All of the Nacogdoches delegates were relative newcomers to Texas. Rusk and Potter had arrived in 1835 and Taylor in 1828. Roberts, a veteran of the Fredonian Rebellion, had arrived in 1826. Three of them preformed important services for the temporary governing body and later for the Republic. Rusk was named secretary of war, participated in the Battle of San Jacinto that brought the revolution to a successful conclusion, served as a brigadier general in command of the Texas army, was a member of the Congress of the Republic, and was elected chief justice of the Texas Supreme Court.

Potter was chosen interim Secretary of the Texas Navy, commander of the Port of Galveston, and member of Congress. Taylor served as chief justice of Nacogdoches County and as county treasurer. Roberts, on the other hand, returned to Nacogdoches and reentered the mercantile business.

Even the threat of impending warfare did not appreciably stem the flow of immigrants from the United States. During 1835, for example, 822 Entrance Certificates were issued at Nacogdoches. Within a period of two months that year at least forty-five of those immigrants settled in Nacogdoches.

On the eve of the revolution, during the winter and spring of 1835-1836, volunteers continuously poured through Nacogdoches on their way to fight for Texas independence. Coming, as they did, from the United States and from other areas of East Texas, their numbers severely taxed the limited resources of the town. Most of the men who enlisted in Nacogdoches were from the American south, with the largest number of them from Tennessee, although some hailed from Pennsylvania, New York, and New Jersey.

On March 6, 1836, a company of Nacogdoches volunteers was organized under the command of Captain Hayden S. Arnold. This unit, the First Company, 2nd Regiment of Texas Volunteers, participated in the Battle of San Jacinto on April 21 and were disbanded June 6 at Goliad by Thomas J. Rusk. Arnold, a native of Tennessee, came to Texas in December 1835 in time to take part in the Revolution and later serve as a member of the Congress of the Republic.

Some individuals have claimed that Nacogdoches financed the Texas Revolution. Its citizens raised funds to purchase guns, contributed money and horses, and subscribed to generous loans to the revolutionary government. One citizen, Adolphus Sterne, pledged to purchase fifty rifles for the first fifty volunteers. They were claimed by Captain Thomas H. Breece's company, the New Orleans Greys.

A young German immigrant who was a member of the New Orleans Greys recalled vividly the type of treatment that awaited volunteers passing through Nacogdoches. When the Greys arrived in Nacogdoches after darkness had settled on the town, they knocked on Sterne's door and found a hot meal of roast beef, venison, and other game awaiting them. After dinner, they shared four bottles of Rhine wine; then proceeded to visit the Mexican coffee house. There he was astonished to see a crowd of men, women, and young girls, all smoking cigars, others gambling in a smoke filled room, and still others watching two Mexican entertainers perform.

Before the New Orleans company left, the townspeople treated them to a feast. A 150-foot board table was spread with food of every description, including a large black bear with the flag of the Mexican Constitution of 1824 in its teeth. The next day they received horses and supplies to send them on their way to the Siege of Bexar and death for many of them at the Alamo and Goliad.

As the Revolution progressed and the Texians suffered defeat and massacre the troops of Santa Anna continued to march steadily toward the east while those of General Sam Houston retreated relentlessly eastward ahead of them, causing residents of central and western portions of the Republic to flee in panic eastward toward the Sabine River and safety in the United States. Known in Texas history as the "Runaway Scrape," this steady desertion virtually depopulated its eastern section.

As news of the victory at San Jacinto reached them, many of those who had fled gradually returned to their homes and resumed their lives as citizens of Texas. Nacogdoches had served as one of the principal staging points for those who came to Texas to assist in the Revolution and for those fleeing and returning before and after San Jacinto.

The County

As soon as peace was proclaimed, one of the first actions of the Congress of the Republic of Texas was to divide the territory of the nation into a series of counties. In this they were following the pattern of local government in vogue throughout all of the American south. The Mexican municipalities of Liberty, Jefferson, Jasper, Sabine, Shelby, and San Augustine, each included in the old Department of Nacogdoches were established as original counties of the Republic. The County of Nacogdoches was reduced to the remainder of the area east of the Trinity. In time at least twenty additional counties would be created in whole or in part from the original area of Nacogdoches County.

Each county was governed by a county court presided over by a chief justice elected by the Congress of the Republic and two justices of the peace elected by the qualified voters of two of the precincts into which the county was divided by the commissioners court. The first Chief Justice of Nacogdoches County was Charles S. Taylor (1836-1839). He was followed by William Hart (1839-1843) who earlier had been a Justice of the Peace (1838-1839). Hart was one of Anglo-Americans who entered Texas after the Revolution. The third and last Chief Justice was William Wilson Wingfield (1843-1846), a native of Virginia who had also immigrated to East Texas after the Revolution.

The three members of the county court, chief justice and two justices of the peace acted as the governing body for the county. As such, they were responsible for the "superintendence and control of the public roads, bridges, and ferries and for the care of the indigent, lame, blind, and poor persons who were unable to support themselves." In 1845, Congress changed this arrangement by creating a commissioners court composed of four commissioners and the chief justice, all elected for two-year terms. At least two of the original four commissioners were William C. Graham and David Muckleroy. Graham and Muckleroy both immigrated in 1837. The latter would go on to participate in the Mexican War and to serve in the Texas State Legislature.

Bartlett H. Simpson (1837-1839), Thomas D. Brooks (1837-1839), Elijah Gossett (1837), William H. McDonald (1837-1839), John Grigsby (1837), and William Simms (1837) were the original Justices of the Peace. Each of these men, except McDonald, about whom little is known, had been born in one of the southern states and arrived in Texas between 1834 and 1839. Two of them were veterans of the Texas Revolution, one, Brooks, having fought at San Jacinto.

Other county officers required by the Constitution of 1836 were a sheriff, a coroner, and a convenient number of constables each elected for two-year terms by the area's qualified voters. David Rusk (1837-1846) was the first and only sheriff of Nacogdoches County during the time of the Republic. David, a brother of Thomas J. Rusk, came to Texas from Georgia in 1836. He was a veteran of the Texas Revolution and took part in the Battle of San Jacinto as a member of Captain Hayden S. Arnold's company of volunteers.

Other remarkable individuals among the more than thirty who served as sheriff of Nacogdoches County since David Rusk's tenure, include R. D. (Dick) Orton (1867-1873), who had the near impossible task of maintaining law and order during the reconstruction period and who in 1880-1881 was again elected. Captain Milton Mast (1873-1880), who followed Orton gained notoriety when he captured the infamous outlaw Bill Longley.

Sheriff Orton chose Andrew Jackson (John) Spradley as his chief deputy during his second time in office. Spradley retained this office until 1882 when he was appointed sheriff to fill the unexpired term of John Orton who resigned. He was defeated in 1884 by his brother J. M. (Matt) Spradley but was returned in office in 1898 to serve until 1914. Spradley gained a reputation as an astute detective and often assisted other officers in solving difficult crimes throughout East Texas.

In 1954, following the death of her husband, Walter Ernest McClain, while in office, Arminda M. Jones McClain was appointed Sheriff to fill out the remainder of his term, thus becoming the only female sheriff in the history of the county.

John Lightfoot, first elected in 1960, achieved the distinction of serving the longest consecutive period of time (over twenty years). William P. Chissum, William Caldwell, and Lemuel B. Brown filled the office of coroner during the time of the Republic. Men who were elected constable included Edward Fitzgerald, John Ford, A. C. Graham, E. E. Hamilton, J. G. Parker, and A. Waters.

To serve as their representatives in the First Congress of the Republic of Texas, the voters of the Nacogdoches District chose Robert Anderson Irion as their Senator, and the voters of Nacogdoches County chose John Kirby Allen, Hayden S. Arnold, and Haden Harrison Edwards as their first three Representatives. Irion, a pioneer physician, was born in Tennessee and practiced in Mississippi before coming to Texas in 1832. He later served as Secretary of State (1837-1838) of the Republic then resumed the practice of medicine in Nacogdoches.

Allen came to Texas from New York with his brother Augustus C. in 1832 where they became very successful real estate dealers. In 1836, after participating in the Texas Revolution, John K. with his brother Augustus C. founded the City of Houston on Buffalo Bayou. Haden H. Edwards was the son of Haden Edwards, the empresario. A Virginian, he came to Texas in 1825 with his father and later took part in the Siege of Bexar and in several Indian campaigns.

Nacogdoches experienced a period of untroubled calm as new national and local governments were organized and began to function; but that condition was not destined to endure for more than two years. Most citizens of Mexico did not recognize the independence of Texas, considering the defeat at San Jacinto as a temporary loss, and her leaders continued to make plans to reclaim the errant province. However, foreign affairs, including war with France, kept the Mexican government from taking action in the years immediately following San Jacinto.

In addition, a significant number of Mexican nationals living in Texas were dissatisfied with the outcome of the revolution and resented having to become citizens of the predominantly Anglo-American Republic of Texas. The principal one of those persons in Nacogdoches was Vicente Cordova. He was a resident of Nacogdoches as early as 1826 when he was active in local affairs. He later participated in the Battle of Nacogdoches, served as the town's alcalde, regidor, and primary judge.

Cordova was an outspoken opponent of the movement for Texas independence who, in 1836, made an effort to recruit volunteers from the Nacogdoches area to resist the Texians' bid for separation from Mexico. Failing that, in the summer of 1838, organized a group of dissatisfied Mexicans and their Indian allies to recapture Texas for the Mexican nation. Cordova gathered his forces together at a camp near the Angelina River. Reports that the local Mexicans had taken up arms reached the town in late summer.

The preacher and congregation of a small rural church came into Nacogdoches to notify authorities that the rebel force had gathered, and soon thereafter a party of the town's citizens searching for stolen horses also discovered and reported the assembled force. John Durst and a party of scouts were dispatched by General Thomas J. Rusk to locate Cordova's men. The scouting party discovered them camped across the Angelina River in present-day Cherokee County.

Rusk issued a call for volunteers to suppress the uprising. Approximately 1,000 men responded to the call. Ultimately General Rusk and his forces defeated Cordova's Indian allies in a battle fought in present-day Anderson County. Meanwhile, Cordova and his forces camped on the upper Trinity River. On assurance of Mexican support, Cordova broke camp in March

1839 and marched toward Mexico.

March 28, 1839, reports reached Colonel Edward Burleson that the rebels were located near Mill Creek in Guadalupe County five miles from the town of Seguin. The Texans attacked killing approximately thirty, wounding Cordova, and ending the uprising. Some of the rebelling Mexicans returned to the Nacogdoches area; where a few were tried for treason but only one convicted. Some, however, forfeited their land and other property. Antonio Menchaca who was convicted and sentenced to be hanged was pardoned by President Mirabeau B. Lamar before the sentence was carried out.

The Cordova Rebellion, coupled with President Lamar's hostility toward Indians living in the Republic, brought about a permanent settlement of the East Texas Indian problem. A treaty negotiated by Sam Houston and John Forbes in 1836 granted the Cherokee Indians and their associated tribes in East Texas land northwest of the old San Antonio Road between the Angelina and Sabine Rivers. Nevertheless, in 1839, soon after President Lamar took office, he abrogated the treaty and determined to drive the Indians from the Republic.

When the Cherokees were ordered to abandon their lands and depart, they decided to fight rather than surrender. In July two regiments of regular army troops and volunteers attacked and after a bloody engagement in present-day Smith County the Indians were defeated and driven into Arkansas. Nacogdoches never again experienced a threat of Indian attack.

Separation from Mexico and creation of the Republic did not bring the problem of smuggling to an end in East Texas. The people of this area continued to oppose any and all tariff levies. The only custom house of the Republic in the region was located at San Augustine, although a clerk was stationed in Nacogdoches. As a result goods were freely imported elsewhere without duties having been paid; but merchants in Nacogdoches were forced to pay the tariffs. They continued throughout the life of the Republic to plead for repeal of the duties but to no avail.

The permanent population of Nacogdoches and the entire East Texas region in the days of the Republic was made up predominately of Anglo-Americans who had never lost their sense of kinship with the people of the United States. Therefore, when talk of annexation arose, they were strongly in favor of the idea of Texas as yet another American state.

The more affluent people of the Nacogdoches area were interested in education for their children, particularly for their sons. They were rewarded in 1845, when the Congress of the Republic chartered Nacogdoches University. Its twenty-year charter required the institution to be open on a equal basis for the education of children of persons of all classes, without regard to their religious beliefs. In addition, the charter mandated that "no religious, sectarian, or other doctrines" were to be taught. The four leagues of land granted to the city by the State of Coahuila y Tejas in 1833 were transferred to the new university; all property of the institution was exempt from taxation for five years; and permission was granted for the addition of departments of law and medicine if circumstances warranted. Gilbert M. L. Smith was appointed the school's first principal, and his wife, Mary Smith, was named an instructor and Miss Mary White designated as the drawing and printing teacher. Sixty males and forty-three females enrolled in the first school term.

The University was governed by a fifteen-member board of trustees. Among the prominent townsmen who served on the Board were Bennett Blake, Charles S. Taylor, Thomas J. Rusk, James Harper Starr, and Frost Thorn. Blake was a native of Vermont who settled in Nacogdoches in 1835 and subsequently served as justice of the peace. He would later become a leading merchant and private banker in the community. Starr, a Connecticut native, was trained as a physician; but after coming to East Texas in 1837, he became involved in land matters, serving as the presiding officer of the Board of Land Commissioners for Nacogdoches. In 1839, President Lamar appointed him Secretary of the Treasury, an office he held for about a year. Thereafter, he became a successful land agent. Thorn was a native New Yorker who came to Nacogdoches in 1824 with Barr and Davenport, and in 1835 he was awarded an empresario contract by the Mexican government. Thereafter, he acquired land holding amounting to thousands of acres, operated at general store in Nacogdoches with partner Haden Edwards, owned a salt mine, and a lumber business. He accumulated a fortune that made him the richest man in East Texas.

 Private subscriptions given by local persons supplemented the land grant, and the University opened its doors in September 1845 in the old Red House just southwest of the Plaza Principal. After seven years at that location, it was housed in a building just across the street for another three years. In 1855 the university was moved some three blocks north to Temperance Hall on Hospital Street where it remained until 1859 when it occupied a Grecian-style red brick structure on Washington Square.

 In May 1855, Haden Edwards, James R. Arnold, and Charles S. Taylor presented William Clark, then Mayor of Nacogdoches, title to 21.5 acres north of the downtown area to be used as a site for a school. Designated Washington Square, in 1859, it became the location of Nacogdoches University. The Civil War disrupted classes, and during the early war years the building was used by local women to teach classes for little children. For at least two of the war years, it was also utilized as a hospital and headquarters for Confederate soldiers and in the immediate post-war period was the headquarters for Union soldiers stationed in the town.

 From 1870 to 1873, Sisters of Notre Dame of the Convent of the Agonizing Heart of Jesus operated a school in the building.

The City of Nacogdoches had invited the nuns to reopen the university, and invitation accepted their convent was moved to Nacogdoches. In 1874, however, the convent was moved to Clarksville; but one of the nuns, Sister Josephine Potard, chose to remain among the Spanish-speaking people of Nacogdoches. Thereafter, from 1874 to 1878, she taught classes in one room of the building, but in 1878, she purchased a house and lot on South Street where for two more years she continued her classes. Finally, in 1880, she left Nacogdoches, moved to the Moral Community west of the town where she cared for the Spanish-speaking Catholics of the area for the next thirteen years.

The university's 1845 charter continued in force twenty-five years, was renewed in 1870, and in 1873 leased to the Masonic Lodge for operation as the Masonic Institute for the following fourteen years. In 1887, it was leased to Keachi College of Keachi, Louisiana. The renewed charter expired in 1895, and in 1904, the building and grounds were deeded to the Nacogdoches School District to be used for "educational purposes only and for white children only."

The economy of the county was based on cotton and slavery. Most of the 197 slave owners in the county owned only one or two, but at least twenty owned ten or more. In 1840, John Durst with thirty-nine was the largest slave-owner in the county. It was, thus, rapidly coming to resemble the typical rural community of the American South.

The City

For the period from the end of the revolution to June 5, 1837, in Nacogdoches the Mexican scheme of municipal government headed by the alcalde and the ayuntamiento attempted to provide a measure of management and ensure that normal operations continued. An 1837 act passed by the First

Congress and signed by President Houston officially incorporated the City of Nacogdoches. The statute called for a government consisting of a mayor, a board of eight aldermen, a treasurer, a secretary, a tax collector, and a constable. It also mandated that all city officials be citizens of the Republic and owners of real estate within its limits. It further required all residents of the town to keep hooks, ladders, and buckets ready in case of fire.

In the election held after this 1837 statute was enacted, Thomas J. Rusk was chosen as the city's first mayor, while Henry Raguet, C. H. Sims, John S. Roberts, Frost Thorn, Kelsey H. Douglass, James H. Starr, and Adolphus Sterne were among the first aldermen selected. This slate reads like an honor roll of the town's leading citizens.

A clergyman from Ohio visited the city December 31, 1841, where he discovered a large crowd assembled to attend a funeral and to witness the trial of a man charged with committing murder a few days earlier. The town, he recalled, contained about 300-400 people living together in a mixture of Spanish and American houses situated on a plain of white sand between two small creeks. The precise population of the town and of the county at this time cannot be determined because no census was taken between the last Mexican count in 1835 and a state census conducted in 1847.

The city streets were initially surveyed about 1840 by Captain A. A. Nelson and names given each of them. The south side of town along Pilar Street to the east was the most popular location for residences at this time. Along West Pilar only a few buildings could be found from the square to Banita Creek. At that time evidence indicates that the old Spanish Camino Real ran down Pilar Street and went on westward around the south side of Irion hill which was then too steep for ascent. The area now occupied by the train depot was surrounded by dense woods and thickets of briars. The boys of the old town had "swimming holes" all along this stretch of Banita Creek as well as others in La Nana Creek on the town's eastern side.

What in later days became known as North Street was then the Henderson Road. It started from the northwest corner of the public square running along present-day Pecan Street, crossing modern Hospital Street, then out into open fields. Some of the community's leading citizens had homes among this road, including Judge William Hart, Thomas J. Rusk, and George M. Adams.

Throughout the life of the Republic (1836-1846) the town continued to be a "gateway" for the steady stream of Anglo-Americans crossing the Sabine River headed for the interior of the new nation. It also was a market town, serving both the local inhabitants of the area and the immigrants who passed down the King's Highway.

From 1821 to the eve of statehood for Texas, life in Nacogdoches resembled that of many frontier southern communities. The principal staples of diet were corn, (flour could rarely be had at any price), and a wide variety of meats, including domesticated animals such as cattle, oxen, goats, hogs, and sheep and wild game of many varieties, such as deer, bear, raccoon, opossum, squirrel, turkey, and duck. Moreover, an abundance of fresh vegetables, such as peas, beans, squash, pumpkins, and potatoes were grown in local garden patches.

Residents could obtain wild peaches, blackberries, persimmons, pomegranates, and melons in the forests surrounding the city. They could also harvest nuts, including walnuts, hickory nuts, and pecans in the nearby woods.

In the 1820's mercantile stores opened that stocked imported goods from Natchitoches, New Orleans, San Antonio, and the interior of Mexico. These stores made hardware and fancy foodstuffs available by 1830. Travelers and well as permanent residents praised the water to be found in

Nacogdoches. Residents also drank quantities of milk, corn wine, coffee, and whiskey. Tradition has it that Nacogdochians cherished their whiskey as a means to help them relax and their coffee to keep them awake.

Clothing for residents often presented a problem. An observer commented in 1830 that apparel ranged from virtual nudity to genteel costume. Because the area was peopled by a variety of ethnic groups and social classes, their dress reflected the tastes and styles of Indians, French, and Anglo-Americans. Dress for the majority of the residents was often of the plainest sort, buckskin was a common sight as were homespun linen shirts.

Spanish architecture naturally dominated the structures erected in Nacogdoches during the formative years. The majority of family dwellings were <u>jacales</u> formed by driving pickets or stakes into the ground and fastening them on top by a plate which supported a simple gabled shingle roof. Spaces between the pickets were plastered with the local red clay and then roof line extended to protect them against the rain. Often these plastered walls were covered by an outer layer of stone or adobe. Since most were small, they contained only one door and probably no windows. There were rarely any partitions or innerwalls. This type of housing constituted the norm until the 1820's.

Some stone buildings were constructed in Spanish Nacogdoches but they were rare. Since there was little or no surface stone, rock had to be quarried along the banks of La Nana and Banita Creeks. The Stone House built by Gil Y'Barbo is the best known of these structures. It was a simple two-story building with a two-story porch covered by a transverse gable roof.

Before 1820 the size, style, and proximity to the town square of residences were dictated by the prominence and wealth of their owners. Probably the largest dwelling in town was the six room structure erected by the Zaccatectan priests. Wealthier residents had the luxury of a water well and a patio within the walls of their home.

After 1820 architectural patterns in the town came to resemble those that had evolved in the American South modified slightly to fit local conditions. Basically, a house was constructed of rough or adzed logs fitted together into a rectangle by means of dovetail or rabbeted joints. They were chinked with mud, clay, and moss to help make them watertight. They generally faced either north or south to take advantage of the prevailing winds. Covered almost always by a simple gabled roof, many had porches producing a double-angled roof line.

At the same time, the more affluent members of the community such as Adolphus Sterne and John S. Roberts built frame houses with mitered timber frames and flushing in walls with clapboards. Colonel Piedras had an unusual framed house constructed on Pilar Street between present-day Pecan and North Streets near the site of the old Catholic Church and cemetery. It combined the palisade with frame construction. Its lumber was purchased from Peter Ellis Bean's saw mill. It was framed with large vertical beams, and then thin laths of wood were tacked over the framing and plastered with adobe. Its walls were protected by large roof eaves on all sides, enabling the house to survive until the 1890s when its was torn down. The adobe used to plaster the walls was made from the red soil of Nacogdoches, causing the structure to be called "The Red House."

Throughout most, if not all, of the period of the Republic the Nacogdoches community continued to grow and prosper, and it seemed destined to retain its ranking as one of the major cities of Texas. However, worsening economic conditions in the Republic and in the United States combined with increasing geographic isolation were instrumental in radically altering that pattern of evolution.

CHAPTER FIVE
THE STATE

After almost a decade of procrastination, the Congress of the United States passed a joint resolution offering annexation as an American state to the Republic of Texas. European nations such as France, Germany, and England attempted to forestall this merger along with the Republic of Mexico, but popular sentiment in the Republic and in the United States in favor of annexation forced Presidents John Tyler and Anson Jones to take action.

Without waiting for authorization from the Congress of the Republic, President Jones called for the election of delegates to a convention to draft a proposed constitution for Texas as an American state. Congress later met, voted to accept the offer of annexation, and approved the call for the election of delegates. In that election, held July 4, 1845, Thomas J. Rusk, Joseph L. Hogg, and Charles S. Taylor where chosen to represent Nacogdoches County in the convention. Rusk was unanimously elected to serve as president of the convention.

Joseph Lewis Hogg, father of Governor Jim Hogg, was a native of Georgia who came to Texas from Alabama in 1839. He was elected to the Texas House of Representatives in 1843 and to the Senate after annexation. He later became a veteran of both the Mexican War and the Civil War.

After a session of fifty-six days, the Convention of 1845 drafted a constitution and issued a proclamation calling for all the counties of Texas to hold an election to vote on the question of annexation and adoption of the proposed state constitution. By an overwhelming margin, voters approved both propositions, and President Jones immediately called for an election to chose new state and national officials.

Whereupon Isaac Parker of Houston County and Joseph

L. Hogg of Nacogdoches County were elected as state senators from District 4, composed of Nacogdoches and Houston Counties. John Brown, Haden H. Edwards, and David Muckleroy were chosen to represent Nacogdoches County in the lower house of the state legislature. Along with their colleagues in both houses, they chose Thomas J. Rusk and Sam Houston as the state's first U.S. Senators. Two other citizens of Nacogdoches filled positions of importance. William Beck Ochiltree became the first judge of the Sixth Judicial District and Richard S. Walker its district attorney.

The Marketplace

While much of Texas experienced boom times in the years between annexation and the outbreak of civil strife in 1861, Nacogdoches did not share in that prosperity. Rather rapidly its earlier growth periods were demonstrated as by products of the unusual conditions brought about by Spanish and Mexican regulations that made it a major entry point for persons coming to Texas. When those regulations were no longer in force, the isolation of a town located in the forests of East Texas soon revealed that it could not retain its importance as a market center for the entire region.

Its principal flaw was that it no longer lay on a well-traveled transportation route. The old San Antonio Road, once its main link with areas east and west, had deteriorated into near impassable conditions during much of the year. It had no waterway, the closest even the smallest steamboats could occasionally come was Patonia, sixteen miles away on the Angelina River near the mouth of Dorr Creek in Nacogdoches County.

From 1844 to 1883, steamboats were a principal means of transporting cotton produced in the area to ports on the Gulf of

Mexico and bringing back goods for the people of Nacogdoches and the surrounding communities. The river was navigable for only six to nine months in wet years, in dry years often less than six. Annexation also opened the Gulf Coast to trade and prompted both settlers and businessmen to select places such as Galveston and Houston rather than inland towns and villages.

A nineteenth century historian of the Nacogdoches community lamented that for some fifty years before statehood the old town had been the scene of much business activity, furnishing supplies and merchandise to a variety of permanent settlers and transient immigrants. But, he explained, as years passed developments in transportation--railroads, steamboats, and ships--routed people around and beyond Nacogdoches and thereby stripped her of her strength by taking away the advantages of her geographic location along the main road to Texas.

As a result, Nacogdoches gradually became a sleepy backwoods county-seat town not unlike thousands of such places throughout the rural South. A Norwegian immigrant, visiting in 1845, praised the town for the manner in which it cared for the poor and needy. She reported that no poor relief was needed in the town and that no beggars were seen because anyone who wanted to work could earn a living and those really in need received ample assistance without begging for it.

She also praised the freedom and equality she found in social relationships and public matters. Presumably she chose to ignore the obvious differences between the free white people and the submerged black slaves and the more subtle distinctions between Anglos and Hispanics.

The fundamental honesty of the people of the town also impressed her. Thievery, she asserted, was despised and rarely practiced. Houses seldom had locks on doors, some not even doors. Residents left their residences unlocked both day and night and often left things out on the sidewalks without fear of loss.

A state census taken in 1847 shortly after annexation revealed that Nacogdoches County had a population of 4,172 persons, of whom 1,228 were slaves and an additional twenty-seven were "free persons of color." Among the latter was William Goyens, who at his death in 1856 owned some 12,432 acres of land in Nacogdoches, Angelina, and Houston Counties and six slaves. John J. Hayter, newcomer from Madison County, Alabama, owned the most slaves with sixty-four, followed by John Tomlinson, who claimed twenty-five.

The county then contained four villages or towns large enough to have post offices: Nacogdoches, Douglass, Melrose, and Flournoy. Nacogdoches with 402 residents, 299 white and 103 slaves, was the largest of these. The county's population was clearly predominantly rural and would remain rural for many decades to come.

A visitor passing through the town at this time recalled that Nacogdoches presented an agreeable appearance. The people, she maintained, were refined and intelligent, much like those she was accustomed to meeting in the older states of the South. She reported a good number of professional men, merchants, and mechanics. A school was in operation and there was evidence of some organized religion.

At about this time, John S. Roberts moved his mercantile business into the Stone House, opened a grocery and saloon that he continued to operate for more than twenty years. His wife, Harriet Fenley Callier Roberts, had begun acquiring ownership of the Stone House in 1842, when she purchased one-half interest in the building from Juan Mora and his wife Maria Carmel Y'Barbo. After having passed through the ownership of a number of Nacogdoches residents, by 1846 Rebecca Danzey Fenley, sister-in-law of Harriet, secured the remaining half interest. She, in turn, sold her portion to Harriet.

Saloon-keeper Roberts and his Old Stone Fort Saloon became well-known local attractions. Roberts shrewdly traded on his reputation and the mysterious quality of the old stone building to attract his clientele. One of his contemporaries recalled that the saloon-keeper commissioned an itinerant painter to paint a sign for the front elevation of the building. The sign attracted attention from all who passed by. It boldly, if inaccurately, proclaimed "Old Stone Fort. Erected A. D. 1619," possibly endowing the structure with the name by which it is known today.

The first legislative session following annexation created a sizeable number of new counties. As a result, in 1846, Nacogdoches county was reduced to the area included in its contemporary boundaries. In addition, in 1848, the City of Nacogdoches was again incorporated and two years later its corporate limits were reduced to include only the territory within a one-mile square with its center at the county courthouse.

In 1837, the Stone House served as the first courthouse for Nacogdoches to be succeeded by a building located on the corner of North and Hospital Streets originally built to house a church. This second courthouse was utilized from 1840 to 1847 when it was sold to the county and moved to the center of the Plaza Principal in the center of downtown. It was a two-story square wood frame structure facing north. The main door had a platform landing on the outside with steps leading to it on the east and west.

By 1850 most townspeople were aware that this building was in such disrepair that inclement weather would force the court to adjourn. Thereafter, enough repairs were made that wind and rain were kept out, but since the building had no stove or fireplace, in cold weather the court was forced to move to warm quarters. Despite the need for a new courthouse, when the county commissioners court determined to build a new building on the square, Mayor A. A. Nelson and the Board of Aldermen protested vigorously supported by citizens of the town who did not want to sacrifice their public square for such a purpose. Instead, they wished to have it utilized as a hitch lot and community water well.

In 1856, however, fate took a hand in the matter. That year a huge fire destroyed every building on the west side of the square. Fearing such a fate for the dilapidated frame courthouse, city fathers decided something must be done. A third courthouse was erected fronting on the south side of the square near the middle of the block. Built at a cost of $12,000, it was an imposing two-story brick building with a gable front and an extended roof supported by large columns. The lower floor contained five large rooms, a stairway, and a hall running the full length of the building. The upper floor housed the courtroom and district clerk's office. This courthouse was destined to serve for more than fifty years as the seat of Nacogdoches County government.

Another outgrowth of annexation was the Mexican War (1846-1848). A company of Nacogdoches men commanded by Captain James R. Arnold volunteered for service. They joined General Zachary Taylor's army then camped near Corpus Christi. Before hostilities were over, Arnold's company of East Texans participated in two major battles: Monterrey and Buena Vista. A second company was organized and recruited in East Texas. With David Muckleroy as its captain, it was mustered in the U.S. Army in San Antonio.

While a war was being fought and a new city government was being inaugurated, other significant developments were taking place within the old town. Street repair, cemetery upkeep and improvement, digging of drainage ditches, purchase of fire-fighting equipment, bridge repair, and filling of dangerous pits and abandoned wells were undertaken by the city authorities. Footlogs across Banita and La Nana Creeks were provided, while Pilar, Hospital, North, and Main Streets were extended.

City expenses, including civic improvements, were financed by a $1.00 poll tax and an ad valorem property tax that ranged from ten to twenty cents for $100 of value. Excises were levied on merchants, places of entertainment, billiard tables, bowling alleys, liquor, shows, circuses, and public exhibitions of slight of hand.

Throughout the decade of the 1850s new buildings were constructed and existing ones repaired and refurbished. Business was brisk and rent property hard to come by. Parties and balls furnished entertainment for the socially elite, and the local taverns provided meeting places for many of the men of the town.

Townspeople were proud of their university, and these were the years of its greatest prosperity. The outbreak of war in 1861 caused the institution to close its doors, and it never recovered from the adverse effects of the war. In addition to the university, public and private schools were in operation in Nacogdoches, Chireno, and Douglass. In 1861 the Female College was erected as an adjunct to the Nacogdoches University. This structure was a very large, two story frame building built by the Whitkorn architect and contracting firm. It was located on Church Street. The lower story was divided into a number of study and recitation rooms, while the second story was an auditorium used for gatherings of all kinds and occasionally for dances. During the holiday season of 1868 the Female College was destroyed by fire. Fortunately there were no students in residence since it was a time of vacation.

In the years leading up to the bitter years of Civil War, Nacogdoches remained predominantly Roman Catholic in religion, although several Protestant denominations--Anabaptist, Baptist, Presbyterian, Methodist, and Episcopal--began encroaching as early as 1830. A new Cathodic Church was completed in 1847 and ordained priests continuously pastored it until 1876. William Biddle first preached Anabaptist sermons in

1828 in the Tenehaw District on the eastern fringe of the Nacogdoches District.

By 1832 Mrs. Massie Millard was holding Baptist devotions for her family and neighbors at her home in Nacogdoches, and two years later Isaac Reed, a Baptist preacher from Tennessee, began preaching from house to house in Nacogdoches. In 1834, he began holding open meetings in an oak grove north of town. There in 1838 the Union Baptist Church, now known as the old North Church was organized. Also in 1834, Mrs. Annette Lea Bledsoe from Alabama organized a Baptist Sunday School in Nacogdoches.

Z. N. Morrell, a Baptist evangelist from Tennessee, on January 10, 1836, preached the first public Baptist sermon, probably the first public sermon, delivered in the City of Nacogdoches when he found a large crowd gathered for an election. The credit for organizing the first Protestant church in town goes, however, to the Methodists. On October 16, 1837, Littleton Fowler and John B. Denton preached two sermons there, and Denton was granted permission to hold services in the Masonic Lodge hall.

The Episcopalians were the next denomination to arrive in Nacogdoches. Mrs. James Pinckney Henderson, wife of the first governor of the State of Texas, persuaded the denomination's General Conference to send a clergyman to her home town, San Augustine, and to Nacogdoches as well. Reverend Henry Sanson arrived in April 1848 to fill both pulpits. Despite these eager beginnings, until the close of the Reconstruction period some thirty years later Nacogdoches was still regarded as the Catholic center for East Texas.

Until the post Civil War period the city remained a stopover on the Old San Antonio Road. Stage lines traveling between the traditional route from East to Central Texas, from East Texas to Western Louisiana, and from East Texas to

Washington-on-the-Brazos had their headquarters in Nacogdoches. Without a railroad until well after the end of Reconstruction, Nacogdoches County residents relied on wagons for hauling goods to and from market. For example, cotton, the county's chief money crop, was freighted by wagon to Shreveport, Natchitoches, or Grantico on the Red River for transshipment. Individuals needing to travel either rode horseback or took the stagecoach.

Long an entry station for immigrants, the volume of immigrant families began to decline after the Revolution. In the twenty-five years immediately preceding the Civil War, less than 400 families came through Nacogdoches, the largest percentage of them arriving between 1836 and 1841. The majority of these ante bellum immigrant families came from Alabama, Tennessee, and Mississippi, while others arrived from Louisiana, Georgia, Kentucky, Missouri, and Illinois.

In 1850, the first federal census for Texas was conducted. Enumerators reported that the total population of Nacogdoches County was 5,197, including 3,758 whites, 1,404 slaves, and thirty-five free blacks. The typical white household contained some six persons; the average age of all persons in the household was just nineteen years with more than one-third of them under ten years of age. Slightly more than a third of all white residents had been born in Texas, while Tennessee with 666 and Alabama with 488 followed Texas as the place of birth. There were twenty-one natives of Germany and thirteen who were born in Ireland.

The next decennial census taken in 1860 placed the total population of the county at 8,289, an increase of more than fifty-seven percent. Of that number, 5,930 were white persons and 2,359 were slaves. The slave population had grown by some sixty-eight percent over the decade, but their percentage of the total population remained fairly constant at slightly less than twenty-five percent. The first *Texas Almanac*, published in 1857, reported that 1,451,931 acres of land in the county was assessed for taxation at a value of $861,640 or an average of about $0.60 per acre. Town lots in the county were valued at $74,960; while 1,702 slaves were valued at $891,100 or an average of some $524 each.

The number of persons in the average white household had declined to less than six, and the average age rose to twenty years. The age group of less than ten years remained at approximately one-third, the largest of all. By 1860, Texas natives outnumbered all others by more than thirty percent, but Alabama had replaced Tennessee in second position, with Germany continuing to furnish the most immigrants from outside the United States.

In the immediate ante bellum years, the economy of Nacogdoches County was grounded on the small farmer, who owned a few slaves (perhaps less than five), raised crops and livestock to feed his family (primarily corn and hogs), and produced some cotton which he sold for cash. In 1858, for example, of the nearly 40,000 acres under cultivation, more than fifty-two percent were planted in corn, slightly more than thirty percent in cotton, the remaining eighteen percent planted in wheat, sugar cane, and vegetables. Hogs were so numerous that persons attempting a livestock count did not assign a total. Most farmers, in addition, owned at least one horse and one cow, but only a very few owned a sheep or a goat.

Nacogdoches County could boast only a very small number of large landowners or slave owners. In 1850, only eight men owned real estate valued at more than $25,000, of which only one was a farmer. Those with the most real estate were Frost Thorn (more than $100,000) and Archibald Hotchkiss (about $88,000). John J. Hayter was listed as having the largest number of slaves in the county. By 1860, the number of slaves owned by Hayter had risen to seventy-seven and the total number of slave owners from 245 in 1850 to 364, a significant increase. These two federal censuses demonstrated emphatically that farming was the occupation pursued by the greatest number of its inhabitants, but a significant percentage of men listed their occupation simply as laborers. A partial listing of the occupations claimed by the remainder of the working men in the county included clergyman, lawyer, physician, teacher, merchant, tavern keeper, carpenter, blacksmith, tailor, painter, baker, and saddler. Several of the more affluent citizens of the community did not profess any occupation.

In keeping with the rest of the slave-owning South, voters of Nacogdoches County claimed political affiliation with the Democratic Party. In the presidential elections from 1848 to 1856, that party polled well over seventy percent of the votes cast, but not a single vote was cast for the newly formed Republican Party. The election of 1860, however, Democratic voting strength was split between the Southern Democrat, John C. Breckenridge (sixty-seven percent) and the Constitution Union Party's candidate, John Bell (thirty-three percent).

The Homefront

Following Abraham Lincoln's election, over the protests of Governor Sam Houston, the Texas Legislature issued a call for the election of delegates to a convention that quickly declared for secession from the Union. Three men from Nacogdoches were chosen as delegates to the 1861 Convention: William Clark, Jr., a Nacogdoches lawyer and native of North Carolina who came to Texas in 1835, Dr. John Newton Fall, a Chireno physician who came to Texas in 1838, and Haden H. Edwards.

The qualified voters of Nacogdoches County approved the Ordinance of Secession by a margin of 317 for and only ninety-four against. A noteworthy element of the election was the fact that along with ten other East Texas counties, over ten percent of the Nacogdoches County voters opposed secession. Perhaps, the explanation for this opposing vote lies in the fact that it was a county of small farmers with a fairly large Mexican element, most of whom were not slave owners.

On May 13, 1861, a company of ninety men and twelve officers under the command of Captain James R. Arnold were mustered into the Texas militia for Confederate service. By March 11, 1862, more than 700 men were in Confederate military service as members of the state troops or Confederate Army. Most of those men served in the state troops, but some who were in the Confederate Army saw service outside the state in Louisiana, Arkansas, or New Mexico. As a part of the 25th Cavalry, some men from Nacogdoches County took part in campaigns in Tennessee and Georgia.

Throughout the war, citizens of the county endured poor traveling conditions, a shortage of housing brought about by a large number of refugees, and a chronic shortage of ordinary commodities such as coffee, tea, cloth, and shoes. They frequently substituted homemade items, while some turned their hands to making items for their own families and producing goods for the Army of the Confederacy.

The war also stimulated the development of such industries as salt works, ordinance works, jug factories, and iron foundries, some of which were located in Nacogdoches County. For example, in 1862, Rufus McLain and Andrew Hayter constructed an iron foundry eleven miles northwest of Nacogdoches. The plant utilized iron ore extracted from mines around Flowery Mountain. This operation was abandoned after the war probably for lack of adequate financing. In addition, the Garrison area twenty miles north of the town was the site of coal mining operations that also persisted until after the war when they were also abandoned. The economy of the county suffered as a side effect of the war. The taxable value of property declined noticeably from almost $3,000,000 to less than $2,500,000; the number of horses and cattle also declined sharply; and specie (gold and silver money) became very scarce.

After General Robert E. Lee's surrender at Appomattox on April 9, 1865, there followed a period of some three months when Texas had no legal government of any kind. By June 17, however, President Andrew Johnson appointed A. J. Hamilton, an Alabama lawyer who immigrated to Texas in 1846, provisional governor, and two days later Union General Gordon Granger assumed command of the military district in which Texas was situated. Granger immediately declared all that had been done by the Confederate state government null and void and that all slaves were now free.

In accordance with instructions from Washington, Governor Hamilton issued a proclamation providing for the registration of voters and issued a call for a convention to draft a new constitution for the state. No person was eligible to vote or be chosen a delegate to the convention who had not taken the 1865 oath of amnesty nor been eligible to vote in 1860.

Delegates elected to this 1866 Convention were in substantial agreement that their task was to secure the restoration of Texas to the Union with the least amount of change in its existing social, economic, and political institutions. This, however, was not the objective desired by the Radical Republican majority that was elected to Congress in the 1866 national election. In March 1867, under their leadership, Congress enacted a series of radical Reconstruction measures.

These statutes, among other provisions, declared that no legal state governments or adequate protection of life or property existed in the former Confederate states. The work of the 1866 Texas Convention was quashed, and the state once again was without legal government.

The 1861 Confederate Constitution made no changes in the organization or operation of counties and their governments, but the short-lived Constitution of 1866 had given them constitutional status. Under its terms, each county's government was to consist of a county judge and four commissioners elected for four-year terms to be styled the County Police Court. County voters were also to elect for four-year terms a county clerk, county attorney, county sheriff, and four to eight justices of the peace and constables.

Both the 1861 and 1866 Constitutions left the creation of cities and towns to special acts of the state legislature. A general law for the incorporation of municipalities was enacted, but the legislature also continued the practice of incorporating individual cities by means of local legislation.

Under direction of the 1867 Reconstruction Acts elections were required in each Southern state. Steps necessary before elections could be held and yet another constitutional convention held proceeded very slowly in Texas, and it was not until June 1, 1868 that ninety delegates assembled and began work. An election held in November 1869 ratified the proposed constitution. Thereafter, the state legislature chosen under its provisions ratified the Fourteenth Amendment to the United States Constitution, and Texas again became an American state.

This 1869 Constitution did not retain the notion of a county police court. Instead, it called for the election of five justices of the peace to sit as the county court. The office of county clerk was abolished and its duties transferred to the district clerk; the office of county attorney was continued, as was that of county sheriff.

At war's end, Nacogdoches County became a part of the Fifth Military District, and as such was occupied by units of federal troops initially under the command of First Lieutenant Asher C. Taylor and later by Brevet Colonel J. Conrad. During this Reconstruction Era an epidemic swept though Nacogdoches leading to the death of a number of these Union soldiers. Some eighteen or twenty of them are buried in unmarked graves in the cemetery adjacent to the Old North Church six miles north of the city.

The occupying force camped along Banita Creek west of downtown. The sounds of their morning and evening drum beats and the sight of their blue uniforms on the city streets served as constant reminders of the defeat suffered by the South. They were generally treated with respectful politeness by most residents but were not accepted into the best social circles of the town.

Late in 1865 a Freedman's Bureau created by Congress early that year began operation in Texas. The activities of the bureau were confined to supervising the interests of the former slaves. They consisted primarily of relief work, education, labor contract supervision, and court protection. By 1867, suffrage qualifications imposed by the federal government were so strict that only a few white men could qualify, therefore, voters and jurors were generally former slaves.

A local physician who lived in the community during Reconstruction days recalled many years later that Confederate sympathizers were disfranchised, ex-slaves made voters and office holders. The polls were guarded on election days by armed men who kept disfranchised whites away. They were backed up by federal troops. The freedmen were organized into a Loyalty League that held night meetings where they were encouraged to exhibit an arrogant overbearing spirit toward their former masters.

One noteworthy incident marked Reconstruction days in Nacogdoches County. Known somewhat extravagantly as the Linn Flat Raid, it grew out of a clash between the State Police and civilian authorities in December 1871 in the village of Linn Flat. The State Police was a military-style force under the control of Governor E. J. Davis. Members of the force contended that they were not amenable to civil law and could only be disciplined by a court martial. They frequently instigated the freed slaves to engage in lawlessness and themselves committed deed aimed at terrorizing local citizens.

That December day in 1871 Columbus Hazlett and William J. Grayson, members of the State Police, murdered David W. Harvell in Linn Flat. Local citizens and their civil officials were reluctant to take action for fear of retaliation in the form of martial law. Nacogdoches County Sheriff Richard D. Orton and Justice of the peace Gibson Dawson, however, determined to act. In the meantime, on December 19, Constable John Birdwell was also murdered undoubtedly by the same two men. Dawson then issued a warrant for the arrest of Hazlett, Grayson, and five other men associated with them. Sheriff Orton summoned a posse composed of more than 100 men and initiated a search for those accused.

Grayson and Hazlett fled to Austin seeking the protection of Governor Davis. Some days later, a lieutenant of the State Police brought the two men back to Linn Flat. But after days spent in fruitless wrangling between the lieutenant and civil officers, the members of the State Police returned to Austin. In due time, the State Adjutant General accompanied by twenty-five or thirty police came to Linn Flat bringing the wanted men. They were turned over to civil authorities, placed in the Nacogdoches County jail, and quiet was again restored in the county.

White farmers and other employers complained that the freed slaves did not make reliable workers and that many could not be induced to work at any price. The overall effect of emancipation was to bring about a reconstituted social system, taking into account a new body of free laborers. Since those newly freed workers often chose not to work as was their right, thousands of acres as of formerly productive agricultural land lay idle.

As a means of meeting the need for agricultural labor and of getting land back into cultivation, Texans, along with landowners in the remainder of the South, turned in desperation to the share-crop system. Landowners supplied tenants of whatever race or ethnic background with housing, equipment, and seed and took a share of the resulting crop, sometimes as much as two-thirds. This system created a more or less permanent underclass of farmers doomed to life at the near poverty level.

The presence of an undetermined number of Ku Klux Klan members in the county did little to affect the situation. In fact, Klan activity in Nacogdoches County was minimal and gradually came to an end following the passage in 1871 of the Ku Klux Klan Act by Congress.

When the Civil War erupted in 1861 Nacogdoches was a town of little more than 500 inhabitants; although the population of the county had increased by more than 3,000 over its 1850 numbers. The war, its Reconstruction aftermath, an economy based on cotton and corn farming, and the devastating effect of the Panic (depression) of 1873 combined to keep the Nacogdoches area in desperate financial straits in the decades of the 1860s and 1870s. Despite these negative conditions, a hint of optimism about the future could be detected.

The 1867 edition of the *Texas Almanac* reported that Nacogdoches County had twenty schools and twenty churches. Petroleum was abundant in places (such as Oil Springs in the southern part of the county), seeping to the surface. Iron ore was also abundant and there was one foundry, but no railroad. Population was increasing and society was good.

The local newspaper editor echoed this optimism. He recalled that Nacogdoches in the 1870s had a "beautiful and romantic" setting located between two ever-flowing creeks, and lying in a valley between hills that commanded splendid views of the town. Water was abundant and good, firewood was easily obtained as was good pine lumber and bricks of excellent quality, and orchards and gardens thrived.

The Backwater

Despite all such expressions of local pride and confidence, the facts do not quite justify this optimism. The City of Nacogdoches, for example, continued to decline in population, until the 1880 Federal Census revealed that only some 300 persons lived within its limits. Offsetting the loss of town inhabitants was the growth in county population. The 1880 county numbers had reached 11,598 an increase of almost 2,000 since 1870. The average family contained just over 5.5 persons, and the average age of all persons was fixed at twenty years. Over a third of the population, however, remained in the under ten years of age category.

The county's growth rate, however, was much less than that of the state as a whole. Rural trade centers, such as Chireno, Melrose, Douglass, and Garrison, became more numerous and competed with Nacogdoches for the farmer's custom. Nevertheless, because of its designation as the county seat, Nacogdoches continued to be the most important business community.

In the years following the war, a growing number of the area's farmers became involved in commercial agricultural production. The need for cash led them to put additional acres into the cultivation of cotton and corn. As was the case all over the rural South, cotton was about to become king.

In 1880, the county had fifty-four cotton gins that regularly ginned more than 6,000 bales each year. The price averaged about ten cents per pound. Corn was cultivated primarily for home use to feed family and livestock. Other crops in very limited production were oats, rye, barley, and wheat. The typical family had a vegetable garden. Although most families owned at least some livestock, it was raised almost solely for home use. Hogs out numbered their nearest rival, cattle, by a wide margin. As late as 1880 unimproved land in Nacogdoches County could be purchased at $5.00 an acre and the poorest land at less than $1.00 an acre. Common rate of interest on land loans was ten percent.

A positive note was sounded for the community's economy during the decade of the 1870s by the beginnings of the lumber industry in the area. Like commercial agriculture, however, its development was slowed by the expense and difficulty of transportation. As late as 1875, the closest rail line was still fifty miles away at Crockett in Houston County, and the closest even the smallest of steamboats could come to Nacogdoches, on rare occasions, was Patonia sixteen miles away on the Angelina River.

A second promising economic opportunity emerged in the postwar period. As early as 1860 attempts were underway to exploit the crude oil seeps that occurred in shallow sands or shale streaks about fifteen miles southeast of Nacogdoches. In places the crude oil oozed to the surface, and the whole area acquired the name "Oil Springs." As early as 17th Century this surface oil was collected and used for medicinal purposes, and in the 18th Century as a lubricant for wagon and cart axles and to soften leather.

In 1859, the seeps so intrigued Lynn Taliaferro (Tol) Barret that he leased the 279-acre Skillern tract in the area. The Civil War delayed further developments, and it was not until 1865 that Barret, Benjamin P. Hollingsworth, Charles A. Hamilton, John T. Flint, and John B. Earle organized the Melrose Petroleum Company. The firm soon executed three drilling contracts, and the following year struck oil at 106 feet. This first commercial oil well in Texas produced ten barrels of crude each day.

In 1867, a producing well was brought in near Oil Springs by Amory Reily Starr and Peyton F. Edwards. Other wells soon followed making Nacogdoches County the site of the first commercial oil field, first pipeline, first effort to refine crude, and first steel storage tanks. Some twenty years later B. F. Hitchcock and E. H. Farrar organized the Petroleum Prospect Company, which by 1889 had drilled forty wells producing 250 barrels a day. This mild "oil boom" lasted until about 1900 when Spindletop and other more profitable fields were developed. The site of Oil Springs is now a 5.5 acre park.

Rich deposits of red clay in the Garrison area of northeast Nacogdoches County stimulated the development of a pottery plant in the post-war period. In 1891, the Garrison Vitrified Brick Company began manufacturing paving brick, becoming in the process the first of its kind in Texas. The firm continued to operate well into the following century, and in 1946, it was acquired by the Acme Brick Company.

The defeat of the Radical Republicans in the 1874 elections and the adoption of a new state constitution in 1876 actually ended the reconstruction period in Texas. A non-partisan taxpayer's convention had convened in Austin in 1871 to protest the perceived extravagances of Republican Governor E. J. Davis' administration. It called for open revolt against the Radical Republicans. The December 1873 election sent to the governor's office a Conservative Democrat, Richard Coke; while the 1872 legislative elections gave the Democrats control of the legislature where agitation began immediately for a constitutional convention. Governor Coke called for a convention in 1875, and the legislature responded by approving the election of delegates, three from each senatorial district. Delegates chosen in the August election assembled in Austin in September, and eleven weeks later produced a new constitution that was approved in February 1876 by the voters of Texas.

Judge Bennett Blake was the only delegate to the convention who resided in Nacogdoches County. In addition to his two terms as a justice of the peace, Blake had served three terms (1850-1862) as Chief Justice of Nacogdoches County and as a member of the Congress of the Confederate States of America (1863-1864). At sixty-six years of age, Blake was among the three oldest delegates.

This 1876 Constitution significantly altered the way Nacogdoches County and the City of Nacogdoches would be governed. A statute enacted by the Radical Republican state legislature in 1870 allowing the governor to appoint the mayor and aldermen of each incorporated city or town and the aldermen to select all other city or town officials was bitterly opposed by local residents. Although this offensive law was repealed three years later, delegates to the 1875 Convention resolved to prevent its repetition.

After 1876, cities and town having a population of 10,000 or less could be chartered by general law only, while those of more than 10,000 might be chartered by special law. The legislature was authorized to constitute each incorporated city or town as an independent school district. As a result, Nacogdoches would be a general law city for the remainder of the century and beyond.

County governments were to be composed of a county judge and four commissioners, one from each of the four precincts into which every county should be divided. These five persons constituted the commissioners court whose precise powers and duties would be determined by the legislature. It became, in essence, merely an administrative convenience for the state. Despite its name, it was not a court; and it did not try cases.

In addition, the commissioners court was to divide the

county into from four to eight precincts in each of which a justice of the peace would be elected. The office of county clerk was revived, but recognizing that in small counties that did not need the offices of county and district clerk they could be merged. The office of county attorney was retained, as was that of sheriff and constable.

In the years from war's end in 1865 to the early years of the 1880s, in rural areas such as Nacogdoches County the vast majority of inhabitants lived the life of subsistence farmers, that is, they toiled in a self-contained agricultural environment. The farmer hoped his small amount of cleared and cultivated land would produce enough to feed the family. His surplus production was earmarked for food he could not produce like coffee or salt or for necessities such as cloth or plowshares. But as the years marched toward the Twentieth Century, all that was to change dramatically.

CHAPTER SIX
THE PROGRESSIVE ERA

The last years of the Nineteenth Century found Nacogdoches still a rural backwater oriented toward subsistence agriculture and no longer a gateway to the west and center of important historical events. That part of the life of the town was a casualty of economic circumstances, geographic isolation, and the aftermath of the Civil War and Reconstruction. A harbinger of change was the arrival in 1883 of the first railroad line, the Houston, East, and West Texas Railroad. For the first time it became profitable to raise and market cash crops such as cotton, tobacco, fruit, and vegetables, to establish small manufacturing plants such as a cabinet shop and a door factory, and to open the doors of the town's first real bank, the privately owned Wettermark Bank.

Recovery Years

In keeping with the mood of the nation, in the decade of the 1890s and the opening years of the 1900s, many persons in Nacogdoches began looking to a future of infinite expansion and development. Despite the emergence of this new mood of optimism, the American South, of which Nacogdoches was an integral part, was a society in transition, one that had reached a temporary equilibrium. It was compounded of a balance between traditional conservative agrarianism on the one hand and emerging urban commercial capitalism on the other.

One contemporary observer of the Nacogdoches scene noted that the actions of its residents displayed a constant interplay of inertia and change, of progressiveness and conservatism. Change was allowed to intrude, most often, when issues of moral reform and business enterprise were essential ingredients.

A dominant characteristic of the Progressive Era was the steady shift of population from rural to urban areas. Owners of large-scale agricultural operations tended to move to the nearest town to enjoy the comforts of urban living leaving their farms in the care of "hired hands" or tenant farmers--often "sharecroppers." Census data for the City of Nacogdoches and Nacogdoches County reflect the fact that they shared in this phenomenon. The county's 1880 population of 11,590 grew to the 1890 figure of 15,984, an increase of more than twenty-seven percent. The 1900 Census counted 24,663 persons, an increase of more than thirty-five percent.

City population rose from 300 in 1880 to 1,138 in 1890, an increase of more than seventy-three percent, and to 1,827 in 1900, an increase of more than thirty-seven percent. In 1880 the city's share of the county population was almost exactly 2.5 percent, growing by 1890 to more than seven percent, but falling in 1900 to slightly less than seven percent.

A. J. Holt, Baptist minister and ardent prohibitionist, remembered that in 1880 Nacogdoches was a "small town of about 800 people with only one church and that was Catholic. In fact, at least three other churches--Methodist, Zion Hill Baptist, and Christ Episcopal--had buildings in the town. By way of contrast, Holt recalled that the city contained "about thirteen saloons."

In 1892, an observer recorded some impressions of Nacogdoches. The city was described as "a pretty little city of 3,000 [the census count was only 1,138] souls." The Stone Fort was portrayed as being built of "rugged sand-stone masonry" with massive, thick walls, small rooms, ponderous arches that supported an upper story. Its inner rooms were characterized as "dungeon-like." In addition, the city taken to task over its treatment of the three very large Indian mounds it had once contained. By this time, two of them had been leveled by an "over-enterprising city administration" to obtain sand and gravel to fill low places in the nearby streets. The remaining mound was being leveled to furnish fill dirt in a place where a new hotel was to be built. Among the sand and gravel were thousands of human bones.

The Spanish American War declared by Congress in 1898 caused a minor break in the calm of end-of-the-century Nacogdoches. Ten thousand Texans largely recruited in the San Antonio area eagerly volunteered for service. The unit recruited there by Colonel Theodore Roosevelt, known traditionally as the "Rough Riders," became the best-known unit of the Texas volunteers.

An honorary military group already in existence by 1898, calling itself the "Stone Fort Rifles," was converted to Company B of the Second Texas Infantry Regiment and went off to take part in the war. Its officers were Captain James W. Ireson and Lieutenants McNeil Chapman and Robert T. Shindler. Ireson and Shindler were Nacogdoches natives. Non-commissioned officers were: Sergeants W. M. Milne, George S. King, William A. King, C. H. Rulfs, Benjamin S. Lang; and Corporals Robert I. Taylor, George B. Dickens, Eugene H. Mast, John D. Jennings, Louis Byrd, Harry E. Goldbolt, Guess Whitaker, S. W. Fitzmaurice, Melville C. Flournoy, John P. Anderson, Harvey G. Russell, and Abe Parker. The company also included seventy-seven privates, an Artificer, two Musicians, and two Waggoners. These men were mustered out in December 1898 at Dallas, Texas. Not all of these volunteers were residents of the city and county, some were citizens of the surrounding counties, but at least sixteen of them are buried in Nacogdoches County cemeteries.

At the end of the 19th Century, the Nacogdoches community experienced an economic "boom time" to accompany its steady increase in population. The basis of that economic prosperity was "King Cotton." In 1900, the more than 3,000 farms of Nacogdoches County were producing more than 16,000 bales each year. Along with the sharp increase in bales produced went a constant upward trend in the price of cotton on the commodities market. In the first five years of the century a 500-pound bale would be worth from $45.00 to $70.00 to Nacogdoches farmers badly in need of cash.

Growing up around the production of cotton were businesses involved with processing it. By the end of the first decade of the century, more than seventy cotton gins were operating in the county, while the Nacogdoches Compress & Warehouse Company stored thousands of bales annually, and a local cotton oil mill processed 5,000 to 7,000 tons of cottonseed.

Processing raw lumber and lumber products was the most important local industrial enterprises. Just after 1900, the largest lumber operation employed more than 400 Nacogdoches residents. In addition, six or more small sawmills and a large planing mill were operating in the county. The largest lumber processing operation was E. B. Hayward Lumber Company, organized in 1904 and by 1906 running at a daily capacity of 125,000 board feet. It was located east of town near La Nana Creek. Other lumber and lumber-related industries operating in 1906 included the Nacogdoches Crate and Box Factory, Nacogdoches Show Case and Hardwood Manufacturing Company, Banita Hardwood Manufacturing Company, and the Craven Lumber Company. By 1914, these various lumber operations employed an estimated 750 to 800 men.

Around the turn of the century both private and public banking institutions appeared in the community for the first time in its history. Prior to that time banking services had been provided by private business firms such as Barr and Davenport and Starr & Amory or by private individuals such as Judge

Bennett Blake. They provided a much needed source of funds for both agricultural and industrial activity.

The two earliest banking institutions in Nacogdoches were A. Wettermark and Son, a private banking firm with branches in Nacogdoches and Henderson, and the First National Bank, one of the first publicly chartered banks in Texas. This very early national bank was organized by John P. Davidson, a native of Alabama who came to Texas in 1849, and had as its first board of directors J. W. Shipman, James P. Sutphen, Gus Levy, J. E. Mayfield, and Davidson. Chartered in 1890 and capitalized, at $50,000, it closed its doors after less than a decade, liquidated its assets, and left the Wettermark firm as the only bank in town.

The Wettermark Bank was organized in 1883 and the management of the Nacogdoches branch placed in the hands of Colonel Benjamin S. Wettermark. Unfortunately, in January 1903, this bank also failed as the result of the reported embezzlement of more than $500,000 by its manager. The Colonel fled the city, was never apprehended, and restitution was never made to stockholders or depositors.

Wettermark's defection brought about a serious, almost crippling financial setback for the city and its surrounding rural area. Nevertheless, Nacogdoches did not remain long without banking services, a second national bank was organized in 1901, the Commercial National Bank, by T. J. Williams of Beaumont, Pete and H. H. Youree of Shreveport, W. B. Chew and James A. Baker of Houston, and R. S. Lovett, president of the Southern Pacific Railroad. E. A. Blount acquired controlling interest in the firm in 1902, became its president, and named F. Hal Tucker its cashier.

Later, in 1910, when the State Legislature created the State Guaranty System for insuring bank deposits, Commercial Bank relinquished its national charter in favor of a state charter and membership in the guaranty system. Still later, in 1937, following the creation by Congress of the Federal Depositors Insurance Corporation, the Commercial Bank again secured a national charter.

A third national bank for the city, the Stone Fort National Bank, was chartered on February 14, 1903. In a few months Captain Ira Link Sturdevant, Charles Hoya, William Usrey Perkins, and John J. Hayter, residents of Nacogdoches, purchased the bank's stock, Sturdevant assumed its presidency, and he held that position for the next forty years.

In 1908, the Farmers and Merchants State Bank was chartered as a guaranty-fund firm. George F. Ingraham was named executive vice president in 1910 and directed the bank's operation until 1919 when it was merged with the Stone Fort National Bank. The three banks in business prior to 1914 did an aggregate annual business of more than $12 million and in the process loaned farmers and merchants money to operate in a competitive market with a greater return on their investments.

By 1883 the Houston, East, and West Texas Railroad had begun offering passenger service to Nacogdoches residents. In fact, citizens of the town had deeded hundreds of acres of land to secure both passenger and freight service. Later the Texas and New Orleans Railroad completed its branch from Beaumont to Dallas. By 1903, it had reached Nacogdoches, intersecting the Houston, East, and West Texas line there. By that time both lines had been acquired by the Southern Pacific Railroad system.

Two short-line railroads were also in operation by 1902. The Angelina County Lumber Company had constructed the Angelina and Neches Railroad that crossed the river and ran on to Chireno in southern Nacogdoches County by 1900, and two years later it was joined by the Nacogdoches and Southeastern built by the Frost Johnson Lumber Company that ran from Nacogdoches through Woden on to Oil Springs.

A manufacturing firm that contributed more materially

than most to the growth and prosperity of the town early in the century was the Mahdeen Company founded in 1912 by J. L. Needham and Frank S. Aikman. Needham was a local barber with a dream, and Aikman was a drug salesman from New York with considerable business acumen. Together they turned Needham's hair tonic, labeled Mahdeen, into a firm that expanded rapidly and soon marketed its product throughout the United States and parts of the world. Prior to Needham's death in 1918, Aikman purchased all shares in the business. The new owner directed the firm's business activity from an imposing brick building that had been erected on the south side of the square until 1939 when death cut short his career.

A 1906 description of commercial activity in Nacogdoches declared that the town had eighty brick business houses, doing a total of $1,500,000 in retail business each year. In addition, the Nacogdoches Grocery Company; W. T. Wilson Wholesale Grain, Hay, and Flour Company; East Texas Commission Company; and other wholesale enterprises grossed some $1,250,000 in annual sales. Two banks, three fire insurance agencies, a long distance and local telephone exchange, an electric light plant, a cigar factory, and a steam laundry were other notable businesses operating in town.

The Taliaferro Cigar Company was housed in a two-story brick building on North Pecan Street adjoining Cox Hardware at the corner of East Main Street. Tobacco was stored on the first floor and cigars rolled on the second floor. The two buildings shared an elevator that was still intact late in the 20th Century. By 1905 the Nacogdoches cigar company was producing some 100,000 cigars a month with most of the leaf tobacco supplied by Nacogdoches area farmers.

In 1906, Andrew W. Hunt and Tilden Tilford founded Tilford-Hunt Lumber Company which came to specialize in the manufacture and export of timbers used as mine props in both the

United States and Mexico. The firm was later reorganized as the Lacy H. Hunt Lumber Company, continuing in operation until Lacy's death in 1969. By that time, Hunt had closed out the firm's sawmills, but it continued in the export business.

Widely known local business establishments included Mayer and Schmidt, owned and operated by two German immigrants, John Schmidt and Abraham Mayer who arrived in Texas in 1878. They opened their first store in Henderson that year but moved the business to Nacogdoches in 1880 locating it at North Fredonia and East Main Streets. The firm ran into financial difficulty in 1929, as a result of the stock market crash that year. John Schmidt died on 24 July 1934, and his son, Herbert J. Schmidt closed the Nacogdoches store and declared bankruptcy. Phillip Henry Schmidt, nephew of John, worked in the Mayer and Schmidt Nacogdoches store until January 1932 when he resigned his position and founded his own business, which is still in operation by descendants today.

Also, Cason, Monk & Company, a partnership originally formed in 1893 by D. K. Cason, Charlie Richardson, and others, specializing in hardware, furniture, and undertaking, occupied a building on the corner of Pecan and East Main Streets. In 1906 this firm merged with the near defunct Mayer and Schmidt operation. Thereafter, under the leadership of R. C. Monk, the enterprise added a grocery department, abandoned its furniture department, and moved to its permanent location on East Main Street.

The city's leading drug and jewelry firm Stripling, Haselwood & Company grew out of a partnership organized about 1894 by Sam B. Stripling, a trained pharmacist. The firm occupied a building on Main Street. In 1901, the business was reformed into a partnership made up of Stripling, R. W. Haselwood, and Thomas E. Baker. Baker soon left the partnership to become president of Commercial National Bank.

Haselwood, the only jeweler and watch repairman "for many miles around" remained with the firm until his death in 1935. There after, Stripling maintained and expanded the business until his death when other members of the family continued its operation. A disastrous fire in 1905 destroyed its original building and its contents; whereupon Stripling had the Blount Building erected on the site according to his specifications.

At the outset of World War I in 1914, six or more hotels offered accommodations in Nacogdoches. The Baxter Hotel, built about 1890, was located on West Main Street east of Banita Creek. Other hotels located near the depot were the Banita and Wilson Hotels. Diedrich A. Rulfs, a talented German architect and builder, designed and constructed the Redland Hotel, a red brick structure of three stories and eighty-five rooms. Located downtown on East Main, it became a popular spot for lodging, dining, dancing, parties, and card games.

The Nacogdoches school system in pre-war days consisted of a high school, a ward (elementary) school, and a school for "colored" children. Some 1,200 pupils attended the free public schools for a period of eight months each year. Although the Texas Constitution mandated that separate but equal schools be maintained for white and black children, the Nacogdoches school for black children consisted of one four-room building serving only 125 students in all grades, an indication that many of those children did not attend school.

In 1914, when the city's population stood at approximately 3,500 persons, seven churches were enclosed within its boundaries and there were an unknown number of others in the county's rural areas. The largest denominations were the Southern Methodist, Southern Baptist, Episcopalian, and Catholic. Their strength can be indicated by a campaign conducted in 1905 under the leadership of A. J. Holt, the Baptist minister, and W. W. Watts, the Methodist pastor, who together conducted a campaign against the sale of alcoholic beverages. A local option election growing out of their activities brought prohibition to the county.

From 1899 through 1914, two newspapers furnished Nacogdoches residents with information on area, state, and national events. *The Redland Herald*, edited by W. S. Davis for most of the period, and *The Daily Sentinel*, established by R. W. Haltom and W. H. Harris. Earlier, the *Gaceta de Texas* published one broadside May 25, 1813; the *El Mexico*, one issue in June 1813; *The Texas Republican*, a few issues in 1819; *The Mexican Advocate*, some issues in 1829; *The Texas Chronicle*, a year of issues between 1836 and 1845; and the *Nacogdoches News*, three years of issues after 1846. In 1875, Richard D. Orton launched the *Nacogdoches News*, which his nephew, Robert W. Haltom with his brother Giles later bought and renamed the *Nacogdoches Star*.

The first local newspaper to publish on a continuing basis, *The Daily Phone*, was established by William H. Harris and Robert W. Haltom. Harris had been part owner of *The Plaindealer*, a weekly newspaper started by Sheriff A. J. Spradley in the early 1890s. The first issue of *The Daily Phone* came out July 24, 1899, and after only six months its name was changed to *The Daily Sentinel*. Four years later, the *Sentinel* owners incorporated as the Nacogdoches Printing Company which was directed by R. W. Haltom, Giles Haltom, and A. F. Henning.

The Sentinel ultimately acquired its competition, and in 1936 Giles Haltom leased it to Stanley Irvine and Bill Colvert doing business as the Irvine-Colvert Publishing Company. They employed Nelson Fuller as editor and publisher and a local boy, Victor B. Fain, as a cub reporter. Eight years later, W. S. Davis bought *The Sentinel* and soon sold it to a group of local citizens who formed the Herald Publishing Company. The original stockholders included R. G. Muckleroy, Sr., J. Elbert Reese, A.

J. Thompson, Navarro Cox, Edward Tucker, and Gillette Tilford.

The next year, Fain purchased stock in the firm and for the following forty-three years served as *The Sentinel's* editor and published. In 1950, the paper moved into the first floor of a new building on North Fredonia in the downtown area. The principal stockholders at that time included R. G. Muckleroy, J. Elbert Reese, Navarro Cox, and M. A. Anderson. Near the end of the century, in 1989, the operation was sold to Cox Enterprises of Atlanta, Georgia, Victor Fain retired, and Roland Nethaway became editor and publisher.

In 1901, the oldest landmark in downtown Nacogdoches, the Old Stone House (Fort) was purchased by Charles and William Perkins and torn down to make way for their drug business. Workmen carefully marked and stored its stones on a strongly-worded request by Cum Concilio Club, a local women's group. Six years later with funds obtained from members, friends, and the Texas Legislature, a small one-story structure utilizing some of the stones was erected on the northwest corner of Washington Square, a block or so north of downtown. It was not, however, a replica of the original building.

In the early years of the century the old brick courthouse located on the south side of the square began to deteriorate noticeably. For that reason, in 1911, after a petition that garnered hundreds of signatures and the offer of a building site by E. A. Blount, voters approved the construction of a new building; work began that year; and the building was occupied the next year. This fourth courthouse for the county was a two-story brick and concrete office-style structure with three rows of windows. It was located on the southwest corner of Main and North Streets.

One of the most alarming prospects confronting the town's residents was the ever-present threat of an uncontrolled, perhaps uncontrollable, fire. The August 1840 event when fire destroyed the entire west side of the town square was only one of a number of costly conflagrations. Until 1907 the city was forced to rely on "bucket brigades" composed of citizens armed with buckets and ladders to combat fires that broke out within the city limits.

The first decade of the twentieth century alone produced at least five prime examples. The earliest occurred in 1903 when fire destroyed a two-story brick building located on the corner of Main and Church Streets and all the wooden structures to the west. In all some eight buildings were leveled and five others damaged, including the Opera House, the Wallace Hotel, and the Commercial National Bank building.

The following year the Central Hotel, located on the corner of Hospital and North Streets and two small houses between the hotel and a nearby livery stable were destroyed and Frost Thorn's home, one of the city's finest residence, and the town's entire business section threatened. Neither of these, however, compared with outbreak of December 23, 1906 when the row of buildings on the north side of the square was consumed.

On July 1, 1907, the Burk-Crain Furniture Company on West Main Street was destroyed, followed in August by the destruction of the La Nana Lumber Company, the Methodist Church, and the Boger and Dooley residences. Finally, in January the following year, a fire of incendiary origin broke out on the second floor of the Davidson Building located on the north side of the street one block east of the square threatening once again the entire downtown area.

Principally as a result of these episodes, the city's residents demanded the organization of a city fire department, construction of a new city water works, the installation of fifty fire hydrants, and the purchase of two, two-wheeled hose carts. By the end of June 1907 a fire department had been organized and its officers selected. Never adequately supplied with equipment, this first arrangement did not endure.

Finally, a second fire department was launched in 1908 with Captain I. Link Sturdevant, local banker and city booster, as its president and fire chief. The department purchased the Hoya lot on the south side of the square in December of that year, and two years later occupied a two-story brick building designed to house the department's equipment and City Hall. The department owned two horses and a horse-drawn hose wagon and employed one full-time fireman to tend them. In addition the town's fire fighters consisted of Chief Sturdevant, five officers, and twenty-four firemen, all volunteers.

Located as it was between the flood plains of two small, winding streams, Nacogdoches experienced periodic flooding. In 1902, for example, a steady rain began during the day, turned into a deluge that evening, and continued for some twenty hours. At its peak, flood waters rose to a height some eighteen inches above any previous high-water mark. Total rainfall was gauged at 14.22 inches. No lives were lost, but scores of residences were damaged, telephone poles and lines were downed, and the town's railroads lost bridges and roadbed. At one point the water reached a depth of three feet at the corner of Fredonia and Hospital Streets.

Social life of Nacogdoches residents at this time centered around church-related activities, school events, and home entertainments. On relatively rare occasions, theatre companies stopped over for one-night stands. To facilitate theatre productions and other such events, John Schmidt in 1888 erected an Opera House. It was situated on the second floor of a building at Main and Church Streets.

Silent movie houses made their appearance in 1909 when the Royal Theatre opened its doors along with the Airdome that presented films outdoors. In 1910 the Lyric Theatre replaced the Royal and was in turn replaced in 1913 by the Ideal. In addition to silent films, tent shows began coming to town in 1905, setting up most times on a tract of land located on the corner of Hospital and Fredonia Streets.

The old Opera House was the scene of a dramatic event in the lives of the world-famous Marx Brothers--Zeppo, Chico, Harpo, and Groucho. While filling an engagement composed of standard dramatic material and musical numbers, their act was disrupted by a runaway mule on the downtown streets and through the square where it began to kick a cart to pieces. For the performers, desertion by their audience was the last straw; after months of one-night stands, heat, insects, hot chili, sleazy boarding houses, and indifferent audiences, the four brothers, in frustration, began to engage in wild, zany antics. When the audience returned they discovered the Marx boys burlesquing any and everything and immediately began roaring with laughter. Their long, successful comedy career was underway.

One of most spectacular occurrences of the time was the opening in 1909 of a park located on the east side of La Nana Creek, covering about fourteen acres, fronting some 700 feet on Main Street and running south along the bank of the creek. It was surrounded by solid wall fence on the west and south, a net wire fence with a single vehicle gate and a pedestrian entrance along the front, and the creek on the east. A twenty to twenty-five foot driveway divided the grounds from the entrance to the south fence line. On each side of the drive a hedge separated it from grass lawns, while a boardwalk flanked by rows of cape jasmine ran from the pedestrian gate to the south, and in the center flower beds were planted.

In the center of the park were mineral wells with pavilions over them, high curbs and pumps, and other conveniences for the thirsty folks who tried the waters. Beyond the wells, rows of hitching posts were installed and over the whole grounds seats and swings were provided. South of the wells, a picnic grove with running water, moss banks, grassy plots, grapevine swings, and other rustic attractions were located to tempt those seeking recreation.

Robert Lindsey and June C. Harris purchased the property, formed a stock company, and undertook the project. The idea was suggested by Charlie Bird, a well-known African-American, who had owned part of the land and whose water well produced the mineral waters that park was designed to exploit.

Lindsey and Harris had the water analyzed by state chemists and local physicians who reported that it contained properties of exceptional medicinal value equal to the already famous waters of Mineral Wells. Investors believed that the wells and park could be developed into a famous health resort. They named the park Aqua Vita, acting on a suggestion offered by Dr. Joseph E. Mayfield, a local physician.

Formal opening occurred April 27, 1909. Railroads offered special opening-day rates for those wishing to attend. Despite a downpour of rain the night before and showers during the day, a crowd estimated at 3,500 to 5,000 visited the park during opening-day ceremonies. The advent of World War I and lack of financial and other necessary support from the community led to the failure of this ambitious venture and Nacogdoches never became a health resort.

As World War I approached, Nacogdoches could boast of some steady, if not spectacular, progress in keeping with the spirit of the times. Railroad transportation had reached the community; state and national banking institutions had been chartered; and some local industry had been launched. Population almost doubled, job opportunities had improved, and agricultural income expanded. Nacogdoches seemed destined to enter an era of impressive growth based on the steadily growing demand for agricultural products. Meanwhile, the coming wartime would create a period of suspended animation.

The War Years

Between 1900 and 1914, Nacogdoches' population almost doubled from 1,827 to more than 3,400; and along with its growth in numbers the city experienced steady economic growth based on increased agricultural prices brought about by war-time demand. This improvement, however, was only relative, for in 1914 Nacogdoches County remained among the poorest sections of the state. The average farm had only thirty-eight improved acres; forty-eight percent of all farmers were tenants, many were "sharecroppers;" the average farm was valued at less than $1,500; and the average value of all farm animals was not more than $300.

Notwithstanding the relative poverty of the rural areas of the county, during the second decade of the Twentieth Century the city expanded and developed in a number of important directions. A local editor proclaimed that in 1910 the public square displayed an abandoned water well in its center, covered with a dilapidated shelter and partly fenced with a chain. A few dead trees surrounded the well while the remainder of the space was used as a wagon yard. That unlovely picture was to change dramatically during the decade.

Local community leaders and others began a concerted effort as early as 1905 to obtain a federal building for the center of the square. This drive resulted more than nine years later in a special city election at which voters approved a proposal to sell this downtown area to the federal government for its location. Some time later, on June 12, 1915, the city council passed an ordinance approving the sale; most land owners around the site then signed a deed of sale; although some became parties to condemnation suits in the federal court at Tyler.

Next, the area was surveyed and final deeds executed. After some adjustments, a site with four sides of unequal lengths was agreed upon, and in August the federal government paid the $5,000 purchase price and obtained title to the land. Construction work on the actual building, a post office for the city, did not get underway until January 1917 when Graeme McDonald Company of California was awarded a $46,000 contract calling for a light colored sandstone and granite for all stone work and brick for the remainder of the exterior.

The local postmaster, A. Y. Donegan, took possession February 27, 1918. Many of the town's residents were disappointed with the new quarters for their post office. Some told the local editor that its interior did not match its imposing exterior; but most found it more convenient and easier to use than the previous structures had been.

Another serious condition in the downtown area was the condition of its streets. They radiated outward from the public square in a rough gridiron pattern that had been imposed on the original layout mandated by Spanish-Mexican colonial regulations. As late as 1910, they were unpaved and thus often so deep in mud as to halt wagon travel for day at a time while their crossings often became impassable for women and young children. From time to time, the city government had bricks and other filler hauled in to improve those crossings. In the residential areas, residents routinely allowed weeds to flourish in the unpaved streets in front of their homes and needed to be admonished to take the necessary steps to eliminate the problem.

Therefore, street paving throughout the city was thus a major issue. City officials began experimenting with various paving substances in the pre-war years, finally deciding that gravel was the most feasible solution. In August 1914, gravel paving was inaugurated. Mound Street from the S. W. Blount home to Main Street and the streets near the post office were surfaced. Thereafter, in 1915, Pilar Street from the Banita Street bridge to the square was also paved.

Surfacing North Street from Main Street north to the city limits was the next important paving project. To facilitate this operation, the Board of Aldermen imposed a street tax designed to finance further street paving. With revenue from this new tax and small donations by citizens living along the street, in 1915, North Street was paved with local gravel at a total cost of $950. Although a group of local residents challenged the validity of another city ordinance requiring property owners along a street to furnish paving, the regulation was upheld by the local district court and the Court of Civil Appeals.

During these years, the city's government consisted of a mayor elected at-large, and five aldermen also elected from the city at-large. The only other elected city official was the city marshal. In the decade of the 1910s, this later office was regularly the only one for which there was any contest at election time. Other officers were routinely elected and reelected.

The city continued with its paving program through the war years; and by 1918, ornamental street lamps were installed in the downtown area at street corners and the ends of the Main Street bridges. Moreover, the city and concerned citizens had expended $90,000 in paving the business district with pine blocks. This experiment, however, proved unsatisfactory and was not extended beyond the downtown area. Additionally, heavy rains had for many years either slowed or temporarily halted travel into and out of the center of the city. By war's end the city government had provided for two concrete bridges over Banita Creek on Main and Fredonia Streets.

Accompanying the increasing number of automobiles and other motor vehicles in the community was a growing public demand for improved roads. Nacogdoches residents especially wanted a "first class" road to Lufkin across the Angelina River south. By the early months of 1917 that road had been completed to the river, and work begun on a similar one to the Rusk County line on the north.

Needing revenue to finance these and other road

improvements, the county commissioners asked voters to approve an ad valorem tax of fifteen cents per $100 valuation on property within the county. The county was so deeply in debt that much of this additional revenue went to repay existing debts. Near the end of the decade, voters approved an $800,000 bond issue to be used in building hard-surface roads in Nacogdoches County. The state added $400,000 and assumed the task of supervising construction.

In the unpaved section of the city, a municipal street-sprinkling service was available from May to November. At first horse-drawn equipment was used to supply the service, but the advent of motor vehicles prompted the city to purchase a tractor to draw the sprinkling equipment. In 1918, the Nacogdoches street department owned five mules, two street sprinklers, a street sweeper, a grader, and a gasoline-powered tractor. The department was responsible for maintenance of some ten miles of improved streets.

When work began on the new federal building in the center of the square, the city purchased two large parcels of land nearby to serve as a "hitch lot" for wagons and teams and furnished for persons and teams a source of free water. This "hitch lot" remained as a feature of the downtown area well beyond the era of horse-drawn vehicles and became, in later years, a portion of the farmer's market.

As traffic increased on city streets and county roads, traffic regulations became a necessity. In 1915, for example, city ordinances mandated a speed limit of six miles an hour in the downtown square and twelve miles an hour on other city streets. State statutes limited speed to eighteen miles an hour on roads and highways. City ordinances also required drivers to slow down and honk at all corners, keep to the right, and avoid blocking passways when not in use. In 1916, parking on Main Street adjacent to the square was banned along with certain other designated streets leading to the square.

Another set of ordinances enacted in 1917 and 1918 restricted the presence of livestock in the downtown area. In general, horses, mules, cattle, and other livestock were banned from an area bounded by the railroad, Hospital Street, Church Street, and Fredonia Street.

Throughout the decade city officials, newspaper editors, and other concerned citizens urged property owners--without much success--to install sidewalks to promote pedestrian safety, improved appearance, and free mail delivery. To encourage compliance, the city put down a five-foot brick walk 300 feet in length along its property on Main Street from the Banita Creek bridge to the downtown area. The county cooperated by laying a brick walk around lots near the courthouse. Well into the Twentieth Century sidewalks remained as uncommon site in residential areas.

As late as 1910 the residents of the city depended almost exclusively on private wells, cisterns, and a pond just north of the city square to supply water for any and all purposes. The need for an adequate, dependable, and healthful source of fresh water was obvious to city officials as well as other residents. Therefore, early in 1914, local citizens subscribed to half of the cost of drilling another artesian well with the city providing the remaining half. This well completed in March, joining three other such wells in the same area of the town. They were located about one-half mile north of the courthouse near the light plant, the railroad tracks, and Banita Creek. Some four years later enough wells had been drilled to double the city's supply of pure artesian water. A reinforced concrete water storage tank with a capacity of 130,000 gallons was also constructed in 1916 near the light plant and city wells in the northern section of the city.

Another pressing concern for Nacogdoches residents at this time was the collection and disposal of sewage. Following a survey conducted by civil engineers in 1917, a plan was devised to create a sewer system that as far as practicable would extend to most parts of the city. The mayor and council assured local taxpayers that the system could be put in place without additional taxes. Work began soon thereafter and by March 1918 the new system was completely installed. All residents living within 150 feet of any sewer line were required to have connections made and cease using the existing privies, cesspools, water closets, urinal basins, slop sinks, or other such receptacles. When the United States entered the World War I Nacogdoches had in place some nine miles of sanitary sewers, reaching all parts of the city and connected with a sewage disposal plant.

At the same time, public utilities in the city included a city-owned waterworks, a municipal electric system, and a privately owned telephone system. The original electric plant had been privately owned and operated, but it was ultimately acquired by the city and numerous important improvements added.

Public transportation consisted of a small passenger bus known as a Jitney and affectionately called "the Cricket" by local townspeople. Its schedule called for the bus to traverse the North Street and Mound Street loop, then go west to the Union Depot near Banita Creek and return. Passengers boarded from the curb at any point along the route. Fare was five cents a trip.

A German immigrant invited to Nacogdoches by John Schmidt arrived in town in 1890 and almost immediately made an impact on the architecture of the town. Diedrich Rulfs, architect and builder, brought with him Victorian styles that were romantic, flamboyant, rich, ornate, and elaborate. Gothic motifs, gabled roofs with elaborate decorations, stained glass windows, and the like were all part of his contribution to the visual in Nacogdoches.

In 1917, for example, the old courthouse on the south side of the square was pulled down to make way for a new three-story and basement structure designed by the German architect. The Mahdeen Company occupied the basement, the third floor, and an office on the first floor; the Garage Company, a Ford Motor Company agency, filled the remainder of the first floor and a portion of the second; and the W. T. Wilson Grain Company offices, occupied the remainder of the second floor.

Between 1890 when he arrived and his death in 1926, Rulfs also designed elegant residences for Roland Jones at Church and Hospital Streets; for J. C. Harris on Virginia Avenue; for S. W. Blount and Tolbert Hardeman on North Mound Street; Tom Summers and Lee Hardeman on North Church Street; and for Eugene Blount on North Street. Additionally, two church buildings also demonstrated his creative talents: Christ Episcopal Church, almost totally Gothic in style, originally stood on the southwest corner of Washington Square but later was moved northward to the corner of Mound and Starr Streets. The second, Zion Hill First Baptist Church, located on La Nana Street immediately north of Oak Grove Cemetery, was a blend of Gothic and Victorian elements.

Residential construction proceeded so rapidly that new additions to the city's original residential sections became necessary. In 1919, one was opened on Walker Street near downtown, another in Harris Heights named Sunset Addition west of the city, and a third along a street running west from Virginia Avenue southwest of the downtown area. Hundreds of new homes were built at a rate rarely matched at any time in the city's history.

A compulsory school attendance statute enacted by the Texas Legislature in 1915 requiring all children between the ages of eight and fourteen to attend school--sixty days the first year, eighty days the second year, and 100 days every school year thereafter. The Nacogdoches public school system did not have the physical facilities to house the number of pupils who would be attending classes beginning with the 1915 school term. To provide them in August 1915, the Board of Trustees of the Nacogdoches School District called a bond election. By a margin of four-to-one voters approved the issue of $45,000 in bonds and a school tax of fifty cents per $100 valuation on property within the district to construct additions to the high school building for white children, the West End Elementary School for white pupils, and the school building that housed black students. In addition, a new brick building was erected on North Church Street to accommodate other white children.

Walden's Business College, the city's first commercial school, opened in the fall of 1917 with approximately forty students enrolled. At the height of its operation, more than 100 students attended its classes.

When rich oil deposits were discovered north and south of Nacogdoches County in the early years of the Twentieth Century, attempts were made to revive production at Oil Springs south of the city. Adding impetus to the "oil fever" was the ten-barrel per day well brought in a few miles southeast of town, almost due south of Melrose. Deep test wells were dug, and by 1918 a number of them produced up to fifteen barrels per day. War-time restrictions and the discovery and development of wells producing great quantities of a better grade of oil in Pennsylvania brought the Nacogdoches oil boom to an end.

Although a war with Mexico threatened in 1914 and a general European war broke out the same year, both in 1914, neither of these developments appeared to capture much attention or cause much concern in Nacogdoches. Interest began to increase in late 1916, and the declaration of war proclaimed by Congress on April 5, 1917 launched the town and county into almost instant action. In only a short time, a mass meeting held at City Hall provoked the organization of home-guard military company that enlisted seventy-five volunteers within a few days.

A Selective Service Act passed by Congress in May required all men between the ages of twenty-one and thirty to register for service in the nation's armed forces. Some 2,500 young men in Nacogdoches County complied, including 713 who resided in the City of Nacogdoches. The draft itself was inaugurated in July and in September the first twelve local men were called. Dave L. Thomas, W. B. Hoffmeister, Eskridge Box, W. N. Booty, William L. Balch, Willie Moore, Robert Bledsoe, and Fred E. Thrash of Nacogdoches; Fred G. Westfall and Roy T. McLemore of Garrison; Charles Carter of Sacul; and Jesse G. Wheeler of Appleby became the first contingent to be drafted. A Military Exemption Board composed of newspaperman Giles M. Haltom, Judge V. E. Middlebrook, and Dr. A. A. Nelson reviewed all requests for exemption.

White and black draftees were inducted at separate times and trained at different locations. The first group of black men from Nacogdoches did not depart until late October when forty of them were ordered to Camp Travis in charge of Matthew Waters, a local minister.

In June a National Guard Company for Nacogdoches County was organized with Captain Charles L. Shindler and Second Lieutenant Orland Patton as its original officers. The unit became a Coast Artillery Company of 150 men who would be exempt from the military draft. Captain Shindler was a veteran of the Spanish American War, and Lieutenant Patton had attended a military school. Within a week some 200 men had volunteered and awaited their physical examinations before being mustered into service. In January 1918, this company was converted into a heavy artillery unit with new officers. Known thereafter as Battery F, 4th Field Artillery, the company was sent overseas in July. Later reorganized as Battery F, 64th Field Artillery, they returned to Camp Bowie in April where discharges awaited them. Also recruited in Nacogdoches was a cavalry company of 105 men, and an Infantry Regiment of between 100 and 200 men under the command of Captain Richard B. Walthall.

Wartime brought about some hardships and restrictions for all persons living in the United States. Peacetime production of articles of trade and other commodities was very sharply curtailed, and government regulations prohibited any work which might interfere with the manufacture of war materials. Residents of Nacogdoches, for the most part, responded to these unprecedented controls with little grumbling, regarding them as sacrifices necessary for the war effort.

The Food Administration, administered by Herbert Hoover, was authorized to fix the prices of staples, license food distribution, coordinate purchases, supervise exports, prohibit hoarding or profiteering, and stimulate production. Nacogdoches residents soon became accustomed to efforts to reduce food waste and limit food consumption, The advent of "Wheatless Mondays," "Meatless Tuesdays," and "Porkless Thursdays" prompted many of them to experiment with new and unusual foods.

The Fuel Administration, directed by Harry A. Garfield, created "fuelless Mondays" and other measures designed to conserve the nation's supply of coal and other fuels. Daylight saving time was another innovation designed to increase production and conserve fuel supplies. A War Labor Board controlled wages and hours in certain designated industries, banned strikes contrary to the public interest, and oversaw the production of war materials. A War Finance Corporation supervised war loans, while urging all Americans to support the war effort by underwriting "Liberty Loans." Nacogdoches residents responded readily and subscribed to all quotas assigned to them.

The night of April 26, 1919 featured a banquet and dance celebrating the homecoming of the first contingent of Nacogdoches veterans, most of whom were members of the local artillery company. The banquet was held on the Washington Square school campus, after which those wishing to take part in the victory dance assembled on East Main Street near the mercantile establishment of Mayer & Schmidt. Both were pronounced a "great success," although the festivities were marred somewhat by a vigorous protest lodged against the post-banquet dance. Local ministers and many church groups strongly opposing dancing at any time leading them to boycott the dance.

The outbreak of a virulent influenza epidemic in the winter of 1918 dampened the joy of victory. Local officials proclaimed that the disease brought about the greatest death rate in the county's history. Combined with spells of rain, the epidemic cost the lives of more than 100 persons.

During the war years, the city government dealt with a number of social problems. Vagrancy, for example, was viewed as a persistent evil, and city officials urged county law enforcement officers to arrest any and all idle persons. Traveling carnivals were banned from operating within the city limits, since they were seen as demoralizing and as a drain upon the resources of the citizenry. A curfew was imposed, requiring all children under the age of sixteen to be off the streets by nine o'clock each night, because children roaming the streets at night were believed to be unnecessarily exposed to corruption. Finally, county voters approved by a margin of more than 300 votes a constitutional amendment that would ban beverage alcohol statewide, because the majority regarded it as a dangerous threat to the social health of the community.

Local women organized a suffragette club in 1915 and called for an amendment to the state constitution granting equal suffrage for men and women. When such an amendment was proposed in 1919, Nacogdoches voters rejected it by the narrow margin of thirty-seven votes. The Nineteenth Amendment to the Constitution of the United States, however, mandated equal suffrage, and women began voting in the county in the 1920 elections.

By war's end Nacogdoches was gradually emerging from its post Civil War status of a "backwater" county seat trade center into a new more promising period in its history. The old city's visual image had been enhanced by a new post office on the square, numerous new business buildings and residences, a network of paved streets, concrete bridges over both creeks, new and enlarged school buildings, and new church buildings. The quality of life for most residents had been upgraded by a sanitary sewer system, an adequate artesian water system, and a modest fire protection system.

WORLD WAR I BATTERY SERGEANTS, 64TH ARTILLERY COMPANY

[1st row, l to r] Weeks, Nacogdoches; Smith, Nacogdoches; Fauset, Med. Sgt, Pittsburg, PA; Meador, Nacogdoches; Mast, Nacogdoches; Mettauer, Chireno; Muller, Nacogdoches; Cordell, Garrison; Rawls, San Augustine; Reese, Nacogdoches; Mentzel, Galveston; Rhodes, Beeville; Perkins, Nacogdoches; Herbold, Sgt. Major, Cleveland, Ohio; Davison, Nacogdoches; and Hess, Texas City, Texas

CHAPTER SEVEN
THE TRANSITION ERA

The years that bridged the span between the two Twentieth Century world wars became a time of transition, of accelerating change. Mass production and other technological developments brought about a flood of consumer goods that made it possible for millions of Americans to enjoy an easier, more pleasant life. The key ingredients in this transition from Nineteenth Century to Twentieth Century America were the steady movement of people from rural areas to cities and towns, the emergence of the gasoline driven automobile as the fulcrum of their existence, and the gradual substitution of a new set of urban values for those of their rural past.

Many Americans were trapped between those two value systems. The Puritan system of their past emphasized hard work, sobriety, and restraint. Throughout the years between the wars this set of values prevailed, albeit with some difficulty, in rural areas such as the Nacogdoches community. But at the same time another system arose to challenge the old Puritan tradition. It featured new diversions for people and tempted them to play, to be entertained, to take part in a wider range of activities even if some of them were illegal. It also encouraged them to throw off many of the old restraints and live a more liberated life style.

In 1920, the population of Nacogdoches stood at 3,546 an increase of less than 200 over the 1910 figure, representing less than thirteen percent of the total population of the county. Ten years later the city had a population of 5,687 which represented almost nineteen percent of all persons living in the county. These figures would increase in 1949 to 7,538 in the city or more than twenty-one percent of the county's population figure. Steadily, if not dramatically, urbanization was emerging in this East Texas community. Just at the end of the first of those wars, Nacogdoches was described as a sleepy pinewoods town serving as county seat and marketing center for a rural agricultural community. In a region of small farms averaging less than forty acres in cultivation that depended heavily on cotton production and lumber operations, per capita wealth fell far below the national average. By the time the United States entered World War II in 1941, the city had become more than the agricultural marketing and processing center that it had been for more than fifty years. It was emerging as an educational hub with a steadily expanding influx of industry.

Education

The event that triggered the development of Nacogdoches as an education center for the East Texas region was the acquisition of Stephen F. Austin State Normal College. Although the college did not open its doors to its first class of students until 1923, efforts to obtain an institution of higher education for the city actually began in March 1915 when the Texas Legislature authorized the creation of a normal college for East Texas and charged the Texas Supreme Court with the responsibility of locating a site. The court declined to accept this responsibility, declaring that locating an educational institution was not a function of the judiciary.

Two years later, the Legislature enacted a statute that again established a normal school and, in addition, mandated that it be located east of the 96th meridian. The same act appropriated $180,000 to allow the college to begin operations, $150,000 being earmarked for buildings and $30,000 for maintenance.

Realizing the need for something to stimulate growth, Nacogdoches citizens exerted a concerted effort to have the new college located in the city. A 209-acre site one mile north of downtown was obtained, largely as the result of donations and other contributions that included free water and electricity. In 1917, near the time America entered the world conflict, a Locating Board, consisting of the governor, the state superintendent of public instruction, and the board of regents of the state's normal colleges visited twenty-seven East Texas communities before settling on Nacogdoches as the most appropriate site.

The onset of war and wartime restrictions delayed action on the normal college project. In fact, a special session of the Texas Legislature in late 1917 repealed the appropriation allotted for the buildings and their maintenance and thus postponed indefinitely putting the proposed college into operation. In the immediate post-war years, popular sentiment discouraged the creation of new regional institutions of higher education. By 1921, however, interest was again sufficient to revive the notion of a normal college for East Texas. The Board of Regents of the state normal colleges at its May 1921 meeting authorized construction to begin in Nacogdoches as soon as funds became available.

That same year the state legislature appropriated $175,000 for construction of administration and classroom buildings as well as $15,000 for campus improvement for the college; but Governor Pat M. Neff item vetoed this appropriation. A special session of the Legislature meeting in 1922 restored over $120,000 of the vetoed funds. Whereupon bids were solicited, a contract negotiated, and construction begun on what became the Austin Building. Credit for the restoration of the funds and other necessary actions in getting the project underway is frequently assigned to Eugene H. Blount, local banker and political figure.

Moore Construction Company of Ranger, Texas began construction in September 1922 with September 1, 1923 projected as the completion date. The initial building plans called for an administration building with a boiler house to supply steam heating. Excessive rainfall and the resulting sea of red mud, along with other problems, caused unforeseen delays. The contractor, realizing that the terms of the contract could not be fulfilled and the building ready by the deadline called for in the contract, abandoned the project. A second contract was executed the same year, but not until May 1924 was the Austin Building finished and ready for occupancy.

Much earlier, in July 1917, the board of regents named Alton William Birdwell as the first president of Stephen F. Austin State Normal College. Whereupon, President Birdwell began the search for suitable faculty members. He was a veteran teacher and administrator, having taught in 1892 at Pleasant Ridge, a small rural school in Smith County, and until 1899 at Pine Springs and Noonday, other Smith County rural schools. At that time he was appointed principal of a Tyler elementary school where he served until 1904 when he was elected to a two-year term as county superintendent of schools for Smith County. Still later he was appointed principal of Tyler High School serving in that position until 1909 when he became superintendent of schools at Troup in Smith County.

The following year, Birdwell was appointed an assistant professor of history at Southwest Texas State Normal College at San Marcos. From 1911 to 1922, he became a professor of history, head of the history department, and dean of the faculty at the San Marcos school. In his academic career he had attended undergraduate classes at the University of Texas at Austin, the University of Missouri, the University of Chicago, and Vanderbilt University. He received the A. M. degree in 1916 from George Peabody College for Teachers in Nashville, Tennessee. After becoming president of the Nacogdoches normal college, he was awarded an honorary LL. D. by Southwestern University at

Georgetown, Texas.

Dr. Birdwell retired August 31, 1942 after serving as president of Stephen F. Austin for just over twenty-five years. A tribute paid him after his retirement pointed out that under his leadership SFA became a reputable teacher preparatory institution.

Looking back on the first four years of operation, Dean Thomas E. Ferguson, English professor and dean of faculty, recalled that at the opening of its first academic year on September 18, 1923, the Austin Building was still under construction and that classes began in a shack erected on the Nacogdoches High School campus. Superintendent R. F. Davis, he recalled, generously allowed the college to use rooms at the high school when available and to keep its building open longer hours to accommodate college classes. In those trying and somewhat unusual circumstances, the 402 students who registered for the fall 1923 semester inaugurated the academic life of the college.

Dean Ferguson remembered the original faculty as a group of men and women--twenty-four teachers and administrators--in the prime of life, thoroughly trained in their respective fields, and enthusiastic about their opportunity to prepare teachers for the region. Some of the more noteworthy members of that original faculty included C. E. Ferguson, mathematics and registrar; Edna Wilkins, typing; Robert (Bob) Shelton, mathematics and coach; Ida Pritchett, music; Ruth Mays, Spanish and dean of women; Karle Wilson Baker, English; W. Fletcher Garner, history and government; and Virginia Broadfoot, physical education for women.

A wooden building, a crude temporary structure, forty by sixty feet in size, served as the original administration building, library, and athletic equipment storeroom. Known affectionately as "The Shack," it was located, for convenience, on Washington

Square near the high school building. The local Chamber of Commerce under the leadership of Carl Monk, president, and H. L. Knight, secretary-treasurer, provided the funds necessary to build this hastily erected temporary structure.

In addition to the classes held in high school facilities and "The Shack," others were conducted in the rebuilt Stone House then also on the high school campus, outside under the trees when weather permitted, the basement of the First Baptist Church, and the Old Nacogdoches University Building located on Washington Square.

The normal college, comparable to those elsewhere in the state, was composed of three units: the normal school, the sub-college department, and the demonstration school. Sub-college classes were offered for students who qualified at the tenth and eleventh grades. They might also enroll in college-level classes for which they were qualified. Demonstration school classes were initially open only to students at the first and second grade levels. They were supervised by faculty in the college's education department and functioned as a practice (training) school for students planning a future teaching career.

The first school year (1923-1924) was highlighted by the completion of the Austin Building and a change in the institution's name, from Stephen F. Austin State Normal to Stephen F. Austin State Teachers College, the name it bore until 1948 when it was again changed to Stephen F. Austin State College. Some 21 years later the name was changed once again to Stephen F. Austin State University.

Assisted by students and faculty, workers moved the college to its North Street campus, much of it into the just-completed Austin Building. This structure was a three-story fireproof building, situated at the end of a long vista lined with stately pines. Later concrete sidewalks would also lead from North Street to the front of the building were laid down. "The

Shack" was also moved to the new campus where it was used to house the physical education department until a gymnasium could be built.

Local citizens continued to support this educational institution during its formative years. In 1924, for example, Frank S. Aikman, president of the Mahdeen Hair Tonic Company, donated $12,000 that was earmarked for the construction of a gymnasium. Named for the man who provided the funds to build it, Aikman Gym, a large wooden structure, served as gymnasium and physical education classroom building until 1961 when Shelton Gym on Raguet Street was completed.

A football field, named in honor of President Birdwell, was also constructed that year. Located on Raguet Street near its intersection with College Street, it was the scene of games until 1946 when Memorial Stadium further south on Raguet Street was completed in time for use for football season that began after the close of World War II.

Steady growth in population in Nacogdoches and the East Texas region between the wars resulted in steady increases in college enrollments. From the official count of 245 students registered for the first semester of operation, numbers increased to almost 600 during the spring semester of 1927, and to more than 1,000 in the 1929 spring term. The depression years saw a steady decline, however, until during the spring semester of 1940, less than 700 were enrolled.

In keeping with the mode of operation of most other colleges in the state, Stephen F. Austin began with classes offered on a quarter system with three quarter terms and two six-week summer terms each year. In the 1933-1934 school year a two-semester and two six-week summer term scheme was introduced. Because in the years between the wars it was primarily a school dedicated to the preparation of teachers and since beginning teachers could obtain temporary licenses after only one year of college instruction, enrollments for the summer terms regularly outnumbered those for the regular terms, often by a margin of almost two to one.

Growing numbers in the student body meant that the school's physical facilities were soon outgrown, causing President Birdwell in 1925 to petition the Board of Regents for permission to build and funding for additional classrooms and laboratories. The board responded by approving plans for a second three-story brick and concrete building and allotting $200,000 for its construction. When completed it was designated the Thomas J. Rusk Building in keeping with the Austin Building that had also been named for a famous statesman of early Texas. It initially housed the Demonstration School on its bottom floor, classrooms and offices on the second floor, and the library on the third floor.

The number of faculty members also increased with additional student enrollment. From the original twenty classroom teachers in 1923-1924, the number grew to fifty by 1927 and in 1931 to seventy. Although the number declined slightly during the depression years of the 1930s, by 1941 it had again risen to almost ninety persons. The Demonstration School expanded its offerings from grades one and two to grades one through eleven on the eve of the war. The sub college gradually merged with the Demonstration School and in time disappeared.

In 1926, more students also enabled the college to organize the first Lumberjack Band under the direction of J. T. Cox, who for many years directed all school bands in the city. This first college band was composed of twenty members and practiced under the trees lining the Vista.

Despite the depressed economy of the surrounding region during the 1930s, enrollment at Stephen F. Austin State Teachers College was seriously affected for only one year, 1933-1934; thereafter it rebounded and continued a steady rise until the outbreak of World War II. Although some ninety-five percent of the students attending the college were members of East Texas farm families where wealth was slight, they were able to attend the local teachers college because it practiced a program of economy. There were no fraternities, sororities, ribbon societies, or social clubs, and fees were held to the minimum. In 1923-1924, for example, students were not required to pay tuition, only a matriculation fee of $12 for a twelve-week term. Dormitories and other college housing were not furnished and no college-operated food service existed.

Enrollment was also aided by a state statute requiring by the opening of the 1934 school term all teachers in the state's rural schools to have completed at least two years of college-level work. This requirement stimulated enrollment in the summer sessions, and for some years thereafter students attending summer sessions regularly outnumbered those attending either of the regular fall and spring semesters.

In an attempt to keep up with continued growth and long-standing needs, additional physical facilities were created from 1930 to 1939. In 1934, the first dormitory, Wisely Hall, was completed. This facility that housed men only was named for J. H. Wisely, the college's first auditor. Located on College Street north of the Austin Building, its basement housed the first college cafeteria, feeding both men and women as economically as possible.

The Women's Recreation Center, a wooden structure located on Raguet Street just south of Aikman Gym, was constructed in 1935 to provide separate quarters for women's physical education. In 1936, a replica of the Old Stone Fort as it was regularly known by this time was erected on the campus just west of Raguet Street. In 1938, classrooms and laboratories for the departments of chemistry, physics, biology, and agriculture were provided in a three-story brick Science (later Chemistry) Building located just south of the Rusk Building.

In 1939, the first dormitory for females, Gibbs Hall, named for Eleanor H. Gibbs an early art professor, was finished and the college cafeteria moved from Wisely Hall to the first floor of the new dormitory. It was located on Raguet Street just south of the reconstructed Old Stone Fort.

The 1940 fall semester saw Stephen F. Austin enroll a record 914 students, claim nine new buildings, and offer more student activities than ever before. The next year, however, in keeping with many other colleges and universities all over the nation, it faced a bleak and quite uncertain future when war again disrupted operations.

That Nacogdoches was similar to most other rural southern communities of the time and shared their dedication to traditional values was illustrated in a variety of ways. It was a "church-affiliated community." in which almost everyone, including most students, regularly attended church on Sundays and at other times during the week. In 1923 when the college registered its first class, there were eight Protestant churches in Nacogdoches with a total membership of 2,265 in a town of just less than 3,500 persons. The First Methodist Church, South and First Baptist Church (Southern Baptist Convention) together claimed more than 1,500 of those members. The Catholic congregation numbered only slightly more than one hundred.

Among the older and well-established congregations of the time was Sacred Heart Catholic Church established in 1847 on North Pecan Street by the Right Reverend John Mary Odin, Bishop of Texas. Catholics of the Nacogdoches Parish worshiped at this site for ninety years until a new building was constructed at the corner of North Street and Mimms Avenue. Fathers L. C. M. Chambodut and J. C. Neraz pastored this parish from 1847 to 1864.

Christ Episcopal Church was established in 1848 and from that time to 1852 when a wooden building was built on the lane from Main Street to its front door (present-day Church Street) conducted worship services in the county courthouse. Frost Thorn donated the lot on which the first church building was constructed. In 1888, the congregation purchased a site on the southwest corner of Washington Square on which a "modern brick building" designed by Vestryman D. A. Rulfs was erected. In 1940, the structure was torn down and rebuilt at its present location at the corner of East Starr and Mound Streets.

In 1884, Luther Rice Scruggs initiated Baptist missionary work in Nacogdoches leading to a building being constructed two years later on North Street where, in newer and much enlarged facilities, the congregation worships today. This first building was also designed by D. A. Rulfs. The home missionary program of what is now known as the First Baptist Church led to the establishment of Fredonia Hill Baptist Church on South Street and Calvary Baptist Church once located on East Main Street but today located on Northeast Stallings Drive.

First United Methodist Church traces its origins to the missionary efforts of the Reverend Littleton Fowler who preached in Nacogdoches in 1837 and the following year founded a "society" of local Methodists. The Reverend Samuel A. Williams became the first minister at that time. The group thereafter built a place of worship on lots near the corner of Hospital and Pecan Streets where the congregation gathered from 1860 to 1887 when a new building was constructed on Hospital Street across from the earlier site. This structure was destroyed by fire in 1907, rebuilt, and occupied in 1910. Today, at the same site, the congregation occupies a new and expanded structure.

In 1836, the Reverend Samuel Bacon organized a Presbyterian Sunday School in Nacogdoches, and two years later the Reverend Richard O. Watkins took over the school and in 1840 launched a church, but this congregation disbanded in 1849. Many years later, in 1886, the First Presbyterian Church, U.S., was organized and a building for it erected in 1889 at North Fredonia and East Hospital Streets. In 1893, a second Presbyterian church known as Main Street Presbyterian, Cumberland Synod, was organized and a building constructed at Main and Mound Streets. Much later, in 1930, this congregation built a second structure at North and Powers Streets and renamed itself Westminster Presbyterian Church. Also in 1893, the Presbyterian Church, U.S. A., organized and constructed a building on East Main Street. The later two congregations merged in 1907, but in 1940 this group disbanded, some thirty-six members organizing the Grace Bible Church and the others going to Westminster Presbyterian.

Sometime before 1879, the Reverend Lawson Reed organized the "Union Church" to minister to the African Americans of the Nacogdoches community. His efforts were strongly supported by the town's Methodist and Presbyterian congregations. That year Frank and Ellen Walton donated two acres of land on La Nana Creek and Park Street where a small church was constructed. Today this site is the location of a small well-kept cemetery. In 1890, the congregation purchased a plot on Logansport Street north of Oak Grove Cemetery where a more modern building was built. The congregation by then known as Zion Hill First Baptist Church sold this building in 1913, and the following year built a newer structure designed by Diedrich A. Rulfs on the same site. Today the congregation worships in a building located on East Stallings Drive.

The community's social life tended to revolve around activities under the direction of the city's two dominant Protestant denominations, Methodist and Baptist. Following all church services, friends lingered to visit and most chose to refrain from indulgence in unsuitable pleasures and unnecessary work. Churches sponsored bazaars, silver teas, and other affairs open to the general public and usually were well attended.

Later in the century, however, other varieties of social institutions were gradually added. In 1894, for example, Mrs. George (Estelle V.) Davidson conceived the idea that the married women of the town could benefit from an organization to "improve the mind, foster worthwhile city projects, and enhance the social graces." From this notion grew the first local study club. Named *Cum Concilio*, it was formally organized by fifteen of the town's leading society matrons. Over time, club members were instrumental in preserving some of the stones and timbers from the Old Stone Fort, establishing the first city library, and landscaping the Memorial Hospital grounds, among other projects.

Fifty years later, the matrons of *Cum Concilio* sponsored a junior study club for younger married women of the town that was organized as the Heritage Club. A second club for younger married women that chose the name Dilettante Club was organized in 1957-1958, also sponsored by *Cum Concilio*. In 1962, the Dilettante Club sponsored the Literati Club to study and pursue the fine arts. Nearly a decade later, in 1971, the Dilettante and Literati Clubs combined to sponsor the Koinonia Study Club to awaken interest in literature and topics of general information and social concern.

In the mid-Twenties men of the community acquired a new social institution to enhance their leisure hours. A County Club and a nine-hole golf course were created in 1926 located on the east side of Highway 59 a few miles south of the town. The original club house burned in 1964 but rebuilt. In 1979, an additional nine holes were added and a swimming pool provided for members and their families. Of course, in time, women were allowed to make use of the facilities.

College-related social activities soon appeared, however, to offer students and townspeople alike other opportunities to be entertained, enlightened, or distracted. Three music clubs appeared during the first year: the Treble Club (women), the Glee Club (men), and the Choral Club (both sexes). Four literary societies emerged: the Anne Birdwell Club, the Blue Bonnet Literary Society, the Thomas J. Rusk Literary Society, and the Stone Fort Literary Society. A dramatic club, the Karle Wilson Baker Dramatic Club, was organized and gave its first performance at Christmas time. A college yearbook, the *Stone Fort Yearbook*, was founded; and the following year, a school newspaper, the *Pine Log*, appeared.

Intercollegiate athletics soon took shape under the leadership of the "father of SFA athletics," Coach Robert (Bob) Shelton. Shelton fielded competitive football, basketball, and baseball teams, although in the early years the college had only very primitive facilities for any sport. Agriculture professor J. H. Hinds initiated a track program and became its first coach.

The Twenties were a time when Nacogdoches citizens routinely encouraged their sons and daughters to attend colleges and universities elsewhere than the local teacher training institution. Often they enrolled at schools as far away as Harvard, Yale, Bryn Mawr, Vanderbilt, the University of Virginia, the University of the South, the University of Mississippi, or Louisiana State University. Most, however, elected to attend Rice Institute, Baylor, Texas A&M, or the University of Texas at Austin.

When these college students who had been exposed to cultural diversity and the changing mores elsewhere returned home for holidays, they often brought guests and exposed the town to excitement it had not known. Parents vied with each other to provide entertainment for children and visitors. During the Christmas break, for example, a New Year's ball sponsored by the Elks' Club became the most important social event of the year. This cotillion was held on the second floor of a building on Fredonia Street directly behind Swift Brothers & Smith's Drug

Store. Half the space was devoted to a dance floor, while the remainder housed a billiard room, a card room, a parlor, and lounges.

Big name bands were imported and formal dress required. Girls wore the stylishly new short gowns of the Jazz Age. Well-known local matrons and socially-oriented dowagers as well as a few husbands filled the chairs that lined the ballroom's four walls. A grand march led by the official marshal, usually the president of the Elks Club, and his lady opened the affair. At intermission college men frequently withdrew to enjoy a smoke or report on athletic events, while girls retired to the lounge to primp, engage in the customary gossip about boys, or relate their plans for the coming school term.

Social life for those students attending Stephen F. Austin was not quite so grand. It was enhanced to some extent by a group of college-oriented businesses situated on North Street within walking distance of the campus. Jimmy Partin's College Coffee Shop, located near the corner of North and East College Streets, was probably the most popular of them. Partin often hired male college students on a part-time basis to help them with expenses, paying them twenty-five cents an hour and free meals and tips. Students would bring their dates to the coffee shop, play the Jukebox, buy Coca-Colas and other soft drinks, sit around tables or dance, laugh, and otherwise entertain themselves.

All-college dances were held on occasion in Aikman Gym, and students would walk their dates to the coffee shop for refreshments or come by after the dance was over. An old piano in the rear of the shop was frequently manned by Tom Lucas, the town's best pop pianist and a member of the Johnny Crawford dance band. At the end of the decade, the Austin Theatre, the first talking motion picture house in Nacogdoches, opened its doors; and English teacher Mary Jane White organized the Karle Wilson Baker Theatre Guild each furnishing additional entertainment opportunities for students.

Some indication of the continuing importance of churches and church-related activities in the lives of the students who attended Stephen F. Austin can be gathered from the foundation of Bible Chairs near the campus. In 1929, the Wesley Bible Chair, located on College Street north of the campus, was established. H. T. Peritte, Presiding Elder of the Nacogdoches District of the Methodist Church, South had begun the groundwork as early as 1926, but his death delayed creation for a time. However, Ed J. Harris, his successor, carried the project to fruition.

Until a suitable facility could be constructed, a temporary classroom was provided in her home by Mrs. H. T. Perritte. Classes where held in her living room for several months. When the new building was ready, the college loaned student armchairs and a teacher's desk. During its first term, forty-nine students enrolled for Bible classes taught by George J. Steinman, a Methodist minister. In time, other Bible Chairs and denominational student facilities joined the Methodists along East College Street.

Industry

From its inception, the economic life of the Nacogdoches community was dominated by agriculture, which in turn was dependent on the uncertainties of the weather and the fluctuations of the commodities market. Following the close of World War I, a modest amount of diversification slowly emerged. Aware that change was necessary if the town was to make any sort of economic progress, local business leaders and their allies in 1919 organized the Nacogdoches Chamber of Commerce as a vehicle for progress.

In October of that year, a group of leading business and

professional men along with other civic-minded residents, under the leadership of local attorney Arthur A. Seale, met at the county courthouse to initiate organization of the chamber. Its organizing Board of Directors included Seale, Carl Monk, J. J. Grieve, Albert Brewer, Thomas E. Baker, F. B. Sublett, and Oscar Matthews, all prominent local men. Within weeks more than 200 individuals became members.

In the beginning, most of the Chamber's effort was directed toward improving the life of the rural families in the market region. Information concerning better farming techniques, soil conservation, diversification of crops, and how to escape domination by out-of-state marketing were stressed at a series of meetings. At the same time, J. H. Hinds, Stephen F. Austin agriculture professor and president of the Chamber, began a campaign to obtain a hospital for the city and to inaugurate a fair for the county.

During the decade hospitals made their appearance in the town. Somewhat earlier, in 1910, the Tuckers--Drs. Stephen Blount Tucker, Francis Henry Tucker, and Fred T. Tucker--converted the entire first floor of a home on Mound Street into Nacogdoches' first hospital. In 1918, Dr. Woolam Ira M. Smith purchased the property and operated a hospital there for some years. Thereafter, Dr. Smith converted his fourteen-room home on North Street into a hospital known as the Nacogdoches Sanitorium. After his discharge from the U.S. Navy following the end of World War I, Dr. Charles Thomas Smith returned home to join his father in the operation. Sometime after 1916, Dr. J. M. Woodson operated a hospital for African American patients. The building was on Shawnee Street, and was later used as the Sid Roberts Funeral Home. Although in addition to Dr. Woodson, at least three other African American physicians practiced for a few years in the town, Dr. Robert E. Hanson began his lengthy practice among those residents of the town.

THE STORY OF NACOGDOCHES

By 1928 the city had sold the land on old Tyler Road, site of the old electric power plant using the funds obtained from the sale to build the original City Memorial Hospital on Mound Street. The decision to sell the city's electric power plant to Texas Power and Light Company generated a bitter political controversy. The issue was resolved by a city-wide referendum, resulting in an eight-vote margin in favor sale. W. E. Baker, R. C. Monk, Roy Gray, Joe Goldsberry, Hal Tucker, and Hilliard Stone were named to the first Board of Directors of the hospital.

The decade of the Twenties saw its efforts rewarded by the coming of several new and important businesses. One of the earliest of these was established by a returning navy veteran, Lawrence Crawford Hunt, who helped launch a small retail plumbing shop which rapidly expanded into a wide-ranging wholesale plumbing supply house. After Hunt gained control of the firm it soon grew into a multi-million dollar enterprise. With its headquarters in Nacogdoches, the supply house ultimately established branches in Conroe, Texarkana, and Mt. Pleasant in Texas and extended its trade territory from Houston, Texas to Little Rock, Arkansas.

Also early in the decade the Mize brothers, B. H. and W. A., came to Nacogdoches and opened a successful dress-making factory. Located on North Street near downtown, the plant at its peak employed approximately 200 women in the production of Mize Modes and Meda Moon labels. The firm ultimately marketed its products throughout the United States.

In 1929, near the end of the period R. W. McKinney, who recognized the potential in highway construction, formed the firm of McKinney and Parmley to tap that potential. Two years later after his brother Jack McKinney joined the firm, R. W. McKinney purchased Parmley's interest in the company and reorganized it into the R. W. McKinney Construction Company. Within the lifetime of the brothers the company engaged in highway construction in Texas, Ohio, and Kansas. Moreover, under the direction of Jack McKinney, the firm expanded operations to include drilled and belled-pier foundations for large structures.

What was undoubtedly the most important industry established in Nacogdoches at any time appeared in 1930. Successful almost from the first and maintaining that success over more than sixty years the Texas Farm Products Company was organized by M. S. Wright, Sr. Growing out of his knowledge of and contacts within the commercial fertilizer industry, Wright learned that large amounts of fertilizer were spread on East Texas farms whose soil was depleted of natural growth elements by persistent planting of crops. Nacogdoches County farmers alone, he was informed, plowed under 12,000 tons annually.

Wright and his eldest son, Steele, left Virginia to try their luck in East Texas. Although they knew no one in the community, they soon met with and convinced Captain Ira Link Sturdevant, president of the Stone Fort Bank, and other potential investors that their plans for a fertilizer plant in Nacogdoches had great potential.

Thereafter, on January 15, 1930, Texas Fertilizer Company capitalized at $30,000 was formed with W. U. Perkins, as its president, M. S. Wright it vice president and general manager, and Studevant, A. T. Mast, Sam Stripling, and Sam Hayter as directors. Steele Wright, who had studied commercial art, took the basic Texas star and ring used by the Texas Highway Department as its logo, added a triangle with the ring touching its three sides, put the words Lone Star on the two upright sides creating the company's trade mark.

Following the 1930 spring fertilizing season M. S. Wright sought a way to add to the company's operations. He hit upon the idea of combining the manufacture and sale of fertilizer with the operation of a feed mill. Mill production began about a year later, allowing the firm to begin a program of diversification. The addition of a cornmeal grinder permitted the plant to produce two grades of corn meal, a high grade marketed as Lone Star Cream Meal, and a lower grade labeled Lone Star Pearl Meal. The firm obtained cottonseed meal from the Nacogdoches Cotton Seed Oil Mill and sold it to the growing number of dairy farms in the region. Finally, the company actively promoted the commercial production of truck crops such as tomatoes and watermelons and marketed them under the label of the Lone Star Produce Company. Within six years, however, the firm reverted to the production of its basic sales items, feed and fertilizer.

At that time the firm's president, W. U. Perkins, in poor health and at an advanced age, sold his interest, and it was reorganized as the Texas Farm Products Company. Between that time and 1942, M. S. Wright purchased all the outstanding shares of stock in Texas Farm Products, and it became a family owned and managed enterprise.

Two other noteworthy commercial ventures were founded in Nacogdoches in the Thirties. One, the Bennett-Clark Company, manufactured bentonite, a clay formed by the decomposition of volcanic ash that had the property of absorbing vast quantities of water and expanding to several times its normal volume. Used in a number of manufacturing operations, Bennett-Clark sold bentonite in the international market. Purchasers ranged throughout the United States, Canada, England, Poland, India, Mexico, and a number of South American nations.

The other, Airline Motor Coaches of East Texas, was founded in 1939 when C. D. Thomas, Sr., N. B. Bunting, G. W. Hyde, Raymond Hammond, and Clarence English consolidated their small motor bus lines. English became the firm's president with Thomas as its vice president and public relations officer.

The next year, after a second merger involving the

Houston, Humble and Livingston Line, Thomas became president of the business, Bunting vice president, and Hammond traffic manager and superintendent of operations. Other mergers followed during the decade along with purchases that enabled the bus line to offer potential customers regular schedules to Houston, Shreveport, Longview, Beaumont, Marshall, Huntsville, and Brenham. At the close of World War II, Thomas and other stockholders sold the business in 1946 to Dixie-Sunshine Trailways of Dallas.

Disasters

Fires and floods plagued Nacogdoches residents between the wars, as they did most small towns of the time. Much of the original town was situated in the flood plain of two converging streams of water and without an adequate flood control arrangement. This combination of circumstances meant that on those occasions when heavy rainfall ensued the threat of flooding was ever present.

Adolphus Sterne's diary records two of these disasters that occurred in the time of the Republic of Texas. In 1841 and again in 1843 the two creeks rose to alarming heights, although the waters did not actually reach the town itself and no lives were lost. Floods surely came to threaten the city in the years between those reported by Sterne and the end of the century, but no records are extant to document them.

The local newspaper that began publication in 1899 recounts that in 1902 a twenty-hour downpour brought water to a point some eighteen inches higher than ever before reported. No lives were lost, but property damage was extensive. Scores of residences were ravaged, telephone poles and lines downed, and railroad bridges and roadbed destroyed. All town bridges except the iron bridge that had been erected on Main Street were lost.

Twenty years later, in 1922, a four-hour deluge converted the La Nana and Banita Creeks into raging torrents. Greatest property loss was confined to the banks of Banita Creek. The Southern Pacific Railroad station was inundated, the South Street bridge across the creek was dislodged and hurled against the railroad bridge in its path wrecking it. Electric and water service was suspended for several hours. Residential losses were greatest in the low area between Church and South Streets. A number of businesses were badly damaged. But again no lives were lost.

The next year a cloudburst fell near Neidmore, six miles north of the city, sending a wall of water down Banita Creek. Residents were warned by an alert railroad crew and evacuated the low-lying areas along the creek. Again residences in the creek's flood plain were badly damaged, and businesses in the area of the Main Street crossing suffered considerable loss. Every home along the creek south of that crossing was flooded. The rising water caused the Mayo dam east of the city to give way and drove La Nana Creek to flood stage.

Three years later, in 1926, a cloudburst inundated the city itself causing Banita Creek to overflow once again and cover its flood plain. No lives were lost, but businesses and residences below South Fredonia Street were hard hit.

An eight-inch downpour in 1940 again sent both creeks out of their banks and flooded their plains. Waters reached the Texan Theatre on Main Street and water swept into the Airline Bus Terminal on Hospital Street. Less than a year later, in 1941, a nine-inch deluge failed to send the creeks out of their banks, because their beds had been straightened and cleared of accumulated rubbish. Buildings along Church Street were flooded, and Fredonia Street from the bus station to Hughes Street was a solid sheet of water.

Between the wars, major fires continued to trouble residents on the average of four or five times each year. For example, the old Ladies Home at Pilar and South Streets was damaged by fire from a defective flue in 1920, and another broke out in the basement of the Co-operative Furniture Company located at the southwest corner of the square the next year. There were few fatalities, but in 1926 a fire that destroyed the Banita Apartment Building claimed the lives of Florence Whitton and her sister Kate.

Perhaps the most costly conflagration occurred in 1927 when the H. E. Stone Lumber Company burned, resulting in losses estimated at more than $75,000. A 1937 outbreak threatened the downtown area when a wide-ranging fire in the 200 block of Main Street destroyed at least eight buildings.

Fire fighting was still the responsibility of a volunteer fire department under the leadership of Captain Sturdevant and after his retirement of Elmo C. (Bud) Feazell. The department was remarkably effective for the time, keeping all losses of life and property at a minimum.

Government

Recognizing the need to modernize the city's government and administration, in 1929, the Nacogdoches City Council appointed a thirty-six member committee of community leaders to draft a new city charter. Included in that number were businessmen, professional men, educators, local officials, and housewives. A. A. Seale, a prominent local attorney and civic leader, was chosen to chair the committee. To facilitate the completion of its task, a seven-man sub-committee under the direction of Judge A. T. Russell was chosen to prepare a working draft for committee consideration.

Russell's group sought input from local citizens and soon produced a draft which was adopted by the full committee, and March 2 designated as the date for a special election to allow voters to adopt or reject the proposed charter. Copies of the proposal were distributed to all qualified voters in the city for them to read and study. A comfortable majority voted for adoption, but the vote was light indicating that most citizens had little or no interest in the details of city government.

The new charter replaced the existing city council consisting of a mayor and five aldermen elected at-large with a city commission composed of five persons, three to be elected at-large in odd-numbered years and two in even-numbered years. The group was to select one of its members to serve as chairman and mayor. If the commissions chose to do so, they were authorized to hire a city manager.

Robert C. Monk, a hold-over alderman, Elbert Reese, and Cates Burrows were elected commissioners in the 1929 election. Hold-over members, Hilliard Stone and Roy Gray, continued to serve until the 1930 regular election.

Overview

Throughout the years from 1920 to 1940, Nacogdoches residents and individuals living in the surrounding area congregated downtown near the post office, banks, retail businesses, theatres, and other assorted enterprises on a regular basis. By simply going to town they could confidently expect to meet old friends and exchange the latest news and gossip. Until 1923, the entire business district, including the square was paved by crude wooden blocks that swelled into odd sizes when wet, offering jagged edges and creating a real hazard for automobile traffic.

That year they were replaced by red bricks which in time became the pride of the city. By 1939 most of the downtown streets were either paved or bricked. The Works Progress Administration provided paving for North Street and other

THE STORY OF NACOGDOCHES

streets, causing Nacogdoches to begin taking on a "modern" appearance.

As World War II loomed, Nacogdoches was certainly a community in transition. Cotton and lumbering were being slowly overshadowed by dairying, stock farming, poultry production, and diversified farming. Area farmers were making strides in soil conservation, forest conservation, and reforestation. Per capita income for rural and city families was gradually increasing. The war, of course, shoved all steps toward further modernization aside and directed the attention of the community toward wartime conditions and activities.

VISTA OF STEPHEN F. AUSTIN STATE UNIVERSITY ABOUT 1957
AUSTIN BUILDING IN BACKGROUND

CHAPTER EIGHT
THE IMPACT OF GLOBAL WAR

Nazi Germany's invasion of Poland in 1939 followed by the Pearl Harbor surprise attack by Japan in late 1941 brought to an end the rural agrarian dominated life that Nacogdoches had known since its earliest beginnings. In 1945, following war's end the town and community experienced a series of changes destined to alter its character and expand the horizons of its citizens.

Lifestyle

During the war years, 1941-1945, Nacogdoches experienced most of the changes common to small towns throughout the United States. American life was profoundly and unalterably changed by such events as selective service for millions of Americans, most of them young and healthy; demographic shifts, especially in the distribution of population; shortages of goods and services, induced by the demands of a total war effort; inflation, the product of increasing purchasing power made possible by higher wages and profits; greater agricultural production, fueled by expanded wartime demands for food and fiber; and technological advances, the result of concentration on science and scientific pursuits. Many a small town went into a decline from which it never recovered even after the war was over. Nacogdoches, although affected in some measure by all these developments, escaped that fate by a combination of fortuitous circumstances.

The war introduced profound changes in the lifestyle of all the residents of the Nacogdoches community. Price controls aimed at combating run-away inflation were instituted by Congress in early 1942, and in April the newly-created Office of

Price Administration (OPA) froze prices on hundreds of items of consumer goods at their highest level in March and established rent controls on living units in virtually all communities. Later that year, in October, wages and salaries of many workers were also placed under the control of the national government, as were prices of farm products.

Congress sought also to limit consumer spending by placing controls on income, sale of war bonds, and sharply increased rates of taxation. Shortages of consumer goods, rationing of many commodities (notably food, gasoline, and automobile tires), and prohibitions on installment purchases also inhibited consumer spending.

The impact of all such wartime policies was dramatized for residents of Nacogdoches in May 1942 when they participated in a totally unique event in American history. They gathered at local buildings to register for food ration cards and thereby initiate the nation's first rationing system. They were issued War Ration Card 1 which entitled them to purchase a limited amount of sugar at a fixed price. Additional amounts of sugar for canning purposes could be obtained upon approval of the county's rationing board.

The following months brought rationing of tires for automobiles and other vehicles, causing the County Commissioners Court to cancel additional issues of county road bonds for a period of ten years thereby halting road construction for the duration of the war. Commissioners believed that rationing of tires and gasoline would sharply curtail use of county roads and curb demands for road construction and repair. Scrap rubber drives were launched and some 175,000 pounds collected in the county within a few weeks. The purpose of those drives was to permit the reclamation and recycling of rubber in short supply brought about by restrictions on imports of raw rubber.

A rationing board for the county was created and began

operations in October 1942 to oversee the legally mandated rationing of such items as coffee, gasoline, and shoes. When the war ended in mid-1945 gradually, item by item, rationing was abandoned, until by the end of 1946 it was essentially withdrawn on all items, and daily life for most residents of the Nacogdoches community could begin to resume something resembling its prewar pattern.

In 1940 the city's population stood at just over 7,500 with some 35,300 persons residing in the county. Stephen F. Austin State University's 1940 fall enrollment had reached a record 914 students, but those figures would soon be drastically altered. In September of that year the United States Congress passed and President Franklin D. Roosevelt signed the Selective Training and Service Act, the first peacetime military draft in the nation's history. As a result, when the Japanese attacked Pearl Harbor in December 1941, all American males between the ages of eighteen and forty-five were liable for military service. Soon more than 16,000,000 had signed up and draft notices began to be sent to all eligible men.

By the end of 1942, for the first time in its history, the nation began permitting females to serve officially in its armed forces. At war's end some three years later, a total of 216,000 women had enlisted, and approximately 15,000,000 men had been "called to the colors."

Most, if not all, Nacogdoches County families were affected in some way by the military draft system. By April 1942 approximately 40,000,000 men had registered for war service, this number represented virtually every man in the United States between the ages of twenty and sixty-four. The previous month the first draft lottery had initiated a system by which 9,000,000 men ultimately would be classified for military service. Etoile resident Thomas Jefferson Farr drew the first number for Nacogdoches County, followed by James P. Irvine and John

Clifford Smallwood, both residents of Nacogdoches.

Men between the ages of eighteen and twenty were required to register by July 1942, and following that date men who reached their eighteenth birthday were directed to register as soon thereafter as possible. Family men and those employed in activities essential to the war effort were deferred in the early stage of the World War II draft. Congress and President Roosevelt promised that men with families would not be called until the pool of eligible single men had been exhausted. In February 1943, manpower demands dictated that family men be drafted unless they were certified as necessary to the war effort.

Many of the Nacogdoches men and women who served in the armed forces and left town and county never returned, although soon after war's end some 2,000 veterans did return. Many of them came home having had experiences that expanded their outlook and changed their perception of the good life for all Americans. These individuals along with a considerable number of others who came to live in the community in the post-war era, would be instrumental in bringing about significant changes in life in the old East Texas county-seat town.

The shift from peacetime to wartime production induced many men and women to abandon their native towns and farms to relocate in the large industrial centers of the nation where industries geared to war production offered jobs paying wages far above those available to them "back home." Many of the men and women who entered the armed forces as well as those who relocated to enter the industrial work force were destined for a variety of reasons never to return to their pre-war homes and occupations. Most notably a large number of women never returned to the traditional roles that females had played in pre-war society.

Those developments, in turn, produced a shift in population to an extent unknown in the nation's history.

Naturally, urban population increased dramatically while rural population steadily declined, touching off a trend that continued for decades. In the case of Nacogdoches, many of its residents of 1940 relocated in Houston and Beaumont. From 1940 to 1950, the population of Nacogdoches County declined to just over 30,000, a loss of more than fourteen percent; while the population of the City of Nacogdoches increased to more than 12,000, an increase of almost sixty-four percent.

In spite of New Deal programs created in the 1930s that were designed to reverse the downward spiral of income for all agrarian Americans, Nacogdoches County agricultural producers did not benefit to any appreciable degree. Between 1930 and 1940 the value of agricultural crops produced in the county declined by some fifty percent. Decades of intensive cash crop farming, especially cotton, had sharply reduced the productivity of their land. Moreover, the machines and chemical additives that enhanced the productivity and profit of large scale farms in western and southern portions of the state were not practical in eastern sections. They fared best on level terrain and large scale operations, not on the smaller and more irregular terrain of farms in the Nacogdoches area.

As a result, the agricultural segment of Nacogdoches life was vitally affected by a number of wartime developments. By the close of hostilities in 1945, income from cotton production in Nacogdoches County had declined sharply; but income from dairying had increased by 400 to 500 percent; and income from poultry production brought about by the introduction of large broiler houses had more than doubled. Much of this increase in farm income had come about by the utilization of modern machinery, increased use of fertilizers, and several years of ideal growing conditions.

Agricultural productivity in Nacogdoches County was further aided by the development and introduction of effective remedies for the many livestock maladies brought on by the area's warm moist climate and improved methods of pasture management. Literally hundreds of acres of farm land which had been devoted to cotton production for decades was taken out of cultivation and dedicated to stock farming and dairy operations.

New Deal agricultural policies offered tempting subsidies to agrarians who took cultivated acreage out of production. These programs prompted Nacogdoches County farmers to cease cultivating their most marginal land, turning it to pasturage or timber production. Since much of that marginal land had been cultivated by tenant farmers in Nacogdoches County where sixty percent of all farmers were tenants, the economic impact of this trend brought about serious relocation and reemployment problems for literally scores of county residents.

Many of those tenant farmers became urban dwellers attracted by job opportunities and good wages offered by war production industries. When the marginal land they had once cultivated was withdrawn from production, the number of farms in Nacogdoches County declined by more than fifty percent in the years from 1930 to 1950 and the number of cultivated acres were reduced by an even greater percentage. Numbers of rural residents in Nacogdoches County fell from nearly 28,000 in 1940 to 18,000 at the time of the 1950 census with most of this reduction occurring during the war years.

Cotton as the county's most important cash crop followed by the milling of lumber both declined in importance in those same years. They were gradually replaced by the steady increase in dairy operations, so that by 1950 some 230 Grade A dairies were located in the county. In addition, poultry production and beef production also advanced as sources of agricultural income.

While rationing created perhaps the wartime's greatest impact on the people of Nacogdoches, a critical labor shortage began to develop by mid-1942. Farm labor exhibited the first serious shortfall, prompting city and county officials to call upon every available man, woman, and child to help in producing and gathering crops. The situation became so critical that one rural resident remarked to a local newspaper reporter that so many men had left the county for employment in defense plants and to military service that there were hardly enough men left in the rural areas to keep the devil at bay. Another local farmer related that in his rural community there were only two young men engaged in farming and that farm labor in that community was provided by older men, women, and children.

At the same time, serious shortages also developed in volunteer firemen in Nacogdoches and teachers for the rural schools in the rural areas. In most other areas of the civilian work force, shortfalls did not develop until after war's end.

Almost certainly the most extraordinary occurrence in the community's wartime experience was the location of a prisoner-of-war camp for German soldiers near Chireno in the eastern part of the county. A severe ice storm and a destructive tornado were instrumental in bringing on this development.

During the night of January 13-14, 1944, intense winds, heavy sleet, and the accumulation of ice on exposed surfaces brought about one of the worst ice storms in East Texas history. Thousands of loblolly and other species of soft pine trees were destroyed. Lumbermen in the area estimated the tree damage alone at approximately $16,000,000, and they also announced that injured tress would have to be harvested within six months or their commercial value would be forfeited. Experienced East Texas timber cutters were in very short supply, because most of them were in military service or relocated to better-paying employment in war and other industrial plants.

Joseph C. Kircher, forester in charge of the U.S. Forest Service's Southern region, along with officials of the Southland Paper Mill, the Angelina County Lumber Company, and the Frost

Lumber Company worked out a practical solution to the timber growers' problem. They appealed to the national War Manpower Commission for permission to construct prisoner-of-war camps and to bring in German war prisoners to supply the necessary labor. Twelve such camps were erected in the Pineywoods of East Texas, one of which located near Chireno.

This eastern Nacogdoches County community was chosen as a site for a camp because large sections of the surrounding thick pine forests were owned and worked by two of the lumber companies and because Chireno was located almost in the exact center of the area hardest hit by the ice storm. In addition, Chireno afforded excellent transportation facilities for hauling the cut timber to mills for processing. In 1912, the Angelina Lumber Company had constructed a rail line from Lufkin, through Etoile in the southern part of Nacogdoches County to Chireno.

By mid-May the Chireno Camp was finished covering some thirty acres, of which five were devoted to the camp's compound. The facility housed 250 prisoners. Lance Mettauer, a Chireno native, served as overseer for the German timber cutters. He took them to work each morning and pointed out the trees to be harvested. He had no fear of the prisoners and soon developed a close working relationship with many of them. The Germans worked these forests for some two years, during which time prisoner labor reached it peak in July 1944 when more than 5,700 man-days were spent in forest operations. In late 1945 the number of prisoners at the camp began a sharp decline, and the camp was phased out of existence early the next year.

This historical ice storm was followed in January 1945 by a powerful tornado that tore through the western section of Nacogdoches, killing a number of residents and destroying large amounts of property. Approximately fifty prisoners from Camp Chireno were dispatched to assist in clean-up operations in the aftermath of the storm. With the arrival of these German soldiers, the people of Nacogdoches came in contact with ordinary German young men. Most of them saw that the soldiers were lonely young men and not too different from their own male relatives and friends.

This killer tornado struck during the night hours, cutting a two-mile path through the city, claiming seven lives along the way, injuring an additional seventy-five persons, and leaving widespread destruction in its wake. Within a very few minutes the tornado snapped off eighteen-inch pine trees, collapsed houses, garages, and barns, and plunged the city into darkness. The Texas Power and Light Company sub-station that supplied power for the entire city was in the twister's direct path and was quickly demolished. City Memorial Hospital, the city fire station, and the private dining room of the Liberty Hotel where many injured were taken for treatment were supplied power by emergency lighting equipment from both Nacogdoches and Lufkin.

Some unexpected developments grew out of the location of the German camp in the Nacogdoches community. For example, the American soldiers assigned to guard the prisoners often left the camp at night to visit young females in training at the WAC school on the college campus, some creating lasting relationships. Moreover, some of the prisoners became so attached to East Texas and its people that they genuinely desired to remain when the war ended.

Under the auspices of the national government, a Civilian Pilot Training Program was created by the Nacogdoches Flying Service utilizing the facilities of Stephen F. Austin State College. Thomas Baker, Dan Leahey, and George Wanamaker operated the service and trained the civilian pilots. The project did not continue in operation for an extended period, but as an outgrowth the City of Nacogdoches selected a site for a new airport, a 400-acre plot carved from the Reggie Wilson farm located west of the city. The original airport had been a smaller plot situated some one or two miles down the Spanish Bluff Road from the newer facility. The earlier site had been cleared and made ready for use in 1933, but it had never been utilized on a regular basis.

In cooperation with the War Department, the City of Nacogdoches secured allocation of a Works Progress Administration (WPA) project and construction on the new field was begun in 1942 when four dirt runways were finished. The next year the WPA terminated its participation, and the city, without sufficient funds to continue, abandoned the project for the duration of hostilities.

College Life

Along with hundreds of college and universities throughout the nation, Stephen F. Austin State College experienced some serious "hard times" during the World War II years. From a record high of some 900 students for the fall semester 1940, its numbers began a steady decline to less than 800 the following year, and to a war-time low during the fall semester of 1944 when it was reduced to just over 300. As male students left the campus to enter the armed forces, the number of female students also declined. Many simply went home to wait out the war or to occupy themselves with war-related activities.

As might be expected, the college's focus shifted from the preparation of teachers for the schools of the area to an all-out attempt to aid in the war effort. Another unsettling development occurred when Dr. A. W. Birdwell, SFA's first and only president announced his retirement in 1942 after some twenty five years as its chief executive. He was succeeded by Dr. Paul L. Boynton, a Texas native then on the faculty of George Peabody College for Teachers.

A nationally renowned psychologist, Boynton began his

THE STORY OF NACOGDOCHES

academic career in 1916 when he enrolled at Rice Institute (now Rice University). After a short stint there, he transferred to Texas Christian University and later to Sam Houston State College in 1928 where he received a B. A. degree. The same year he then entered upon a teaching career as a high school principal, coach, and history teacher in the Lufkin, Texas public schools. In 1921, he moved to Wichita Falls, Texas, where he was employed as a junior high school coach and part-time classroom teacher. Two years later, he was awarded a master's degree in psychology from George Peabody College. During the time he pursued graduate studies at the Nashville institution, he taught one summer session at Appalachian State Teachers College, in Boone, North Carolina.

After receiving his master's degree, Boynton accepted a teaching position with the Department of Psychology at the University of Kentucky, becoming between 1923 and 1930 an instructor, assistant professor, associate professor, and acting department head. In 1927, he obtained the Ph.D. degree in psychology from the Nashville graduate school, and three years later was appointed professor and head of the department of psychology at George Peabody. He served in that capacity until 1942 when he left to take up his duties as president of the Nacogdoches college.

Before he came to Nacogdoches, Paul Boynton had gained national recognition in the field of psychology, having authored or co-authored books, monographs, and articles in his major field. In addition, he was in demand as a consulting psychologist by schools and hospitals.

As one of his first acts upon assuming the Stephen F. Austin presidency, Boynton pledged that the college would channel all its efforts toward assisting the war effort. He encouraged young men and women to stay in college and finish a degree. He pointed out that teachers of mathematics, science, and vocational subjects were badly needed, and he fostered a project of streamlining the student's college schedule to enable him to finish a degree in three instead of the traditional four years. Knowing that books for servicemen were needed, he encouraged the college to serve as a regional depository, and its library personnel sorted and packaged thousands of donated books destined for centers for servicemen.

Under his leadership, all male students were required to enroll for some physical activity course each semester. Those courses were designed to improve the physical condition of males so they could meet military standards and thus help prepare them for the transition from civilian to military life.

The college also declared a moratorium on intercollegiate football for the duration of the war, citing manpower shortages and transportation problems as the principal reasons. Competition in intercollegiate basketball was continued with Stanford W. McKewen, who later became the college registrar, named to replace Bob Shelton as coach. To replace intermural football, a strong program of intramural physical activities was launched, and all male students encouraged to participate as a part of the wartime physical fitness effort.

As was the case in most colleges, traditionally, SFA had fielded an all male band, but wartime conditions forced a reassessment of this policy. J. T. Cox, college band director, began recruiting females and demonstration school students and carried on that part of the music program as best he could. The drama program did not fare so well. One play was produced in the 1941 school year, and operations were suspended for the duration of the world conflict.

Viewed from any perspective, Boynton was faced with the task of fighting a battle of survival for the college. In 1942, he elected to hasten to Washington, D.C. to petition the War Department to locate a training facility of the Women's Army Auxiliary Corps, later renamed the Women's Army Corps, on the nearly deserted SFA campus. His petition was granted and in February, 1943, an Army Administration School, WAC No. 1, got under way in Nacogdoches.

The bottom floor of the Austin Building was devoted to the Army school's offices and classrooms; the bottom floor of the Science Building given over to headquarters offices and its second floor to the school's infirmary; and the Women's Recreation Center converted into the post exchange. Wisely Hall and Gibbs Hall served as barracks for the women enrolled in the school, while the Band Hall was converted into living quarters for the post's permanent enlisted personnel. As a result of these arrangements, resident civilian students were compelled to seek lodging in private homes and apartments in town.

So much classroom space was allotted to the training school that college classes were scheduled whenever and wherever vacant space could be found. Many classes met in the offices of the instructor, while others occupied vacant classrooms in the Demonstration School.

The WAC School located at Stephen F. Austin State College was the first of its kind to become operational. The first female recruits arrived on campus in February 1943 fresh from basic training in Des Moines, Iowa. This first class was made up of 250 women who joined the approximately fifty permanent cadre assigned to their training operations. Before the program was terminated in 1944, more than 2,000 uniformed personnel, male and female, were stationed on the college campus.

During its lifetime, twelve classes graduated from the Nacogdoches training school. New classes began every few weeks so that there were always approximately 600 WACs on campus at any one time, most of whom were natives of one of the nation's northeastern states. Training was arduous. Classes, drill, and related activities occupied almost every minute of the recruit's time Monday through Saturday. Reveille was sounded at

6:20 a.m., followed by classes morning and afternoon and close order drill several afternoons each week. Taps was sounded at 10:30 p. m.

Some sixty different subjects made up the school's curriculum. Typing, correspondence, and preparation of reports were emphasized. Classes continued for a period of six to eight weeks before graduates were dispatched to other duties.

One of the WACs stationed briefly in Nacogdoches during this time recalled that they were not the only students occupying the campus. They shared its facilities, she remembered, without much contact between the two groups. Socialization was discouraged, not by rule, but by the lack of time and opportunity. She also remembered that Nacogdoches created for her a special mood. Although everything was in short supply for the civilian population, they shared with the women in the military freely and with an open spirit making the recruits feel "right at home." The WACs likewise made a lasting impression on local residents and helped to widen the horizons of many of them.

The Wac school proved to be a near life-saving operation for SFA. It went a good way toward rescuing the college from the enrollment and financial crises brought on by the war effort. The war's end was followed by an upturn in the fortunes of SFA and other colleges and universities throughout the nation, for in 1944, Congress enacted the Servicemen's Readjustment Act popularly known as the GI Bill of Rights. Among its other provisions the statute offered living allowances and tuition payments to college-bound veterans. This offer encouraged thousands of returning servicemen to chose a college or university, set up housekeeping with their wives and young children in abandoned military barracks moved to college campuses, and embark on a career as "mature students." They were destined to change forever the nature of college life.

SFA shared in the revival this turn of events brought about, for by the beginning of the fall semester of 1946 its enrollment again exceeded 1,000 with male students outnumbering females by a ratio of three to one. Despite a severe housing shortage, hundreds of veterans descended on the college in the 1945 and 1946 academic years.

As a result, by 1946 the college was well on its way to recovery and unprecedented growth in physical plant, educational programs, enrollment, and reputation. One of the most significant developments was the creation of a Department of Forestry, the first of its kind in the state to offer such a four-year degree program. U.S. Representative Nat Patton, U.S. Senator Tom Connally, and a number of East Texas lumbermen under the urging of President Paul Boynton combined efforts to bring about this result.

This new educational program was the culmination of a series of events that began in 1944 when Congress established a U.S. Forest Experimental Station in conjunction with Stephen F. Austin State College. The first step was the transfer of a number of acres of farmland in the area then owned by the Farm Security Administration to the Forest Service. A 2,000-acre plot known as the Blount farm was conveyed to the Forest Service. The State Board of Control and the Texas Legislature then approved the transfer and authorized the creation of a forestry department at SFA. During the summer and fall of 1945 a departmental faculty was assembled, a curriculum created, and housing made available, enabling classes in forestry to begin being offered during the 1946 spring semester.

As means of honoring those men and women who entered the military forces during the global conflict, the City of Nacogdoches and SFA cooperated to establish a memorial. Officials of the college with the express approval of Texas Attorney General Grover Sellers leased college-owned land to the

City of Nacogdoches for the construction of facilities to be owned by the city. The college then granted a long-term lease to the city on some of its property along the east side of Raguet Street. The city in turn pledged to finance and construct an athletic stadium with a seating capacity of 5,000, dressing room facilities and field house, a lighted softball field, tennis courts, and a swimming pool.

A 1946 city election allowed Nacogdoches voters to authorize the city's government to issue $60,000 in bonds to construct the stadium and field houses as the first units of the overall project. The entire project when completed was then designated Memorial Park and the athletic field Memorial Stadium.

All these developments in the life of the Nacogdoches college meant that it would never return to the regional teacher training institution that had been its principal focus since its opening days some twenty years before. The new Forestry Department signaled an expanded scope, and its increased enrollments forecast a more comprehensive mission.

Political Life

Prior to the outbreak of World War II and continuing for some years thereafter, political life in the Nacogdoches community exhibited, in the main, the characteristics of many rural areas in the American South. As result of its geographical location on the western rim of the Bible and Cotton Belts, it was steeped in the traditions of the Old South which colored deeply its attitudes toward politics and participation in political life.

A pattern that featured an amorphous, not well defined, one-party (Democratic) system with most of the internal divisions common to other states that made up the Old Confederacy had grown up over many decades. Its prevailing temper among all its divisions was solidly conservative with occasional injections of rural radicalism, such as Populism. Rural populists sought by democratic means to have government help them cope with the power of big businesses.

One of its key elements--probably the most common--was an innate, unquestioning, fiscal conservatism that most often translated into demands for low taxes and little spending. This commitment meant that all local governments, dependent as they were upon ad valorem taxation of property, were severely handicapped when attempting to provide services for their residents. In the American political culture tradition dictated that landowners resist the levy of all property taxes, and where those individuals made up the dominant voting power, property tax rates were invariably low and their rates increased only reluctantly when crises were acute and increases could not be avoided. Government services, therefore, were of necessity kept to the barest essentials and proposals for new or additional expenditures defeated whenever possible.

In most rural areas, the one notable exception to this resistance to public spending was the construction and maintenance of roads. Texas farmers who were forced to haul their cotton and other commodities to gins and other processing facilities and to local markets for sale many miles over dirt roads, many of which were impassable in rainy seasons, were especially interested in improved roads. City merchants heavily dependent upon rural customers, educators who desired to consolidate small, one-room rural schools into larger more efficient units, and others who wanted better roads for their new and improved automobiles joined farmers in demanding more and better roads. Thus, both rural and urban Texans were in complete agreement in the expenditure of vast sums of public funds for roads and bridges.

Local political campaigns in the years following the Reconstruction Era did not feature divisive issues, except when "moral" questions were involved, especially questions of prohibition and legalized gambling. Races for county and municipal offices normally were uncontested and incumbents regularly returned in office as long as they cared to serve. In Nacogdoches County, for example, Oscar L. Holmes held the office of county clerk for sixteen years (1842-1858); Ephraim Coon served as Chief Justice for three years (1847-1850), District Clerk for two years (1855-1857), and County Tax Assessor and Collector for five years (1860-1865). David Rusk (1837-1846), R. D. Orton (1867-1873, 1881-1882), Milton Mast (1873-1880) and A. J. Spradley (1882-1894, 1904-1906, 1908-1910) held the office of sheriff forty of the years between Texas independence and 1920.

African American citizens, women, and men under twenty-one years of age were legally excluded from participation throughout much of period between the Texas Revolution and the outbreak of World War I. In addition, in many local elections, especially those involving bond issues, only those who paid property taxes were allowed to participate. Grandfather clauses and White Primaries were devices used to exclude African American men and women from casting legal ballots.

Concern with racial issues in Nacogdoches did not generate the heated and sometimes violent consequences that it tended to generate in communities in other areas of the American South and in other East Texas communities. For a variety of reasons including holdover memories from revolution and post-revolutionary days only a relatively small percentage of the city's Spanish-American citizens chose to take part in the political activities.

Local government was, therefore, overwhelmingly in the hands of an easily identifiable Anglo-American establishment. That political grouping was composed, in the main, of bankers, merchants, large land owners, and their allied professional persons--doctors, lawyers, and the like. Together they constituted the "moneyed class" of the community.

Political life, however, began to undergo some gradual but significant modifications during and immediately following World War II. As the city's population steadily increased, the racial, economic, and social composition of the community underwent important alterations. This, in turn, tended to spark opposition to the long-standing political establishment. U.S. court decisions such as the Supreme Court decision in 1944 outlawing the White Primary brought African American voters in the community into the political mix. Returning veterans of both genders likewise became more active in voting and in seeking political office. Later U.S. Supreme Court decisions outlawing all tax payment (such as the Texas poll tax) as a qualification for voting encouraged still other elements of the local citizens to become active participants.

By 1946 there was ample evidence that changes had taken place and were continuing to take place in the lifestyle of the people and institutions of the old town of Nacogdoches. Growing economic prosperity, increased population, recovery of the college, emergence of timber production, all pointed to increased prosperity for many. However, against these developments must be projected some prudent realities. Not every resident of the city and county became affluent or even approached that state. The 1950 census data revealed that almost half of the dwellings in Nacogdoches County had no running water or indoor plumbing of any sort. In short, hundreds of persons in the community were living well below the poverty level as defined by the U.S. Census Bureau.

BURLEY TOBACCO LEAF READY FOR HARVEST, JULY 1909

CHAPTER NINE
THE POST-WAR TRANSFORMATIONS

The flood of servicemen that inundated colleges and universities, continued economic prosperity, rapid advances in technology, and growth of a global outlook were just some of the developments that combined to bring about a number of significant transformations in American life in the years immediately following the end of the Second World War. In the Nacogdoches community those alterations were especially apparent in the areas of public education, municipal government and politics, and public services.

After experiencing the adverse effects of the depression years followed by the war-time crisis, Stephen F. Austin State Teachers College experienced significant changes. Enrollments began to mount from the 1,000 students of the 1946 fall semester to more than 1,500 the fall semester of 1949, and to almost 1,700 the fall of 1955. The G. I. Bill of Rights that encouraged returning veterans to seek a college education, the decision by college officials to provide housing for returning veterans and their families, and the implementation of a much expanded scope to its academic offerings were instrumental in attracting more students. Set over against these influences was President Paul Boynton's determination to maintain the college as an East Texas regional institution.

The impact of the G. I Bill is illustrated by 1949 college enrollment figures that show 482 of the 1,538 students (more than 30 percent) registered for the fall semester were veterans. Its regional nature is revealed in the geographic distribution of men and women enrolled that same semester. Of the 1,538 students registered, 482 were residents of Nacogdoches County, 206 of Angelina County, 124 of Cherokee County, 121 of Shelby

County. This total of 933 students, just over 60 percent, came from Nacogdoches County and three of the surrounding counties.

To meet the housing needs of the scores of servicemen and their families who found that they could not find a place to live in the city, two veteran's housing projects that became known as Veterans' Villages or Vet Villages appeared on campus. Renovated from Army surplus barracks, these first apartment houses, although far from fancy, were adequate to meet the demand for temporary housing.

This influx of returning veterans transformed college campus life in at least two important aspects. Providing housing for them and their families added apartments to the traditional dormitories, a development that would remain a fixture long after G. I.'s had ceased to swell enrollments. Moreover, the older, more mature service men and women launched a trend toward an increased age level for college students, a trend that continued throughout the remainder of the 20th Century.

Increased enrollments also brought about the necessity of greater numbers of faculty members, and thereby initiated a transformation in both the numbers and composition of the teaching staff. Since 1923, faculty members at SFA had predominately been persons with public school teaching and administrative experience with master's degrees. This condition was, of course, the logical outgrowth of the college's mission, the preparation of teachers for schools in the East Texas region. After 1946, the emphasis when filling appointments to the faculty would be on liberal arts and the sciences and upon securing persons with the highest earned degrees in their fields.

Some indication of the growth in faculty can be gleaned from their numbers in 1946 and thereafter. About ninety-five full-time and part-time positions constituted the college faculty in the fall semester of 1946, but this number grew to more than 100 by the fall of 1949, and to 110 by the 1958 fall semester. Thereafter, new faculty members were added at a rate of more than ten each year. Deaths, retirements, and resignations created vacancies that need to be filled, but increased enrollment was the major cause of increased numbers of new faculty members.

When the college opened its doors, two men filled its most important administrative positions: President Alton W. Birdwell and Dr. Thomas E. Ferguson, academic dean and head of the English Department. Birdwell retired in 1942, but Ferguson continued as dean and department head until August 31, 1955 when he was replaced by Dr. Joseph Newton Gerber. Gerber had been serving as dean of the Junior Division and Director of Guidance since 1950, having come to Stephen F. Austin from Northwestern State College in Natchitoches, Louisiana.

Growing numbers of students also transformed the college's physical plant. Additional students registering each academic year created a need for additional classrooms, laboratories, and offices. Without funds available for major construction projects, college officials initially resorted to the acquisition of surplus frame buildings from World War II military installations. At least five such buildings were acquired in 1946 from Camp Claiborne, Louisiana. Three of them were relocated to the northeast corner of the intersection of North Raguet and East College Streets to house classes and offices for the Forestry, Music, and Commerce (Business) Departments. The remaining two were moved to the west side of North Raguet Street and assigned to the Agriculture Department. Each building was furnished with the appropriate chairs, desks, and other equipment.

A reliable and continuing source of funds for construction of permanent academic buildings was created in 1947 when an amendment to the Texas Constitution authorized the state to levy an ad valorem tax of ten cents per year on all taxable property within the state. The proceeds from this levy were dedicated to acquiring, constructing, and initially equipping buildings on the campuses of designated Texas colleges and universities. Among the designated colleges were members of the Texas State College System which included Stephen F. Austin State.

With $225,000 of its initial allocation of funds SFA acquired a student union building and an additional men's dormitory. These structures were converted Army surplus buildings that were located west of Wisely Hall facing College Street. The Student Union building housed the Lumberjack Luncheonette, a games room, a bookstore, the Stenographic Bureau, and a student post office. Later this building, familiarly known as the SUB, was renamed the Birdwell Annex and remodeled into a classroom and office building that also housed the Stenographic Bureau and offices for Student Publications.

Other funds from this first allotment were used to construct a powerhouse behind and slightly east of the Austin Building, a dormitory for women on the south side of the campus, an auditorium and fine arts building located on North Street just south of the Birdwell Building, and a physical education building containing a gymnasium that seated 3,500 persons on a site just south of Memorial Stadium along Raguet Street. When the physical education building was finished in 1951 it was named Shelton Gym in honor of the college's first coach and athletic director Robert (Bob) Shelton. The women's dorm was also completed that year.

Later using funds derived from the constitutionally dedicated fund, in the 1950s Stephen F. Austin embarked on an ambitious building program. In addition, the Demonstration School was eliminated by a mandate stemming from the Texas Legislature requiring that all such schools be abolished. This freed two floors of the Rusk Building for use as college classrooms and offices. In 1954, the Birdwell Building named in honor of the college's first president and located at the corner of North and College Streets was completed. It originally housed the English, Foreign Languages, Geography, History and Government, Mathematics, and Sociology Departments, although in later years it would be renovated and used to house other college departments.

The following year construction began on a much-needed library building situated on a site just east of the Birdwell Building, between it and the Austin Building. It was later named the Boynton Building to honor Paul L. Boynton, the college's second president. Rounding out the construction of new buildings in the decade was the completion of the Fine Arts Building later named the Griffiths Fine Arts Building in honor of an early Nacogdoches family who had owned property just south of its location.

Since it inception college buildings had been forced to depend on windows and air vents for cooling in the long, humid hot weather seasons that often lasted for six months or more each year. In the summer of 1955, however, state funding made air conditioning available for most classrooms and offices. In the older buildings window units at first supplied welcome cooling until larger whole building units could be installed.

The success of the first veterans apartments coupled with the continuing demand for apartments led college officials in 1954 to undertake construction of six new brick veneer apartment houses on Raguet Street, each house containing four units. Eight of the new apartment units had two bedrooms and the remaining sixteen only one bedroom. The old "Vet Village" units having served their purpose as temporary housing were torn down when the new units were ready for occupancy. Two years later two men's dormitories, Units I and II, were erected on Raguet Street near the location of the original college baseball diamond. These one-story structures were constructed of brick and tile.

The original president's home located on Starr Avenue on

the southeast rim of the campus was deemed outmoded and unsatisfactory by 1956 and plans developed for the construction of a new house. By 1957 the new brick two-story home was completed and the older one moved away to make room on the East Starr site. The old house was moved one half block east on Starr Avenue and was used by the Department of Home Economics as a Home Demonstration House.

By late in the 1950s the physical aspects of the campus had undergone considerable alteration. Several new classroom buildings, a new athletic field, a new library, and several new dormitories gave the college a new progressive look.

The most significant transformation in the curriculum of the college was the introduction of an emphasis on agribusiness. The new and singular forestry curriculum inaugurated in 1945 was designed, for the most part, as an aid for East Texas timber growers and timber processors. In addition a new vocational education program was established aimed at preparation of vocational agriculture teachers for the public schools of the region. Finally, a 207-acre farm was acquired for use as a vocational laboratory for students specializing in dairy husbandry.

Two other outstanding events occurred during the decade. In 1949, the expansion of the college's mission and its increasing student body, help prompt the Texas Legislature to rename it Stephen F. Austin State College. The sudden death of President Paul Boynton on August 6, 1958, left it without executive leadership. Boynton had guided the college for sixteen years through some very troubled times. During his tenure SFA's enrollment had with some fits and starts gradually grown from some 500 to more than 2,000 students; the value of its physical plant increased by millions of dollars; and an increasingly professional faculty was assembled.

During the interim while the Board of Regents of the Texas College System undertook a search for a successor for

President Boynton, Dean J. N. Gerber acted as the college's chief executive. Within a very short time, a few weeks, the Board announced that on November 1 Dr. Ralph W. Steen would become SFA's third president. A West Texas native, Steen had spent his childhood in the small rural community of Eula east of Abilene. After receiving his high school education in the nearby Clyde public schools, he was awarded a bachelor's degree by McMurray College in Abilene, and master of arts and doctor of philosophy degrees from the University of Texas in Austin. He then joined the history faculty of Texas A&M University in 1935 and later was named head of its History Department. By the time he was named SFA's president, Dr. Steen had established a reputation as a superior classroom teacher and a national authority on the history of Texas.

The end of World War II saw the public schools of the nation facing a serious, even distressing condition. The depression of the 1930s had sharply reduced school budgets and the restrictions of the war years had not permitted any relief. Much needed new construction and the modernization of existing physical facilities had been, of necessity, postponed for many years. The return of prosperity during the war time might have enabled school districts to acquire the necessary funding, but all nonessential construction and remodeling was not permitted. The result was that in 1946 the United States faced the prospect of a greatly increased school-age population and a badly deteriorated physical plant accompanied by a troublesome shortage of qualified teachers.

Nacogdoches County schools shared in all those problems. In keeping with the traditional arrangements in rural communities throughout the agrarian South, between the end of the Civil War and the Great Depression of 1929 some 158 separate schools had existed for varying periods of time, all small and poorly equipped, many taught by teachers poorly prepared.

In the 1909-1910 school year, for example, sixty-six public schools held classes in the county whose population at the time stood at just over 27,000. That arrangement, although modified slightly after 1930, continued to prevail up to and including the World War II years.

Not until June 1948 did the trustees of the Nacogdoches Independent School District decide that they could initiate a postwar building program and thus begin the transformation of public school education in the community. At that time they asked taxpayers of the district to approve a $100,000 bond issue to enable them to authorize construction of a new West End Elementary School for African American students, a new vocational education building for Nacogdoches High School, and a new gymnasium for E. J. Campbell, the African American secondary school.

E. J. Campbell for whom the school was named was a native of Nacogdoches County and a descendant of slaves brought to the Douglass Community by a Campbell family. He was educated in the Douglass and Nacogdoches public schools and Prairie View State Normal College. He was granted a teaching certificate about 1910 and thereafter taught in Nacogdoches County schools until his death in 1937. For twenty-seven of those years, he served as principal of the African American schools in the city.

July 31, 1948 voters approved this bond issue by a margin of four to one. Whereupon ten acres of land was purchased on Burrows hill near the city water reservoir as the site for the new West End Elementary School. In less than a year, this new elementary school, named the W. E. Jones Negro Elementary School, was destroyed by fire. This tragic event in tandem with growing student population led to voter approval on February 5, 1952, of a another bond issue totaling $850,000. The four to one margin indicated that property owners in the district were aware of the near desperate straits of the local school district.

The funds obtained from this second bond issue were used to construct two eighteen-teacher elementary school buildings for white children, a new high school building for black pupils, a replacement for the burned West End Elementary School, and extensive remodeling of the Central Elementary School building on the Washington Square campus. This renovated structure was destined to serve as the Thomas J. Rusk Junior High School for white children for some years thereafter.

The school board then chose two sites for new elementary schools. A tract of land immediately north of the Raguet Street "Vet Village" was leased from the college and designated as the location of the new north-side Raguet Elementary School. A tract of land bounded by South, Fredonia, and Seale Streets was purchased as the site of the new south-side Fredonia Elementary School.

Continuing the transformation of the public schools of the NISD, in 1952, the trustees purchased approximately five acres of land adjacent to the existing E. J. Campbell campus. On this site a new high school building for black students was constructed, and the older building designated as an elementary school. A $460,000 bond issue approved by a margin of some five to one on May 22, 1956 permitted the district to erect a new gymnasium-band hall for the Nacogdoches High School, nine additional classrooms for the old West Side Elementary School now renamed the Nettie Marshall Elementary School; a new nine-room junior high school for black students, later named the Brooks-Quinn School; a new cafetorium for the E. J. Campbell High School, and purchase the necessary land, furniture, and other equipment.

Although willing to provide new and renovated classroom buildings, gymnasiums, cafeterias, and athletic facilities for all school-age children in the district, Nacogdoches voters were not willing to abandon the traditional old South arrangement of racially segregated schools. In a referendum conducted by the school district in the 1950s, they indicated by a margin of eleven to one their preference for separate schools for white and black children. Participants in only one voting precinct, Precinct Five, favored integration. The voter's action came despite a ruling by the United States Supreme Court some two years earlier (Brown v. Board of Education) that segregated schools violated the equal protection clause of the Fourteenth Amendment to the U.S. Constitution.

In an effort to avoid the necessity of bringing about total integration of pupils within the Nacogdoches Independent School District, in 1959 the Board of Trustees adopted an ability-grouping plan whereby children would be placed in the "teaching environment" where they might receive the "best possible instruction." Grouping was to be based on the past academic record of all students.

Rural school districts in the county also followed the same pattern of development. Many new buildings and other structures were constructed and other important alterations made, but segregation remained the rule. Voters in the Nacogdoches community were willing to go only so far in transforming their educational systems.

When the Texas Legislature enacted the Gilmer-Aiken Bill creating the Minimum Foundation School Program in 1949, another far-reaching change was initiated. Among its many provisions, the new law included a "dominant school clause" requiring any local school district, following the 1946-1947 school year, that failed to operate a school for two successive years must consolidate with an adjoining district where school was being held on a regular basis.

This legislative mandate produced an election held September 13, 1949, in which nine local school districts adjacent to the Nacogdoches District approved consolidation with the NISD. A second election held in 1953 added three more rural districts bringing the total number of districts consolidated to twelve and increasing the size of the Nacogdoches District to approximately 150 square miles. In a move aimed a preventing their forced consolidation with the larger NISD, in August 1959, the common school districts of Central Heights, Union Springs, and Lone Pine were consolidated to form the county's first rural high school district.

In Public Service

Regular population increases between the end of World War II and American involvement in Vietnam in the late 1950s brought about still other modifications in the lives of Nacogdoches residents. The 1940 U.S. Census placed the number of persons living in the City of Nacogdoches at 7,600; ten years later that figure had grown to 12,300; and in 1960 stood at 12,674 persons, an increase of more than sixty-six percent in twenty years. This dramatic growth created five major problems for the city's government: How could the commission best meet the demand for sewer extension, water supply, street paving, garbage disposal, and parking facilities?

For some years the city and adjacent areas had experienced water shortages during drouth periods, but in 1949 an acute shortage placed residents living outside the city's limits on the east in acute distress. They depended upon water supplied by the city and failures left them lacking adequate dependable water. To deal with this problem, the City Commission formulated plans to annex a sizeable area on its eastern boundary lying, for the most part, between the Center and San Augustine Highways. This plan hinged on the willingness of the of a majority of the qualified voters in the area to sign a petition indicating their support. The Commission assured residents that adequate water and sewer facilities would be forthcoming but only when funding was available. By a margin of only eight signatures, the petition failed and the city's annexation plan was rejected.

In the wake of this failure, commissioners determined to employ a qualified engineer to conduct a survey of areas adjacent to the city limits and recommend which sections should be annexed. The following April voters in five contiguous areas that had been recommended for annexation approved, bringing 893 additional residences and 3,662 individuals within the city limits. This series of events marked the beginning of major expansions of the city's territory.

Yet another facet of the city's growth was revealed in a report by the U. S. Census Bureau in 1953, indicating that dwelling units in Nacogdoches totaled 3,675 with about twenty-seven percent of them having been constructed since the 1940 census. New residential sub-divisions brought into being by this steady demand for new housing also altered the physical appearance of the city. In addition to these new residences, some forty new business opened their doors between 1946 and 1948, many in new buildings on new locations, while many older buildings were renovated or rebuilt. Another radical change in the physical appearance of the city emerged in 1948 when the first post-war shopping center was opened.

Inevitably accompanying persistent growth in population and area was a growing demand for water which regularly produced critical water shortages. In 1946, the City Commission responded to the demand by authorizing the drilling of new wells, but they were not completed and in operation until summer of the following year. In the interval water consumption rose to a record high, and Mayor A. J. Thompson appealed to residents to restrict their water usage.

Alarmed and frustrated by continuing water shortages, property owners and other residents of the city voted to authorize the city commission to issue $150,000 in revenue bonds to finance water supply and sewage disposal projects and to complete the construction of previously authorized Memorial Park projects. Only $10,000 of these funds were earmarked for the park project, the remainder was dedicated to water and sewer improvements with revenue received by the water and sewer departments pledged to redeem the bonds.

A new 500,000 gallon water storage tank was completed, and a new pump station, degasifier, and sand trap were installed in 1950; and two years later two additional storage tanks were provided at the intersection of Butt and East Main Streets to facilitate supply for east-side residents and at the intersection of Wells and Townsend Streets to serve south-side residents. Despite these near-heroic measures, by 1958, residents of the city were again registering strong complaints about continuing periodic water shortages.

A new sewer disposal facility was put in operation in 1949, but disposal and treatment problems were ongoing problems for the city administration throughout the next decade, A $975,000 bond issue approved by the city's voters dedicated to improvement of water and sewer systems permitted laying new sewer lines and installation of a more efficient sewer disposal system. By 1960, however, these intrepid measures proved insufficient as a permanent solution to the problem.

Moreover, by 1960, concerned individuals were beginning to recognize that an adequate supply of water for residential, industrial, and related purposes could not be provided by wells. In 1954, for example, voters in Nacogdoches and Angelina Counties approved the creation of the Angelina-Nacogdoches Counties Water Control and Improvement District Number One. They likewise endorsed the development of a lake to be known as Lake Ponta on a site in northwest Nacogdoches County. This man-made lake was destined to supply water to the cities of Nacogdoches, Lufkin, and Henderson. For a variety of reasons, including intercity rivalry and resistance to supplying adequate funding, this water supply source was never constructed. Instead, some years later, City of Nacogdoches voters authorized the construction of Lake Nacogdoches in western Nacogdoches County.

By the overwhelming margin of eight to one, voters in Rusk and Nacogdoches Counties approved a revenue bond issue of $2,400,000 for the construction of Lake Striker in Rusk County. Texas Power and Light Company encouraged the approval of the project by pledging to purchase one-fourth of the water produced. The remaining three-fourths would be sold to support water conservation projects in the two-county region.

Without an efficient and sanitary garbage disposal system, before 1949 residents were forced to handle the problem on an individual basis. That year, responding to the continuous pressure exerted by hundreds of local citizens, the city commission voted to put the city in the garbage collection and disposal business. More than 500 residents had signed agreements indicating that they would support city garbage collection at a cost of $1.00 monthly for twice-weekly pickups. Rates for pickups at business sites would be negotiate on an individual basis. The city having purchased garbage trucks and all other necessary equipment by August that year garbage pickup service was initiated.

Increased traffic on the city's streets and the accompanying problem of adequate parking facilities created yet another perplexing problem for the city administration in the post-war years. By 1948, registered motor vehicles in Nacogdoches County had grown to nearly 5,000. A high percentage of them were driven by residents of the city and virtually all of the rest by rural residents who regularly "came to town" to shop, to attend to affairs at the courthouse, or to enjoy the variety of restaurants, amusements, sporting events, and the like available in the city.

City officials attempted to meet these problems initially by embarking on an ambitious street paving program and an effort to provide additional parking spaces. In 1946, the old "hitch lot" north of Main Street and east of Banita Creek was paved to provide additional parking for the downtown area. The following year, parking meters were authorized by the City Commission for the downtown streets in an additional effort to facilitate parking downtown. Although the meters never successfully kept traffic flowing or appreciably eased the parking situation, they did generate some much needed revenue for the city government. In 1946, alone they brought in some $1,600 each month.

World War II had caused construction of streets, roads, and highways to be deferred until war's end. The City of Nacogdoches, Nacogdoches County, and the Texas Highway Department thereafter faced a critical need for construction and maintenance of existing traffic arteries as well as the demand for additional routes. Better facilities that would enable the more rapid transportation of persons and goods across long distances and that would accommodate the constantly escalating number of motor vehicles were imperative.

The City of Nacogdoches responded, in 1946 by proposing an ambitious paving program to the Highway Department (now the Department of Transportation) in Austin. The city commissioners projected a joint city-state effort to widen and pave North and South Streets from Hospital Street northward and southward to the city limits. To initiate the project, the commissioners agreed to obtain the necessary right-of-way, instructing City Attorney M. M. Stripling to begin condemnation proceedings if necessary to obtain the required pieces of land.

Later that year the city received notice that the project had been approved and that it would be included in the 1947 primary federal-aid allotment.

To give property owners along the route to voluntarily surrender the required small portion of their property, condemnation proceedings were not instituted until August 1947 when thirty-seven of those owners had refused to sign deeds donating the necessary land. Jewel P. Byrd, P. L. Sanders, and Edward B. Tucker were appointed as a committee to provide estimates of the value of the property involved. Condemnation suits were ultimately concluded in June 1949 and work scheduled to begin the following month. Owners were offered payment of the amounts judged fair by the committee. At least thirteen owners refused and instituted suit to contest the decision in their condemnation cases. These appeals along with other legal complications delayed work on the project until in June 1949 contracts were finally executed.

Meanwhile, the city and property owners along Texas Highway 7 from South Street to the city limits on the west, a distance of just over three miles, reached agreements concerning right-of-way. This project called for rerouting the highway and paving its surface. Later, in 1950, when that portion of the highway had been completed, Highway 7, known locally as the Old Spanish Bluff Road, was extended an additional nine miles to the Angelina River.

Rural residents also experienced improved driving conditions. In 1947, the county's first farm-to-market road was constructed from Legg's Store through Cushing to the Rusk County Line. Four years later paved rural roads in the county financed, in part, through the federal farm-to-market road program exceeded sixty-five miles. In 1959, however, this paving program was slowed when by a decisive margin of more than 400 votes county property taxpayers defeated an increase in their ad valorem tax rate designed to finance highway and road development in the county.

Local observers such as Victor B. Fain, *The Daily Sentinel* editor, concluded that war's end found the streets of Nacogdoches at least ten years in arrears. They and other concerned residents challenged the city commission to at least embark upon a modest long-range paving program. Not until 1950, however, did the city administration agree to accept the challenge. At that time a $200,000 bond issue dedicated to street improvements was proposed and approved by voters in a special election. Funds generated from the sale of the bonds were then used to defray the city's share of the cost of paving additional streets and repairing the paving of those already paved. The remainder of the cost of paving and curbing would be provided by levies on the property owners adjacent to the streets.

Paving and guttering of some 25,564 feet of additional streets was covered in a contract executed in 1951, whereupon the city administration announced that the money obtained from the bond issue was depleted and that at least $50,000 in new funds would be necessary to finish paving and guttering streets already approved for hard surfacing. One of the most conspicuous of these paving projects was the hard surfacing of the Old Tyler Road.

Eight years later, in 1959, taxpayers in Precinct One of Nacogdoches County which included all of the City of Nacogdoches voted by a margin of 1,322 to 493 is authorize the city to issue $350,000 in additional bonds to assist in continuing the street and highway expansion program within the precinct. With these additional funds, right-of-way was purchased to develop a seven-mile alternate route across the city, to widen East Main Street, and to extend Park and Butt Streets.

Pre-war Nacogdoches had offered its residents and visitors little in the way of facilities for athletic events, recreational activities, and other diversions. Post-war actions, in some measure, sought to address that problem. In 1946, the first unit of the $150,000 city recreation project, Memorial Park, was completed when Memorial Stadium was constructed. It was formally dedicated to the memory of those men and women of Nacogdoches County and those students of Stephen F. Austin State College who lost their lives in the service of their county during the second World War. The next year a $66,000 swimming pool located just south of the stadium was finished, and plans were underway to begin work on a series of tennis courts.

In keeping with long-standing Southern practices, use of the new pool located on Raguet Street was limited to white persons. As an outdoor facility, it was open from early May until mid-September each year. The pool was operated by personnel from the college, and all net revenue divided equally between the city and the college. Ten years would lapse before a municipal swimming pool open to black persons was constructed. This $36,943 plant was located in Temple Park, in an area cut from the old Frost Lumber Industrial holdings on the south side of the city.

Nacogdoches residents, students and towns people alike, relied heavily upon motion pictures. In 1949, for example, two modern innovations appeared in the community, drive-in theatres. The Redland Drive-in Theatre and the Pines Drive-in Theatre, were erected south of the city. Work also began on two new additional traditional movie houses in 1950: the SFA Theatre located in College Heights on North Street just north of the campus and the Main Theatre on East Main Street downtown. They joined two existing theatres giving Nacogdoches residents four choices. To accommodate African American patrons and comply with state law, in 1955, the Main Theatre added a balcony for their seating and a separate entrance and box office for their admission.

A long-range effort to turn Nacogdoches into an important health care center for the East Texas area was launched in 1950 when bids for a $320,000 expansion of the City Memorial Hospital were approved by the city commission. The city-owned hospital had originally been constructed and put into operation in 1928 with $60,000 in funds obtained from the sale of the municipal power plant. Local residents had contributed furnishings valued at $9,000 for the twenty-bed facility.

In 1938, a small-scale expansion of Memorial Hospital was completed, and in 1946 a large-scale effort was initiated when the Board of Managers for the hospital announced a plan to more than double its capacity. In early 1947, the City Commission approved the board's plan to increase the facility's capacity from fifty-five to 125 adult patients. Commissioners believed that two-thirds of the $250,000 to $300,000 needed would be available through a bond issue and the remaining third secured by a federal grant-in aid. City property-owning taxpayers subsequently approved a $150,000 bond issue, and in 1948 a $100,000 federal grant was made available.

Compliance with conditions laid down by federal regulations for receiving the grant money delayed the start of construction for more than two years, and it was not until late in 1952 that construction was finished. By then the cost of expansion had increased to $500,000 for the new addition that covered some 13,000 square feet and increased adult capacity to ninety-seven instead of the projected 125 persons. Once again, as in its beginnings, many of the hospital's new rooms were furnished by funds made available through contributions from local clubs, organizations, and individual donors.

By 1955 the enlarged facility was operating at or near capacity, and hospital board members began planning for a second major expansion. The city commission, however, delayed endorsing the project for approximately four years. Nevertheless, a third addition estimated to cost $125,000 was undertaken and when finished provided an enlarged dining room, a recovery room, a fourth surgery room, a consultation room for physicians, and five additional rooms for patients.

From the beginning of city ownership and operation of Memorial Hospital a three-member executive committee selected by the fifteen-member Board of Management appointed by the city commission had provided supervision and ongoing management. Membership on this executive committee was later increased five, all members of the larger Board of Management.

Two city-owned and managed cemeteries existed in the immediate post-war years--Oak Grove and Sunset Memorial Park. Private interests had demonstrated some interest in acquiring Sunset Memorial Park, north of town along Highway 259/59, and city officials debated the issue for months before coming to a decision. Finally, in November 1954, the Commission determined to retain city ownership, adopt a perpetual care plan, begin improvements immediately, and promote the sale of burial plots. In doing so, Nacogdoches became the first Texas city to undertake the operation of a perpetual care cemetery.

Prior to 1957, the City Library was located on North Fredonia Street in a building rented from A. T. and H. R. Mast. In December that year, it was moved to 135 North Mound Street to a white house just south of Dr. A. A. Nelson's Clinic. In less than a year's time, it was relocated in the Adolphus Sterne House at 211 La Nana Street. The Sterne property had been deeded to the city in September 1958 by Jennie Mast and Roy and Clara Gray, Joseph T. Hoya descendants. City officials then changed its name to the Hoya Memorial Library and Museum.

Growing concern in the post-war years concerning the activities of the youth of the community coupled with a desire to direct those activities into constructive channels led to the establishment of a youth center and a baseball complex. The youth center, officially designated the Dragon-Net, was opened in 1954 at a location on North Street. It use was restricted to white junior and senior high school students and then only on Friday and Saturday nights. In 1955, the center moved from its original North Street location to temporary quarters on East Main Street. Following a lengthy search, a lot on Hughes Street just east of North Street was secured and work began on a permanent building. A site for the youth baseball complex was obtained south of the downtown area on South Mound Street, and the facility designated as the Little League Baseball Park opened in time for games to be played in the 1953 season.

Despite sometimes strenuous efforts on the part of the city government and property owners in the city, fires and floods continued to inhibit progress. In 1948, for example, a serious fire broke out at the Nacogdoches County Lumber Company sawmill located on the Old Tyler Road, and before it was contained it had damaged a large amount of lumber and destroyed the kiln. More than $50,000 in damage was the official estimate.

Two years later the downtown area was again threatened when Stripling Drug Store's warehouse was destroyed and the store itself badly damaged by fire and smoke. It was again menaced in 1951 when Julius Eichel's dry goods store on the corner of Main and North Streets went up in flames and the entire stock of merchandise destroyed.

A year later four conflagrations erupted in the city causing more than $250,000 in property losses. Stripling Drug Store's warehouse was the site of a second fire in twenty-six months with damages estimated at $100,000. In addition, the attic, roof, and pipe organ of the First Baptist Church on North Street were badly damaged by fire. Near the same time, a blaze at the Hill Top Grocery and Washateria on Highway 21 West destroyed building, stock, and equipment. Perhaps the most dramatic of the year's four fires involved the newly-completed building of the Church of Christ at Mound and Starr Streets which was pronounced a total loss.

The next year a blaze that was visible for a great distance destroyed the mill and finishing house at General Oak Flooring Company located one half mile beyond the city limits on the southeast. The same year saw the Sanitary Laundry and the Western Auto Store located on East Main Street badly damaged with losses estimated at more than $100,000; and the First Baptist Church leveled by its second fire in less than a single year.

Continuing the series of destructive conflagrations, in 1954, several structures were destroyed as fire swept through the Stone Lumber Company plant on then Old Tyler Road. Losses included a planer, two kilns, a mill shed, an engine room, and a boiler room. Then, in 1957, Stewart's Food Center on North Street was badly damaged; Sutton's General Oak Flooring Mill experienced a second blaze; and Julius Eichel's new store on the west side of the downtown square was damaged.

In its attempts to deal with the situation, the Nacogdoches Fire Department was severely handicapped by old, worn-out equipment and insufficient manpower. In 1951 alone 312 different fires were reported. As a result, Nacogdoches taxpayers authorized a $225,000 bond issue dedicated to the purchase of new state-of-the-art equipment.

Geography, nature, and neglect together conspired to keep the city vulnerable to periodic flooding. In 1953, for example, more than three inches of rain fell in thirty minutes during one night bringing about flooding in low places, sending swirling water in low-lying homes, and setting business houses awash. Because the ground was already saturated by frequent serious rains and storm sewers in many areas clogged, flooding occurred in locations that had never before had that experience. High water marks on North Fredonia Street from Main Street to Washington

Square were exceeded; buildings along the street were inundated by six or more inches of flood water. Park, Mound, Bailey, and Raguet Streets were covered with water, and houses in the Hoya-Driver Addition off the Old Lufkin Road also experienced some flood damage.

Four years later, in the early morning hours of April 24, La Nana and Banita Creeks roared out of their banks following a torrential downpour of almost four inches, more than three of which fell in a two-hour period just after midnight. Bridges spanning both creeks were closed for several hours and homes near South Fredonia Street between Banita Creek and its 700 block were evacuated. Every business establishment on East Main from La Nana Creek to Shawnee Street was under water. Pine Street between North and Raguet Streets north of the college campus, Raguet Street north of College Street, and the Little League and Babe Ruth League baseball parks on South Mound were also flooded.

In Political Life

Transformations in numerous aspects of life in the Nacogdoches community, some rapid and dramatic others gradual and even routine, occurred in the immediate postwar years; but in its political life the story was largely "politics as usual." In keeping with other small, rural communities in the American South and Southwest, changes in government and politics came about slowly. When they did take place, it was often after careful deliberation or when forced by court decisions and congressional mandates.

In the decade from 1950 to 1960, for example, eleven annual city elections were held during the first week in April to select the five members of the city commission. Only eleven men, no women, were chosen. During that time twenty-seven positions were up for election, but in no instance was an incumbent commissioner defeated when seeking reelection. In fact, Bieto Beseler served for four terms, a total of eight years; but the norm was a stint of three terms or six years. Just four individuals served as chairman of the commission (mayor): Joe Kinsey, Frank Hathcock, Bieto Beseler, and M. M. Stripling. All of these commissioners were easily identified as members of the long-standing political establishment.

Before being elected as a commissioner, M. M. Stripling had served as city attorney for three terms (1939-1941) and (1946-1951). He was followed by another local attorney, Moss Adams, a descendant of an early Nacogdoches family. Adams held the position for many years, and during his tenure he was instrumental in persuading the commission to authorize a codification of the city's ordinances last codified in 1900. Meade White, a representative of the Municipal Code Corporation of Tallahassee, Florida, a firm specializing in such work was employed and in August 1957, codification was complete and adopted. It provided an indexed list of the city's ordinances that had been scattered among the commission's minutes for more than half a century.

At the beginning of the decade the city had on its payroll only forty-six persons, all under the supervision of Grady Stallings, Nacogdoches first City Manager. In selecting Stallings for the position, the commission began a practice that continued for decades, the choice of a local businessman or other non-professional for the city's top administrative post. Despite rapid growth in the numbers of city employees during the period, Stallings continued to supervise all city workers until his retirement in 1960. He had been employed in 1919 as office manager for the light, water, and sewer departments. Originally, the city he was appointed to serve could provide only about 200 gallons of water a minute, had only a few paved streets, primarily

North Main, Mound, Fredonia, and a few side streets leading from those main downtown arteries, and was without adequate sewer facilities.

To replace Stallings, in 1960 the commission chose J. T. Alders as the city's second City Manager and Cleon Compton as its City Secretary. They officed in a new City Hall that had been constructed in 1953 on the south side of the square to house, in addition, a meeting room for the city commission, the police department, and the central fire station.

The city's government and administration faced a series of issues that they only reluctantly and slowly addressed. Among the most important were widening of streets, especially North and South Streets the principal north-south artery; construction and renovation of city buildings and other structures, such as fire stations and city offices; embarking on an accelerated street paving program, and increasing demand for some sort of zoning ordinance. If the project involved the expenditure of large sums of additional revenue and the consequent increase in city taxes, in keeping with long-standing tradition, the city government responded at the rate of a snail's pace.

School board elections also reflected the practice of electing members from the establishment group. In the decade of the 1950s only seventeen persons served on the Board of Trustees of the Nacogdoches Independent School District. In a least five of the ten elections held during that time, candidates were uncontested and the total voter turnout small, often less than 100 ballots cast for the winning candidates. While women were not encouraged to seek public office, several prominent Nacogdoches females were regularly chosen to serve on the school board. Mrs. C. B. (Ruth) Davis was elected chairman of the board in 1953; while Mrs. J. Frank (Ellen) Beall, Mrs. A. T. (Pat) Mast Jr., and Mrs. Walter (Elizabeth) Scott were others elected thereafter. The dominant philosophy concerning membership on the board may be best expressed in the slogan: "One good term deserves another," for successful candidates regularly served two terms.

An insight into the community's political persuasion were local schools were concerned was illustrated in the Board's 1955 decision not to participate in the national government's surplus commodity program which would have provided certain foods for use in the school lunch program. They were motivated by the belief expressed by many district voters that participation would allow officials of the national government to dictate policies contrary to local wishes, a notion related to their dedication to local home rule for schools.

Only two men served as Superintendent of the Nacogdoches District during the decade: Ernest D. Cleveland and Ben A. Copass. Cleveland resigned after only one school year, leaving to accept the position of Superintendent of the Gladewater School system.

Some inclination on the part of community voters to break away from their post Civil War practice of solid support for candidates of the Democratic Party at all levels: national, state, and local became apparent in the decade. In the presidential elections of 1948 and 1952 they strongly supported Harry S. Truman, Lyndon B. Johnson, and Adlai Stevenson; and in 1954 Ralph W. Yarborough, all Democratic Party candidates. But an omen of change occurred in the 1952 presidential election when Dwight D. Eisenhower polled the greatest number of votes for a Republic candidate ever cast in the county, and in the 1956 election won the county for a Republican candidate for the first time since Reconstruction days.

County and city voters supported the candidacy of Ralph W. Yarborough for a U.S. Senate seat and John F. Kennedy (by the slim margin of 83 votes) for the presidency. In that presidential election many city voters deserted the Democratic candidates in the majority of election precincts by favoring the

Richard Nixon-Henry C. Lodge ticket. Only two city precincts supported the Kennedy-Johnson ticket.

In Nacogdoches, as in most other areas of the state, a new political pattern appeared to emerge. Growing numbers of voters had begun to support Republican Party candidates for national offices while clinging to their traditional allegiance to Democratic Party candidates who were least nominally members of the party for state and local offices. Local candidates who were nominated in the Democratic Party primaries for county and precinct offices and who were incumbents continued to be retained in office, some for as many as twenty years, until they chose not to seek reelection.

A political issue that clearly illustrates the operation of the local political system came to prominence in the 1950s. For many years, a growing segment of the county's residents, especially those living in the city itself, favored adoption of the county-unit road plan. Rural residents under the leadership of their elected county commissioners generally opposed the plan, wishing to continue the existing system whereby county roads in each of the county's four precincts were the responsibility of its commissioner.

In a 1947 special election brought on primarily at the instigation of city dwellers, by the narrow margin of less than 150 votes, county voters authorized the abolition of the "antiquated" precinct system of road and bridge administration and the implementation of a "modernized" county unit system. The unit system called for the employment of a county engineer who would supervise the construction and maintenance of all county roads and bridges. An overwhelming vote favoring the new plan by city voters brought about its adoption over the "bitter opposition" of residents of the rural areas.

A county engineer was not appointed until early 1948 because no funds were available in the county budget to pay his salary. The first engineer, Kenneth H. McMullen, was chosen in 1949 and continued to fill the position until early 1951 when he was discharged by a unanimous vote of the county commissioners court. Meanwhile, almost 1,000 county voters had signed a petition calling for a special election to overturn the result of the 1947 vote. Commissioners responded and an election in November 1950 featuring in a very "light turnout" resulted in voters again voting in favor of the unit system provided for in the Optional County Road Law of 1947. As was the case in the 1947 election, city voters provided the margin of victory.

In January 1951, the Commissioners Court rejected the county engineer's recommendations and voted unanimously to continue to operate the county road system with roads and bridges in each precinct in charge of its commissioner. Being asked to advise them concerning the matter, County Attorney Tom Reavley, later to become a respected federal appeals judge, responded that the commissioners could not legally purchase equipment, hire or fire road employees, refuse to employ an engineer nor dismiss one without good cause. Nor could the Court establish any policy concerning roads and bridges contrary to the 1947 law.

Finally, the commissioners responded to Attorney Reavley's opinion by employing W. A. Thompson as the county's second engineer. Thompson was the resident Texas Highway Department (Department of Transportation) engineer. But as late as the end of the decade, *The Daily Sentinel* announced in a bold headline that the county unit road law had not yet been implemented. County officials, thus, seemed determined to preserve the status quo in spite of all pressures brought upon them. The issue also illustrated the growing division of opinion concerning government operations between county and city voters.

Yet another important event in the political life of the

community during the 1950s was the erection of a new county courthouse. During the summer of 1955 a group of concerned local citizens began organizing a drive to secure approval for the construction of a new courthouse and jail. In November, county commissioners were persuaded to authorize a special bond election calling for the issue of $600,000 in government bonds to finance the project. County voters approved the issue, plans were drawn and approved in 1956, and in 1957 contracts let and construction begun.

This building was erected on the same site but slightly behind the existing structure, necessitating demolition of the old courthouse. While demolition was in progress, the southern wall of the older building collapsed crushing a portion of the new building. An additional complication arose when the demolition contractor abandoned the project after his performance bond expired. The debris he left behind was quickly dubbed "the rock pile" and was not completely removed from the site until September 1959 after a second contractor had taken over the operation. The Commissioners Court finally took possession and moved into the county's fifth courthouse the following year.

Events that transpired beyond the limits of the Nacogdoches community brought about still other significant transformations in the operation of its institutions of government. An amendment to the Texas Constitution adopted in 1954 prohibiting the exclusion of persons from jury duty on account of gender allowed Vera Cloudy to become the first female to serve on a Nacogdoches County jury--a sanity hearing in the county court. Thereafter, the names of other women began to appear on jury panels selected for the Second District Court. Mrs. Otha (Lucille) Johnson of Cushing and Mrs. Lillie Bailey Holmes of Nacogdoches then became the first of their gender to serve on a jury in a criminal case tried in the district court.

A series of decisions handed down by the U.S. Supreme

Court in the 1940s and 1950s banned systematic exclusion of African Americans from both grand and trial juries. In complying, somewhat reluctantly perhaps, five of them were selected for the jury in a civil case tried in the district court. The local newspaper proclaimed that this number constituted more such persons to serve on a civil jury in the county since Reconstruction days.

In Religious Life

In the years since the middle of the Nineteenth Century in Nacogdoches as well as in most rural communities throughout the American South, community social life to a very large extent centered around its churches. In the years during and immediately following the Second World War that situation was gradually being transformed. This change was fueled by technological advances such as television, by improvements in transportation, such as better roads and more efficient motor vehicles, and by an increasing variety of attractions, such as theatres, sporting events, and live dramas and concerts.

That this transformation was gradual almost imperceptible is evidenced by the growth in numbers of church members and places for worship. From 1948 through 1958, nine of the city's Christian congregations erected new and larger church buildings: Fredonia Hill Baptist Church in 1948-1949; First Christian Church in 1949; Mound and Starr Church of Christ in 1950-- destroyed by fire and rebuilt in 1953; First Church of the Nazarene in 1951; Grace Bible Church in 1951; New Hope Congregational Methodist Church in 1953; First Baptist Church in 1956; Calvary Baptist Church (as a mission of First Baptist Church) in 1957; and Perritte Memorial Methodist Church in 1958-1959. The important part that churches still played in the life of the community was indicated by the forty-five or more churches located within the city's limits and perhaps that many more dotted about the rural areas of the county.

In the meantime, First Methodist Church added a two-story brick education building adjacent to its facility on Hospital Street, and two other church groups added to their ministry by establishing Bible Chairs near the college campus. In 1949, the Reverend Glenn Flinn, state director of Methodist student work, announced that a student center for his denomination would construct a center honoring Macon Alston Gunter, a former Stephen F. Austin student who was slain on the Italian coast while serving in the U.S. Air Force. Three years later ground was broken for a new Baptist Student Center. Both of these buildings adjacent to each other were located on College Street across the street from the campus.

At the end of the century other denominations had established student centers about the city. Joining the Methodist and Baptist establishments on East College Street immediately north of the campus were the Association of Baptist Students which ministered to Baptist students other than those affiliated with the Southern Baptist Convention; The Yellow House which accommodated students affiliated with the Church of Christ; and St. Mary's Catholic Student Center which served the college's Catholic students. The Assembly of God Center was located on North Street near the campus; the Campus Crusade for Christ and the Episcopal Student Association had been established on Raguet Street also near the campus; but the Redeemer Lutheran Center was housed on the Appleby Sand Road some distance east of the campus.

Even a casual observer could detect that by the end of the decade of the 1950s, Nacogdoches was gradually being transformed from a small county seat market town in a rural county dominated by small farmers and row-crop agriculture to a growing city emerging as a center for education, and from a rural environment dominated by cotton and other row crops to a record setting producer of poultry and dairy products. It had also begun to acquire a reputation as a focal point for health care, and a favored location for retirement and for tourist attractions.

CHAPTER TEN
THE RECOVERING ECONOMY

Unexpectedly the economy of post-war America experienced more than a decade of growth and prosperity the result of baby boom, military spending, conglomerate corporate mergers, and gradual introduction of agribusiness. The economy of Nacogdoches--city and county--was slow to feel the benefits of this emergent nation-wide affluence. Instead, its recovery was slower and more gradual than many other parts of the state and nation. Indeed, one study of the economic history of the community concluded that significant recovery did not take place until the mid-years of the decade.

Improvement in economic conditions in all of East Texas was slow as the result of three highly significant factors: the Korean War that began in 1950; the absence of adequate paved roads, streets, and highways; and the community's reliance on a strictly undiversified economy. Initially, the onset of the Korean War that seemed to erupt on the heels of World War II was the most influential.

Congress, in the belief that the end of the Second World War would bring about lasting peace-time conditions, had allowed the Selective Service Act of 1940 and its extensions to expire. Growing international tensions in 1948, however, caused Congress to reactivate the system, and that year federal officials projected a draft call of 400,000 men. In due time, approximately 250,000 young men between the ages of nineteen and twenty-five were inducted into the armed forces for twenty-one months of service.

Individuals continued to be called for duty well into 1954 even though a questionable armistice had been agreed upon the previous year. By the close of 1954 almost 900 men from the

Nacogdoches County area had been drafted or had volunteered for military duty. The Korean War, officially denoted the "Korean Conflict," cost the nation more than $15 billion and more than 140,000 casualties. Nacogdoches undoubtedly suffered its share of casualties and paid its share of the cost.

An almost incidental outgrowth of the Korean Conflict was the organization of a Naval Reserve Unit in the local community with Dr. Joseph N. Gerber, a World War II veteran, as its commanding officer. It steadily drew men into its ranks until late in 1953 it had reached the strength of two divisions. Near the end of the conflict, a reserve unit of the U. S. Air Force was also organized.

Aside from these two reserve units, Company D, 386th Armored Engineer Battalion, Texas National Guard, was operational from its base at the Nacogdoches Guard Armory located at the local airport. A new armory building built at a cost of slightly over $66,000 was completed in 1955 on land the city donated to the guard unit.

Agriculture

As the United States entered World War II agriculture was still the dominant element in the economy of the Nacogdoches community. By the war's end, George W. Rice, the local County Agent, reported that during the war years most of the tenant farmers and many of the marginal farmers left the county. He stressed that they either went into the Armed Forces or into the many industrial plants that were built along the Gulf Coast. Of necessity then a trend toward fewer and larger farm units developed, marking the tentative beginnings of agribusiness in the area.

Steady increases in farm income also unfolded in the immediate post-war years. In 1940, gross farm income in

Nacogdoches County was reported as almost $1.25 million; in 1950 it had climbed to over $4.30 million; and by 1960 to almost $13.5 million, an increase of nearly 1,000 percent. Inflation certainly was a factor in this significant twenty-year growth rate, but increased production brought about by greater use of machines, commercial fertilizers, and new management techniques certainly contributed to this outcome.

The decade of the 1960s could without too much exaggeration be called a "boom time" for agriculture in Nacogdoches County. Statistics drawn from the *Texas Almanac* indicate the magnitude of recovery. Farm income at the beginning of the decade was listed at slightly more than $13 million annually, but by 1973 it had more than doubled to just over $30 million. In 1970, the county had been the center of a diversified livestock-poultry industry with more than nine-tenths of its agricultural income derived from livestock, poultry, dairy, and truck crops. The traditional staple cash crops such as cotton and grain had declined steadily in importance. Thousands of acres once given over to row crops had been converted to pasture, more that 2,000 acres in 1959 alone.

In 1961 the county's agriculturists produced 18 million broilers (chickens) and counted some 500,000 laying hens, 200 Grade A dairies, and 45,000 head of cattle. At the close of the decade the chief agricultural output was listed as poultry, eggs, dairy products, beef products, and timber products. Some ninety-five percent of all agricultural income was derived from those sources. A real insight into the transformation could be gleaned from the fact that cotton gins had all but disappeared from the city and county.

Poultry production in the county was given a real boost in 1963 when Purina, in conjunction with a corporation formed by members of the Nacogdoches Chamber of Commerce, announced that the group would construct a broiler processing plant which

Purina would then lease and operate. The new plant was ultimately located on the south side of Butt Street, east of the TN&O railroad tracks. The following year, DeWitt Brothers, Incorporated, entered the poultry production market and thus insured that Nacogdoches County would become the largest poultry producing county in the state. For example, in 1964 alone the six major poultry producers raised 34 million broilers and generated more than $17 million in gross revenue.

After 1946 shortage of farm labor also hastened the replacement of cotton and corn by pasturage and livestock raising, poultry production, and dairy farming as the county's most important agricultural money producers. In the immediate short run, dairy farming established itself as the dominant agricultural activity. By the end of 1950, the annual income from dairy operations in the county exceeded $4 million. The county then contained 301 grade A and twenty-seven grade C dairies. In the long run, however, dairy farms decreased in numbers with some twenty-five percent of them ceasing operations between 1954 and 1958. However, annual income from the production of the remaining farms continued to grow, reaching $7 million by the end of the decade.

The 1951 annual report of the County Agriculture Agent revealed that in early 1949 fifteen broiler houses were engaged in the industrial production of poultry in the county, but that by the end of 1950 the number had increased to 350 with the typical house measuring twenty by 130 feet and holding some 3,000 chickens. By 1953, annual income from poultry production had gone over the $6 million mark. Later reports revealed that it remained at that level for several years.

Although stock farming, poultry production, and dairy farming had become important agricultural pursuits, Nacogdoches County remained a timber producing area. In 1959, 409,500 (sixty-six percent) of its 615,300 acres of land was devoted to commercial forests. This meant that approximately two-thirds of the total land area of the county was producing or capable of growing commercial stands of timber. The County Agent's report for that year, proclaimed that 375,000 acres of Nacogdoches County land was in forest, 160,000 in pasture, and only 40,000 in row crops.

The importance of the commercial production of timber locally was indicated in 1968 when the Long-Bell Division of the International Paper Company selected Nacogdoches as the site for a $5.5 million wood products manufacturing center. The plant which featured total utilization of wood was located on the southeastern rim of the city, annually generating approximately 100 million square feet of plywood, 20 million feet of lumber, and 3,500 carloads of wood chips for use in producing paper.

Business and Industry

January 1946, estimates placed the number of young men from Nacogdoches remaining in the armed forces at approximately fifty percent of the total number involved. In addition, there was a critical shortage of civilian clothing for those being mustered out of service and of housing for them and all others. Anxiety concerning rapidly rising prices for all commodities, of the possibility of a severe depression such as those that followed the end of several past wars, and of the continuation of federal controls disturbed local residents. Despite these conditions, the city's economy steadily improved. In that year, for example, more than $1 million in new construction projects were undertaken, one third of them devoted to new homes and apartments. Moreover, at least fifty new businesses were launched, federal price controls were phased out, and the supply of goods and services increased to meet the level of demand.

At the same time, more than 1,500 persons in the county

drew unemployment compensation--over 1,300 of them returning veterans; but by mid-year of 1947 that number had been reduced by almost fifty percent in both cases. That trend continued throughout the remainder of the decade, and the ranks of the unemployed in the county were reduced to national norms.

Congress stimulated the growth of business and industry in the post-war years. In late 1945, legislation reducing war-time levels of federal taxes was enacted and in 1947 all wartime price controls except those on rents, sugar, and rice were eliminated. Rent control was finally decontrolled in mid-year 1949, and controls on sugar and rice followed in due time.

In 1952, expansion of existing businesses and industries and the opening of new ones was in full swing driven, in part, by the national recovery from wartime shortages and restrictions on materials and prices. Texas Farm Products Company, the city's principal industrial operation, constructed a new feed warehouse at Bremond and West Main Streets. The company had celebrated its twentieth anniversary in 1950 when it employed an average of 133 persons at its feed and fertilizer plants. The fertilizer plant at that time had the capability of producing more than 25,000 tons annually, while its feed mill had a capacity of 200 tons of feed each day.

Lone Star Phosphate Company began construction of a new plant one mile south of the city limits on Shawnee Road. The new plant was owned by men associated with Texas Farm Products: Steele Wright, Joe Wright, Tom Wright, and Glenn Weaver. It was designed to produce twenty-percent phosphate for agricultural usage. A new Dr. Pepper Bottling Plant located on South Street also began operations during the year.

In the latter weeks of the year, plans for a community-owned hotel were unveiled. The area bounded by Hospital, Fredonia, Edwards, and North Church Streets north of the downtown area and south of Washington Square was chosen as its site. The Nacogdoches Community Hotel Corporation was chartered enabling promoters to sell stock and borrow funds. Revenue thus secured would enable them to purchase the land and begin construction. Jack McKinney was elected president of its board of directors at the corporation's organization meeting. R. G. Muckleroy was elected vice president, Ben Ritterscamp secretary, Emery W. Monk treasurer, and Thomas W. Baker assistant treasurer. In addition thirty-five directors were named, and Herbert Wilson of San Angelo, an experienced hotel manager, was chosen as its chief operating officer.

Plans called for the building to contain eighty-four rooms, four office or shop spaces, public and private dining facilities, and the necessary auxiliary and service areas. Its six-story central tower was designed to face the corner of Hospital and Fredonia Streets with seventy rooms and a lobby. A cabana area to provide an additional fourteen rooms would extend in a semi-circle around the central tower. In the area between the cabanas and the main structure a patio and swimming pool would be provided.

By early December 1952 community residents who served as volunteer salesmen had completed sale of $500,000 in stock pledges, assuring that an eighty-four room hotel at a total cost of at least $800,000 could be erected. An additional $360,000 was secured through loans extended by four Texas banks: Second National Bank of Houston ($150,000), Republic National Bank in Dallas ($150,000), Stone Fort National Bank of Nacogdoches ($30,000), and Commercial National Bank also of Nacogdoches ($30,000). Colonel W. B. (Bill) Bates, a Nacogdoches County native and well-known Houston banker, was instrumental in creating this loan package.

In April 1955, a crowd estimated at 6,000 persons attended the formal opening of the hotel. Susan Prentice McKinney, four-year old daughter of Dr. Edgar P. and Katherine Monger McKinney, had suggested the name Hotel Fredonia for the facility. After only four years of very successful operation, the hotel's board of directors proposed a $250,000 expansion. The proposal was quickly approved by the stockholders, and in January 1960 ground was broken, and Oak Terrace formally opened later in the year.

That year a Coca-Cola Bottling Plant was completed on North Street in the College Heights area. Additionally, a bowling center named the East Texas Lanes opened for business in the strip mall known as Northview Terrace further along North Street.

The announcement that H. L. Hunt Products Company intended to locate a chicken canning plant north of the city limits on Highways 259 and 59 added to the growing sense of prosperity in the local community. The Hunt firm took over the existing Ma Still operation and expanded its scope. Pete Still was retained as general manager. Products of the new plant carried the Parade of Homes brand and began operations with 120 employees working one eight-hour shift.

Despite the growing number of successful business enterprises launched at this time, two notable failures were also recorded. Early in 1952, Olin Industries, Inc. acquired the assets of Frost Lumber Company, including the Frost Lumber Mill of Nacogdoches County. Four years later, after selling its lumber holdings in central Arkansas, western Louisiana, and eastern Texas to International Paper Company, Olin Industries left the area. International Paper then announced that it would continue to operate the Frost Lumber Mill. Nevertheless, shortly after this announcement, Temple Associates of Diboll in Angelina County purchased the old Frost mill and offered Nacogdoches timber interests an opportunity to keep it in operation. When none responded, Temple Industries closed the mill, and some 300 Nacogdoches residents lost their jobs.

At nearly the same time, Bassons Industries Corporation,

hailed as one of the nation's largest plastic fabricators, announced in October 1952 that the company would establish a branch plant in Nacogdoches County. Nacogdoches residents were asked to provide some $150,000 to assist in getting the plant in operation. In its turn, the company promised to employ approximately 200 persons the first year and when in full operation a total of 1,000 individuals. By the end of the month the requested $150,000 had been made available.

A ten-acre site originally a part of then old Frost Mill land near the Bennett-Clark plant southeast of the city was chosen for the new plastics plant; but it readily became apparent by mid-1957 that the Bassons Company would default on its promises. Nacogdoches residents, however, were assured that they would receive refunds totaling the $150,000 they had invested. In the end, no refund money was forthcoming, causing the Nacogdoches County Industrial Foundation to file suit in civil court to recover the invested funds. Recovery was not forthcoming, partially as an outgrowth of the bankruptcy proceedings filed by the company in February 1959 and sale of the company's assets at auction.

While new businesses were being established in the community, existing enterprises were expanding their operations. In 1956, NIBCO of Texas commenced construction of the first unit of an expansion plan that in ten years was projected to add 120,000 square feet to their existing plant. Texas Farm Products Company completed construction of a new High Analysis Pelleted Fertilizer plant and commenced construction of an additional fertilizer plant adjacent to the Lone Star Phosphate plant located south of the city on Farm-to-Market Road 1275. Also that same year the Stone Fort National Bank finished a thorough renovation of its downtown building.

The following year, Bennett-Clark announced an expansion program that was projected to double the company's production the first year and more than triple it in thirty months.

This additional facility was located on a thirty-nine acre tract of land immediately north of the original plant on the Shawnee Road.

Accompanying growth in business was increased labor union activity. The first post-war attempt to organize locally occurred in 1947 when the Congress of Industrial Organizations (CIO) began a drive for members at the Frost Lumber Mill. The organizers succeeded in having the union recognized as the bargaining agent for the mill's employees. At approximately the same time, the American Federation of Labor (AFL) won the same recognition at Stone's lumber operation.

An attempt in 1950 to create a closed shop at NIBCO was defeated. In 1952, the Woodworkers Union was reaccredited at the Frost Mill, but in the same year employees at the Burgess Poultry Plant overwhelmingly rejected an organizing effort. Four years later, a second attempt to gain recognition at NIBCO again ended in failure, although this effort was accompanied by a week-long strike.

In the 1960s a renewed interest in the discovery and production of crude oil and natural gas added yet another element to the economic recovery experienced by the community. It began in 1952 when the Delta Drilling Company of Tyler drilled a test well in the Patuxy and Glen Rose sands near Appleby in the Sarah White Survey, about nine miles north of the city. The same year also saw the Humble Oil and Refining Company of Houston sink a test well in the Smackover sands northwest of Nacogdoches three-fourths of a mile from the Trawick community.

Transamerica Oil Company, also located in Houston, in 1964 developed three test wells in the general vicinity of Oil Springs south of the City of Nacogdoches. Then, following a three-year lapse, W. M. Coats of Longview, in independent operator, began drilling at a site below the Douglass community in the western section of the county.

At the end of the decade at least fourteen producing oil wells and several producing natural gas wells generating some $5.4 million in gross income were located in the area around Douglass. In total, thirty wells had been drilled in the county, eleven of which were producing oil and one producing natural gas; over 450 field workers were employed by these operations; and approximately $4.8 billion in income was being generated from the production of 238,000 barrels of crude oil and 33.1 billion cubic feet of natural gas.

During this same time new financial institutions began operations in the City of Nacogdoches. For many years the two downtown national banks had dominated the market, joined in more recent years by two savings and loan associations. In 1933, Thomas S. Davidson had organized and served as chief of operations for the First Federal Savings and Loan Association; and 1956 it was joined by the city's second such operation, the Nacogdoches Savings and Loan Association.

In 1963, however, a group of local investors organized and petitioned the federal government to grant a charter for a third national bank, but their application was refused. Whereupon, thirteen of them turned to the State Banking Commission of Texas seeking a state charter. They were soon joined by twenty-two additional investors who pledged to fund an initial capitalization of $350,000. The charter was approved later that year, and early in 1964 Rowland Vannoy, a native of Temple with twenty-seven years of banking experience, was chosen its executive vice president.

Named the Fredonia State Bank, this financial institution opened its doors for business that spring in a converted business building on North Street west of the college campus. It remained at this temporary location until 1970 when it moved further north and to the east side of North Street between Lloyd and Blount Streets.

Earlier, in 1961, the Commercial National Bank expanded its quarters on Main Street downtown, and the Nacogdoches Savings and Loan Association began construction of a new building on the northern half-block bounded by North Hospital and Pecan Streets. This four-story structure faced Hospital Street and featured an arcade and a one-story western extension soon occupied by Mize Department Store. Some four years later, the Stone Fort National Bank purchased the property just south of its downtown location and embarked on its own expansion program that featured a drive-in tellers window on Pilar Street and a new facade.

During this period, new industries began locating in Nacogdoches. One of the first of these was a plant erected for the use of the Southern Division of Moore Business Forms. The operation has heralded as a new million dollar business in the community. In 1963, production began at this plant located on a twelve-acre site four miles north of the city on Highway 259 and 59 near Millard's Crossing.

Growth of the tourist industry was marked by the addition of three new motels during the decade of the 1960s. The Continental Inn on North Street near the college campus began business in 1963 as did the Caraban Hotel on Highway 59 north of the city. In 1969, a Holiday Inn was constructed on North Street north of the site of the Continental Inn. The Chamber of Commerce recognized that tourism was rapidly becoming a major local industry, announcing that in 1966 some forty-three conventions alone had added nearly $2 million to the local economy.

For many years, but especially in the years after the end of World War II, the supply of rental housing had not met the ever increasing demand. In 1964, some effort was made to address this need. A thirty-four apartment complex styled The Claridge was erected on North Street; and later a rent supplement apartment project was begun in 1968 by the Nacogdoches County

Industrial Foundation aided by a grant from the Houston office of the Federal Housing Administration. Named Oak Hill Plaza, this ninety-two unit complex was located on a nine-acre tract of land at the intersection of Dolph Street and the Looneyville Road.

The first discount store to locate in Nacogdoches--Gibson's Discount Center--entered the business scene in 1966 when a building was constructed for their operations on a five-acre plot on North Street. Somewhat later, in 1972, the city's first shopping center--Northview Plaza Shopping Center--began operations. Originally located in this center were long-time Nacogdoches businesses Beall Brothers Department Store, Brookshire Brothers Grocery and East Texas Lanes. Joining them were new businesses such as Baskin-Robbins Ice Cream, and Otasco Drugs.

Another industry that appeared on the industrial scene was Gay Products. In 1966, this fabricator of aluminum furniture began production in the M. A. Anderson Grain building on the southeastern edge of the city at the old Frost-Johnson Mill property.

By the early years of the decade, the "old Hitch Lot" just east of Banita Creek at Taylor Avenue and West Main Street had become an anachronism. City officials, recognizing this fact, erected thirteen brick-and-steel spaces for the display and sale of farm produce and the area became known as the Farmers Market.

In keeping with their other efforts to stimulate improvements in the business climate, the Nacogdoches Chamber of Commerce determined to "revitalize aviation" in the area. The Chamber was aware that the demand for air travel was growing, that an increasing number of individuals and corporations had acquired aircraft, and that air mail delivery was becoming more popular. As a result, in 1947, Nacogdoches voters approved a $50,000 bond issue for improvements at the city airport. Revenue from the sale of the bonds was dedicated for construction of a paved runway with lights, paved taxi-ways and parking aprons for aircraft, and a rotating flashing beacon for nighttime identification.

Renamed Del Rentzel Field in honor of Delos W. Rentzel, administrator of the Civil Aeronautics Administration in Washington, in 1950, the facility held a formal opening ceremony. Administrator Rentzel was present for the opening and delivered the dedicatory address.

At war's end the only representative of the mass media present in Nacogdoches was its daily newspaper; however, less than a year later two radio stations were issued licenses by the Federal Communications Commission. KOSF, owned and operated by Kelly Bell, a local attorney, was approved to broadcast on a full-time basis; and KSFA, under the direction of W. Casey Fouts, began broadcasting but only during the daylight hours. After 1956, KELS FM, owned by Lee Scarbrough, for a short time operated as an afternoon station. The previous year, a television station, located near Pollock southwest of Nacogdoches was licensed, but it did not begin broadcasting for some two years. During the same time period, *The Daily Sentinel* moved into new and expanded quarters in a two-story building located on North Fredonia Street adjacent to the Masonic Hall. For some time thereafter, the second story was devoted to offices for local attorneys.

Although steady progress was evident in many areas of community life in the post-war years, one era came to an end. In August 1954, the last two-a-day train passenger service was terminated, and the next year all passenger service was suspended. Many old-time residents of the city, including its newspaper editor, lamented that after seventy-two years the community was back where it started where passenger trains were concerned.

As these years of growth and transformation in its overall economy drew to a close, the Nacogdoches community was involved in a dilemma, one that was perplex its residents for the remainder of the century. On the one hand, it welcomed, even sought, the dramatic growth it was experiencing along with its drive to create a new and more modern appearance; but at the time it struggled to preserve vestiges of its historic past, something to demonstrate that it was one of oldest towns in Texas.

THE STORY OF NACOGDOCHES

CHAPTER ELEVEN
THE EXPANSION IN PUBLIC AFFAIRS

At the beginning of the 1960s, public institutions in Nacogdoches confronted a swelling population with all the myriad of demands that accompanied the increased numbers for whom they needed to provide services. Considerable strain was placed on its educational institutions, its water and sewer facilities, its garbage service, and its traffic movement and control systems. Its health care facilities were also stressed, and its political system came under critical examination. Expansion often accompanied by dramatic change became the norm.

Some sense of the magnitude of the task faced by local governments and other public institutions can be gleaned from statistics extracted from the *Texas Almanac* and other sources. For example, the population of Nacogdoches County increased some thirty percent during the decade, from 28,046 in 1960 to 36,362 in 1970; while the city's increase was even more spectacular from 12,674 to 22,544 or almost eighty percent. Much of the city's population growth was the result of the rapidly increasing enrollments at Stephen F. Austin State College. From slightly more than 2,000 students enrolled during the fall semester of 1960, the numbers swelled to more than 10,000 at the beginning of the 1972 fall semester, a remarkable growth of almost 400 percent in only twelve years.

Not only did the city experience outstanding population increases, but its physical dimensions also rapidly changed. A major annexation effort in 1950 brought into the city limits five contiguous areas and more than 3,500 individuals. At that time the city charter stipulated that before contiguous territory could be annexed a majority of the qualified voters in the area had to signify their agreement. A series of annexation ordinances were soon adopted that simplified the procedure and permitted the city commission to annex adjacent territory without the permission of a majority of its qualified voters. The adoption of those ordinances was made possible by a 1961 city charter amendment granting the necessary authority.

The next year, sixteen square miles of contiguous territory were annexed. The annexation ordinance stipulated that a uniform standard width of 600 feet south around Loop 224, 400 feet north of the Southern Pacific overpass, and 600 feet east of Highway 59 north past the overpass be applied and the territory incorporated into the city limits. Most, perhaps all, of the territory adjacent to the city that was not undeveloped farm land was thereby added to the city's physical dimensions. In this way, more than 3,000 persons were added to the city's population bringing it to an estimated 16,000 residents.

In 1972, another annexation ordinance added 3,200 acres to the city's territory, increasing its size by approximately thirty percent. This new area lay along the northeast quadrant of Loop 224 and its incorporation increased Nacogdoches population to more than 22,500 and indicated that much of the city's growth was to the north toward the Appleby community. How, then, did all of this increase in people and territory impact the city's public institutions?

Education Under Stress

Dramatic increases in student enrollment at SFA were the result of a combination of contributing factors; among the most important were a change in its focus from a regional teacher training institution to a multi-purpose state university, a campaign of aggressive recruitment underwritten in large measure by the local Chamber of Commerce, a favorable location nearly equidistant from the metropolitan centers of Dallas and Houston, and an attractive physical setting among stately pine trees enhanced by well-tended shrubs and flowers. A history of the institution points out that in 1958 its enrollment was 2,017, its operating budget was just over $3 million, and its physical plant valued at slightly more than $6 million. Just fourteen years later, in 1972, the enrollment had skyrocketed to more than 10,000, the operating budget to a sum in excess of $17 million, and the physical plant's value to more than $42 million. Much of this development can undoubtedly be attributed to the aggressive leadership provided by President Ralph W. Steen who had assumed the presidency in 1958 following the untimely death of President Paul Boynton.

Enrollments doubled every four years throughout the period. Such rapid increases in numbers of students on the college campus taxed its physical plant, especially its housing and feeding services, its classroom and laboratory facilities, its supply of faculty and student parking facilities, and its student service resources. Expansion of the physical plant thus became the first priority for college officials and friends.

Consequently new buildings were erected continually in an effort to keep up with student and faculty needs. In 1961, two new dormitories were added: North and South Dormitories; in 1962, an Agriculture Building and Warehouse; in 1963 two more dormitories: Dormitories 10 and 13 (Wilson Hall); in 1964, Dormitory 14, in 1965, Dormitory 15 (Martha T. Griffith Hall); in 1966, Dormitory 16; in 1967, Dormitory 17 (Gladys E. Steen Hall) and East College Cafeteria; in 1968, Dormitory 18 (S. A. Kerr Hall) and the Science Building; in 1969, Dormitory 19 (later the Garner Apartments) and the Ferguson (Liberal Arts) Building; and in 1970, Forestry, Music, and Home Economics Buildings.

Funds for the construction and equipping of those buildings were provided, in part, by loans secured from the federal government. Among the housing projects, other than the traditional dormitories, made possible by those loans were 116 apartments for students and faculty completed in 1961, three new dormitories authorized in 1962, and others in 1964 and 1965. A student cafeteria also authorized the later year. When Dormitory 19 was ready for occupancy dormitory capacity on campus had reached almost 5,000 students.

A federal grant totaling $1.5 million provided by the Department of Health, Education, and Welfare in 1966 helped enable the college to construct a new science building. Two years later, a second grant of $734,000 from the same federal agency aided in financing the construction of the Forestry, Music, and Home Economics Buildings.

An amendment to the Texas Constitution adopted in 1965, further facilitated the expansion of the physical plant. The College Building Amendment as it became known levied a state-wide ad valorem tax on property "for permanent improvements at Institutions of Higher Learning" and allocated the funds derived to seventeen Texas colleges and universities, among them Stephen F. Austin State College.

Recognizing the need for more land to the south of the campus on which to erect a series of dormitories for women, in 1961, college officials touched off a protracted controversy. They, along with cooperative city officials, determined to pave Griffith Boulevard and obtain title to Griffith Park. The boulevard running from Raguet Street west to North Street was unpaved and at times awash in mud, and the park virtually unused by city residents. The city had been given title to the land in 1930 by Griffith family heirs with the firm understanding, they believed, that when it was no longer put to that use it would revert to the ownership of the heirs.

Family objections to the paving plan as well as the transfer of title, prompted the SFA Board of Regents to request the Texas Attorney General to institute condemnation proceedings. A number of city residents under the leadership of Jack McKinney, Dr. Stephen B. Tucker, and Roger Montgomery circulated a petition addressed to Governor Price Daniel asking his assistance in preventing the condemnation.

Texas statutes required that an offer to purchase the land in question must be made before condemnation proceedings could be instituted. To comply, in August 1961, college officials offered the city $10,000 and agreed to assume the cost of paving Griffith Boulevard. Whereupon, the City Commission at its regular meeting the following month voted to reject the offer on the grounds that the deed vesting title to the park stated that the donors hoped the property would be forever preserved as a city park and that if it were put to other use the property would revert to the Griffith heirs.

Some two years later, in May 1963, the college administration renewed its offer to purchase the property and announced that reversionary rights had been surrendered by all but one of the Griffith heirs. At the next city commission meeting agents of the college offered $25,000 for the park property, and its offer was accepted. The one heir refusing to surrender her reversionary rights, Mrs. Lavinia Griffith Sanders, steadfastly refused to approve the sale forcing the state to institute condemnation proceedings.

An appraisal commission appointed by the court to determine the value of the property awarded $14 to Mrs. Sanders. She immediately appealed, and when in 1964 her appeal was rejected by the appellate court, college officials proceeded with existing plans to construct a dormitory for women students on the site. In due time, other dormitories would also be erected in this area of the campus.

Major changes in the academic structure of the college were initiated in May 1965 when five schools were created and each of its twenty-one academic departments assigned to one of them. These new schools, later to be designated colleges, were named Liberal Arts, Sciences and Mathematics, Education, Fine Arts, and Forestry. A sixth, the School of Business Administration, was created the following year. Dr. John T. Lewis, III, head of the Department of Psychology, was named Vice President for Academic Affairs; Charles G. Haas, College Comptroller, was later named Vice President for Fiscal Affairs, and much later Dr. Gordon T. Beasley became the first Vice President for Student Affairs.

In 1969, as a result of legislation enacted by the Texas Legislature, the institution's name was changed to Stephen F. Austin State University in keeping with its expanded scope and more diversified programs. The university was withdrawn from the Texas State College System and given independent status. An initial Board of Regents was then appointed by Governor Preston Smith composed of R. E. McGee of Houston as its chairman, Walter C. Todd of Dallas, J. Harold Bates of Houston, Douglas Bergman of Dallas, Mrs. Lera Thomas of Houston, Roy Manes of Beaumont, Sam Tanner of Longview, James I. Perkins of Rusk, and Joe Bob Golden of Jasper.

A much larger student body and a growing physical plant were accompanied by a corresponding growth in faculty and staff positions. At the beginning of the Steen presidency, the number of faculty members totaled approximately 100 individuals including some part-time teachers, but at the beginning of the 1972 fall semester that number had increased to more than 350 individuals. The enlarged faculty was composed of persons with wide-ranging academic specialties and from a growing number of different graduate schools around the nation.

The student body also reflected more diversified backgrounds. From 1923 until the early 1960s, students from Nacogdoches County had constituted the largest geographic grouping; but by 1964, the bulk of the student body came from twenty-five Texas counties with Harris County surpassing Nacogdoches County as the leading geographic area supplying more than 16 percent of all students. For more than thirty years thereafter Harris County continued to contribute the greatest number of SFA students, and in 1970 Dallas County surpassed Nacogdoches County. That year Harris and Dallas Counties accounted for just over thirty percent of the students enrolled.

By 1965 increased student enrollment had reached a level that caused SFA to be designated as "the fastest growing college in Texas." Annual increases of some thirty-five percent were common. In 1960, about eighty-eight percent of SFA students resided within a radius of 100 miles around Nacogdoches, Coincidentally, all SFA students came from just eighty-eight Texas counties, eighteen states, and four foreign countries. By 1966, however, they represented 161 Texas counties, thirty-seven states, and eleven foreign countries. Many, perhaps most, of the foreign students were attracted by the programs of the Forestry Department.

In 1970, the university was embroiled in the only major civil rights demonstration of the period. Mickey McGuire, a resident of Washington, D.C. and a representative of the National Association of Black Students, came to town. Among his other activities, he visited the campus talked with students and teachers, was invited to speak to a number of classes particularly those in the School of Liberal Arts, and began organizing a demonstration to protest the treatment of black persons in the Nacogdoches community.

At approximately 9:30 p.m. on May 13 a march to downtown Nacogdoches was begun, one group coming south down North Street from the university campus and another up East Main Street coming west from the area of Shawnee Street. Police Chief M. C. Roebuck estimated that about 150 persons participated in the march. He later reported that demonstrators established a road block on East Main and refused to disperse when ordered. He also alleged that they broke windows, overturned trash cans, threw bottles, and generally created a disturbance.

Nine persons were arrested as a result of their activities during the demonstration, seven of them were arraigned before Justice of the Peace Carl Burrows. Mickey McGuire was held in jail for federal authorities because he had possibly violated a federal statute forbidding crossing a state line to incite a riot. He was also charged with violations of various state statutes and city ordinances. He was incarcerated in the city jail and his bail set at $107,000. This excessive bail requirement was later reduced by County Judge George Middlebrook and City Judge H. W. Whitten to $11,000 in keeping with state guidelines. That amount was quickly posted, and McGuire released. Ironically, Judge Middlebrook was defeated in the next election by Justice of the Peace Burrows.

The Mickey McGuire incident clearly demonstrated that in the years following the close of the Second World War the social problem that commanded the most attention, especially in the American South, was race relations. Political and social pressures looking toward racial equality intensified, especially after 1948 when President Harry S. Truman issued an executive order fully integrating the armed forces of the nation. Integration at Stephen F. Austin State University was accomplished without fanfare or protest during the summer session of 1964 when the first African American student quietly registered and attended classes. A mature man from Lufkin, he was accepted by faculty and students alike without overt adverse reactions, and the following semesters black students appeared on campus in gradually increasing numbers.

The national movement directed toward ending segregation in public education provoked almost twenty years of controversy in the local community. The 1954 decision of the United States Supreme Court styled *Brown v. Board of Education* had mandated that public schools be integrated "with all deliberate speed." But seven years later that order had not been implemented in the Nacogdoches Independent School District. In keeping with thousands of school children on public school campuses throughout the South, the more than 4,000 students attending classes in the NISD were still segregated according to their race. Indeed, it was not until 1965 that the Board of Trustees of the Nacogdoches district took any sort of affirmative action to end the practice.

At its regular meeting in May 1965, the board adopted a "freedom of choice" plan whose purported purpose was to achieve a desegregated school system. The plan designed to become effective with the opening of school that September permitted all school-age children in the district to attend the school of their choice. The next year, guidelines were handed down from Washington dictating that all desegregation plans must actually break down dual systems and that both students and faculty be fully integrated.

After only three years of experience with its "freedom of choice" plan, Nacogdoches ISD officials were notified by the Department of Health, Education, and Welfare that this scheme was not achieving the announced goal of desegregation. HEW inspectors discovered that less than ten percent of the African American students in the district had elected to attend a formerly all white school.

In order to give the Nacogdoches district time to implement a new plan, the federal department allowed the "freedom of choice" arrangement to continue in place until end of the 1968-1969 school year with the stipulation that all children in the ninth grade be assigned to a single high school and that twenty-three classroom teachers be assigned to service in schools where their race was not in the majority. Finally, in 1969, NISD officials were notified that the district was not in compliance with the federal Civil Rights Acts and that unless it came immediately into compliance all its federal funds equaling about eight percent of its total budget would be forfeited.

The following year, after being cited by the U.S. Department of Justice for failure to desegregate and being served with notice of court action to compel integration, trustees of the district at their August meeting approved an alternate integration plan and submitted it to HEW for review and approval. Approval was granted in time to put the new plan into effect at the beginning of the 1970-1971 school year.

This plan called for all pupils in grades one through five to attend Nettie Marshall, Raguet, and Fredonia Elementary Schools in numbers equal to the racial ratio within the district; children in grades six and seven be assigned to the Emeline Carpenter School; those in grades eight through twelve to Nacogdoches High School. Special education and kindergarten pupils were assigned to the Brooks-Quinn Jones School, and adult education classes, administrative offices, a media center, and other miscellaneous activities were to be housed in the E. J. Campbell Building.

Integration plans figured as the central issue in school trustee elections at the time. Elections for members of the Board of Trustees of the Nacogdoches Independent School District from 1961 through 1968 had followed the traditional pattern. Incumbents were regularly reelected in contests featuring light voter turnouts. When incumbents resigned or chose not to seek reelection, they were often replaced by persons appointed by the board to fill the remainder of their terms. The appointed individuals were then routinely elected at the next regular election. In those eight years, four trustees resigned and their replacements as well as all other incumbents then chosen by voters. No incumbent was defeated who sought reelection.

When the possibility of forced integration mandated by the federal government became an issue, however, the pattern was shattered. In a trustee election in 1969, for example, Dr. Charles Coussons, Branch Patton, and Charles Wright, who ran on a on a resistance to integration platform, defeated incumbents Wilson Muckleroy, Paul (Pete) Smith, and Rowland Vannoy. Voter turnout was uncharacteristically heavy with a record 2,193 ballots cast. The next year's election produced a second record turnout with 2,383 ballots cast. Ed Morgan and Joe Tom Harris, both new board members, were winners based, in large part, on their stand on the integration issue. The 1972 election produced yet another record vote with 3,603 ballots cast. Although integrated schools were now an accomplished fact, these record turnouts are ample evidence of strong and continued citizen interest in the school integration issue.

This troubled time was spanned by the administrations of three superintendents for the district. Ben A. Copass who had served in the office for many years and was in place when the problem arose resigned in 1961 to accept an appointment as director of curriculum at San Marcos Academy, a private school. His replacement was James K. Kearns then serving as superintendent of the Gladewater ISD. In less than a year, Kearnes also resigned to accept a position with the U.S. State Department in the African nation of Nigeria. Lenvill Martin, a native of the Nacogdoches community, a veteran of World War II foreign service, and for a number of years principal of Raguet Elementary School, was then selected as the NISD superintendent.

In the ten years from 1961 to 1971, the student population and the physical plant of the Nacogdoches district increased in size along with the college, the town, and the county. During those years the Gravel Ridge Common School District (1962) was consolidated with NISD as was the Appleby Common

School District (1963).

New physical facilities and improvement of existing ones was began in 1962 when voters in the district approved a $1.45 million bond issue. Six new buildings were under construction the following year: two for the Thomas J. Rusk School on the northwest corner of Washington Square, to house a cafeteria, administrative offices, and classrooms. When these structures were finished, the Red Building was torn down. The remaining four buildings were designed to be used by the new Emeline Carpenter School for black pupils located on the Stewart property on Leroy Street east of the downtown area. One of them became the home of the primary grades, another for the upper elementary grades, another for the junior high (intermediate school) grades, and the other for library, cafeteria, and administrative offices.

A second bond issue of $700,000 approved in 1971 allowed the district trustees to erect athletic and vocational facilities on school district property at the intersection of the Appleby Sand Road and Loop 224. In addition, a portion of those funds was used to remodel a section of the E. J. Campbell Building for use in teaching vocational education courses.

Pressures on Public Services

The years from 1961 through 1973 were times when major decisions faced the city's government and administration. Serious problems demanding immediate action had emerged as a result of rapid population increases, steady territorial expansion, and continuing industrial development. For example, a large segment of its residents continued to press for an adequate dependable supply of water and a satisfactory sanitary sewer system.

By the summer of 1964 the periodic water shortages city residents had been experiencing for several years had surfaced once again. The City Commission elected to deal with the problem by pursuing two avenues, neither destined to provide a permanent resolution: on one hand the commissioners ordered that new wells be drilled and on the other enacted ordinances restricting the consumption of water. Eight new wells were ultimately authorized, but as late as the summer of 1972 supply continued to lag behind demand at times. For example, water use restrictions were imposed during a six-week period in 1964 when no rainfall was measured and again in 1971 when rainfall was well below normal for several months. Another water shortage appeared likely the following summer but was avoided by an early July downpour measuring over seven inches. Nonetheless, by the summer months of 1973, eleven wells attempted to meet the demand for water but periodic shortages still occurred.

Funds necessary to meet the costs of drilling operations, pumping and other necessary equipment, and other costs were obtained by borrowing when necessary. In 1962, time warrants totaling $435,000 were issued, and an additional $950,000 was later approved to secure matching funds from the federal Public Works Program. These funds were used to extend the city's water and sewer services to newly annexed areas. Later voters approved a bond issue to cover the $950,000 in time warrants.

To meet the need for adequate water storage facilities made necessary by increased supplies from new wells, in 1964, the City Council approved construction of a 2,000,000 gallon concrete storage tank. Eight years later the Commission again authorized the construction of storage facilities. Located in and designed to serve the city's growth to the northeast, an elevated tank of 1,000,000 gallon capacity was erected, and a 5,000,000 gallon ground-level tank provided.

The growing realization that artesian wells alone would never be able to solve the water supply problem, caused the Commission in April 1969 to recommended the construction of a man-made lake to serve as a surface reservoir. By a margin of almost four to one Nacogdoches voters supported this recommendation by approving a $3 million bond issue to finance the project. At the same time voters agreed to an increase in the city's ad valorem property tax rate to the legal limit of $2.50 per $100 valuation or a rate of 2.5 percent. A site west of the city on the Loco Bayou was selected and plans formulated to obtain title to the land, begin construction, and have the reservoir completed within six years.

Even with a more than adequate surface water supply provided, as late as 1999, city residents found themselves once again experiencing restrictions on the use of water. City officials announced that the limitations stemmed for inadequate pumping equipment that could not keep the city reservoirs at levels beyond the danger point.

Health officials as well as concerned residents also pressured the city administration to come to grips with the lack of a sanitary sewer system for the entire city. In response, the City Commission launched what it termed "a sanitation campaign" in 1967 by pinpointing the elimination of "pit toilets" as its first priority. City employees were instructed to strictly enforce the ordinance requiring all residences within the city limits to have inside plumbing where sewer service was available. Businesses were informed that sanitary sewer service was required of them as well. As new sewer lines were installed, residents were obliged to obey the sewer ordinance.

At the same time, city officials decreed that in the interest of public health and to eliminate a persistent eye-sore the city dump site located at Richey and Power Streets would be abandoned. For many years, an open pit or ditch at the crest of the hill at this location served as the dumping ground for city trash and other materials. Fires were maintained there on a daily basis causing smoke to fill the air over a wide area of the city. The

Richey and Power Street site was filled, and the city's waste diverted to a landfill location south of Loop 224 and Rayburn Drive.

In 1968, the Commission also took action to control the twin problems of litter and garbage disposal. The first step was to order strict enforcement of the existing ordinance requiring garbage pickup and outlawing burning and other similar disposal practices within the city. The next phase in the program saw the city acquire a fleet of garbage collection trucks and order compulsory garbage pickup throughout the city.

To accompany these actions and to achieve some control over the physical makeup of the city, in 1970, the Commission enacted a zoning ordinance. As an aid in enforcing this ordinance a five-member Planning and Zoning Commission was created. The Zoning Commission was authorized to hear requests for any and all adjustments and make recommendations for the consideration of the City Commission.

Area and population growth meant that an ever increasing number of motor vehicles placed a severe strain on traffic flow along the city's streets and caused a continuing demand for construction of additional streets and bridges. With assistance from the Texas Highway Department, two major paving projects were completed as Farm-to-Market Roads by 1965: the Appleby Sand Road from Starr Avenue northward to Loop 224 and the Press Road three miles south of the loop. In 1966, Taylor Avenue was extended to connect with Pearl Street forming a new north-south route from Main Street northward. The northeast quadrant of Loop 224 was completed in 1970, and in 1971 Park Street was extended eastward to intersect Loop 224 necessitating a bridge over La Nana Creek.

Perhaps the most widely discussed and controversial traffic flow project adopted during this time was the decision to cooperate with the state highway department to construct Loop

224 around the city in order to divert much of the through traffic away from the downtown area, especially the North-South Street corridor. Ultimately designated Stallings Drive to honor the city's first City Manager, loop construction began in January 1963 and the first section completed and opened to traffic in approximately eighteen months. Before work began on other segments, a delegation of twenty-seven residents made up of oil company agents, service station operators, and others whose places of business were located along the North-South Street corridor appealed to both the City Commission and the County Commissioners Court to rescind their actions approving contracts with the Texas Highway Department in which they agreed to secure the necessary right-of-way.

In early 1965, however, the county court reaffirmed its agreement with the highway department and again began securing the right-of-way needed for further construction of the loop from State Highway 21 westward to Highway 259-59 on the north. In about two years, two additional quadrants were under construction: the northeast and northwest segments.

To help ease the traffic congestion that had built up on the North-South street artery, by 1967 the overpass on South Street near the downtown area had been widened to make Highway 259-59 four laned from the "Y" north of the city southward to the Angelina River. In spite of these actions and a "pay-as-you-go" street paving program, the city continued to experience clogged streets especially in the downtown area and a bothersome parking problem also critical in that area. City officials would address these problems, experimenting with a variety of solutions, for decades to come.

With ever increasing numbers of individuals within the city and in the surrounding rural areas came growing demands for adequate state-of-the art health care facilities. In order to meet this demand, more physicians and other health care persons as well as more hospital space were needed. In late 1962, the City Hospital Board requested $800,000 to expand and upgrade its facilities, the City Commission deferred action on the board's request pending the outcome of a bond election scheduled for early the next year. After approval of the bond proposal by city voters, $600,000 in bonds backed by tax revenue were issued and dedicated to hospital improvements.

A federal grant-in-aid was secured amounting to $585,450 later in the year, and the board prepared to construct a new hospital using the existing structure as one of its wings. When completed this project added fifty rooms as well as expanded non-bed services such as infant care and physical therapy. The new portion was built along Tejas Street south of the older segment.

At this point in its history non-resident taxpayers made up a significant percentage of those individuals availing themselves of the services of the city-owned and operated hospital. Increasing numbers of patients from within and without the city as well as sharply rising health care costs caused the Hospital Board to recommend that city commissioners take action to create a county-wide hospital district in order to widen the hospital's tax base. To implement this plan, state statutes required that enabling legislation be enacted by the Texas Legislature. That secured, the proposition had to be submitted to a vote of the county's registered voters, and if approved by them, a second election held to chose a governing board for the new legal entity.

The required enabling legislation was enacted in 1967, and in 1968 county voters approved creation of the new district by the narrow margin of only 165 votes. Voters in the county's rural precincts indicated strong disapproval with only two rural communities approving: Martinsville and Chireno. A proposal to authorize a $460,000 bond issue dedicated to hospital improvements was defeated by the narrower margin of just forty-one votes.

Many persons in the health care community believed that these developments would not adequately meet the existing needs. As a consequence, in 1972 a group of eight local physicians headed by Dr. James R. Russell, a local dentist, and a Dallas construction firm offered to purchase Memorial Hospital. When their offer was rejected, they decided to construct a privately owned and operated hospital on forty-two acres of land near the intersection of Loop 224 and Highway 259-59. In early 1973, Medenco, Inc. of Houston began construction of a three-story 150-bed general care hospital on the site. Later, when completed, it would be named the Nacogdoches Medical Center. Still later, City Memorial and Medical Center would be joined by a third facility, a psychiatric facility (Pinelands Hospital), located on Loop 224 just to the east of Medical Center.

Spurred by the addition of Medical Center, the Board of Directors of Memorial Hospital in 1973 launched an extensive construction program destined to provide twenty-five additional private rooms and intensive care units. Later that year, Mrs. A. T. (Patricia) Mast, Jr. became the first woman to serve on the hospital board when she was appointed to fill the unexpired term of Garrison resident Jim Taylor.

The steadily increasing number of elderly men and women in the community induced concerned individuals to construct a retirement-care facility for the elderly in 1963 on a site near the 1200 block of North Mound and Ferguson Streets. Named Oak Manor, the facility was completed and operational the next year. As the century neared its end, Oak Manor had been joined by at least five other retirement-nursing homes: Austin House, Nacogdoches Convalescent Center, North Place, Rock Haven, and Westward Trails and an assisted living center known as The Arbor.

By the end of the century Nacogdoches had become a

major health care center for Deep East Texas. With three hospitals, several clinics, and some seventy-five or more practicing physicians as well as twenty-five or more dentists, and chiropractors, physical therapists, and other professionals in related fields, patients came from the whole region for their medical needs.

By 1960 the existing post office building situated in the center of the downtown square was clearly inadequate for community needs. The building itself was far too small, and parking for postal patrons severely limited. Moreover, persons who sought postal service added to the already overcrowded downtown streets. At that time, city officials, postal authorities, and concerned citizens urged the selection of a new site and construction of a new post office building. By 1963, a one-acre site located between West Main and Hospital Streets across from the County Court House was secured, plans for a new building approved by local and federal authorities, and a contract for construction awarded. The following year, an enlarged building and a small parking area were ready for use.

After much discussion and thorough investigation, in 1974, the abandoned post office building on the square was turned over to the city and the city library moved to the location. At this time Lee Cage was named City Librarian. Still later, that structure proving inadequate for library needs, the library was again relocated to a portion of the converted Winn-Dixie Grocery Building on North Street.

The need for additional recreational facilities also became apparent during these years. Therefore, in 1963, the City of Nacogdoches obtained a thirty-two-acre plot of land that bordered on Mitchell Branch in the southern section of the city. It was designated as a public park and named Pioneer Park. Thereafter, in 1966, the old Memorial Park swimming pool on North Raguet Street was sold to the college to be used primarily for college classes. By the early years of the next decade, the pool in Temple Park had been vandalized and was rarely patronized. Realizing the need for a new facility, city officials, in 1973, obtained a seventeen-acre site fronting on the south side of Maroney Drive in northeast Nacogdoches near Loop 224 and the High School Football Stadium. Named Maroney Park it became the location of a new integrated city swimming pool and other recreational facilities.

Furthermore, in 1969, a twenty-four-acre plot on East Starr Avenue west of La Nana Creek and just across Starr Avenue from the college intramural fields was purchased by the city as an additional park site. Aptly named Pecan Acres Park, the site had been planted originally as a pecan orchard and many of the original trees still stood.

Two sports complexes made their appearance in the early years of the 1970s. One of them, a 700-acre tract was acquired in 1971 with a view to developing it as a public golf course and real estate operation. The site was just south of and adjoining the Nacogdoches County Club on Highway 59 South. C. D. Thomas, Sr. and his two sons, C. D., Jr. and Richard, along with a group of stockholders formed the Woodland Hills Development Corporation and began creation of what became a championship level golf course.

During the same year, the old Hazel Field Baseball complex on the city's south side had become inadequate for its growing youth baseball program. A site on Loop 224 in the northwest sector of the city was chosen and a youth baseball complex constructed.

As historic landmark after landmark disappeared from the Nacogdoches scene, movements to preserve at least some of them sprang up. One of the oldest historic structures, the Old Nacogdoches University Building located on Washington Square adjacent to the "White Building" was preserved. The building had been erected originally in 1859 by John H. Cate from funds derived from private subscriptions and a grant of land from the Republic of Texas. In 1963, 104 years later, private subscriptions again provided the means whereby the building was restored and opened to the public. It became a valuable tourist attraction and scene of weddings and other social events. The Nacogdoches Federation of Women's Clubs became its caretakers and remain responsible for its operation at century's end.

Changes in Political Life

The community's political life likewise underwent some gradual but far reaching changes from 1960 through 1972, changes that would almost revolutionize local politics. In a special senatorial election conducted in 1961 to select a successor for Lyndon B. Johnson who had been elected Vice President of the United States the year before, Democrat William Blakley prevailed in county balloting in what was described as a light turnout. A clear indicator of change, however, could be seen in the results in the Aikman Gymnasium Precinct which was the polling place for most qualified voters in northeast Nacogdoches. There Republican John Tower was a strong victor. In the regular elections of 1962 and 1964, county voters supported Democratic Party candidates, but in the 1964 elections, signs of the growing strength of the Republican Party were evident in three county precincts: Aikman Gymnasium, the Courthouse, and Goyens Hill. The plurality of votes in each of them was cast for Republican presidential candidate Barry Goldwater. Two years later the trend toward heavier Republican balloting continued, for in the U.S. Senatorial election, the Republican candidate, John Tower, outdistanced his opponents in Nacogdoches County by a decisive margin. Three city precincts, Nacogdoches High School, Shelton Gymnasium, and the Courthouse, were instrumental in providing

Tower with the winning margin. The more affluent northeast section of the city now seemed solidly Republican in its political orientation.

In the 1968 presidential election, the Democratic Party ticket of Hubert H. Humphrey and Edmund S. Muskie prevailed over Republican Party candidates Richard M. Nixon and Spiro Agnew by the slender margin of 114 votes out of a record 3,349 ballots cast in the county. Continuing the trend of diminishing support for Democratic Party candidates, in the 1970 gubernatorial election, Preston Smith, the Democrat, received the most votes, but only a slight plurality, out of yet another record of 6,130 ballots cast. Two years later, Democrat Dolph Briscoe easily out distanced his Republican opponent in county balloting, but more significantly the Republican Party held a primary election for the first time in history and witnessed more than a 100-vote turnout.

That same 1972 election year spotlighted a steadily emerging pattern in political life in Nacogdoches County. In the down-ballot contests for local offices and state-wide races upwards toward the governor's office, candidates nominated by the Democratic Party regularly prevailed, but at the level of national offices Republican Party candidates often received the greater number of votes cast. A clear signal was apparent in the 1972 election when Mrs. Joan Cason, the Republican Party nominee, became the first woman and the first member of her party to be elected to the County Commissioners Court in the county's history.

Between 1963 and 1972, federally mandated reforms in the electoral process also significantly influenced politics and elections in Nacogdoches County and in the City of Nacogdoches. In 1963, the qualified voters of the county helped to defeat a proposed amendment to the Texas Constitution that was aimed at abolishing the poll tax as a qualification for voting, but the next year the Twenty-fourth Amendment to the U.S. Constitution outlawed all taxpaying requirements for voting in elections where officers of the national government were being chosen. Confronted with the inevitable, in 1966, the Texas Legislature repealed the state's poll tax qualification.

The reform process was completed in 1972 when the U.S. Supreme Court and the federal district court in Tyler in a series of four cases declared unconstitutional statutes making ownership of property a qualification for voting, making a year's residence a qualification, and all other state residence requirements of more than thirty days. Later in the year, the Nacogdoches County requirement that college students registering to vote in the county sign an affidavit promising to live in the county after graduation was abandoned. These actions opened the way for increased student participation in all elections held in the city and county.

In 1968, the U.S. Supreme Court in a case arising from Midland County, Texas, applied their "one-man-one-vote" rule to the apportionment of voters in county commissioners precincts. The initial reaction of the local commissioners court was to "wait and see," thinking that perhaps they would not be forced to comply. But in May local commissioners precincts were reapportioned to bring them within the guidelines mandated by the federal courts.

Rural voters, feeling that the number of rural commissioners would be reduced from the traditional three to two or less, obtained an injunction from the Second District Court of Texas that would delay implementation of the realignment. To no avail, for in 1969, visiting District Judge O'Neal Bacon of Newton County, withdrew the injunction and ordered the commissioners to "redivide" the county into four precincts of "substantially equal" numbers of persons. The threat of possible contempt of court citations motivated the local commissioners court reluctantly to reapportion the county into precincts that met the requirement and receive court approval in time for the 1970 elections.

The City of Nacogdoches was also involved in this reform movement. From 1961 through 1971, the long-standing custom of unopposed candidates and uncontested elections remained in place. In that time, only one incumbent failed to be reelected, and two prominent local residents, M. M. Stripling and R. G. Muckleroy, were routinely chosen as chairman of the commission and consequently acted as the city's mayor.

This tradition began to erode in 1972 when nine candidates, the largest slate in living memory, announced for the two open positions on the city commission. In a near record-breaking voter turnout (1,117 votes) one incumbent was returned to office but one was defeated.

Of more significance, however, were the backgrounds of the candidates that announced. Near the deadline for filing their candidacies, ten individuals announced for the two open positions. Among them were four SFA students: Howard Lee Holbert, William Frank Spivey, Jr., James Donald Appling, and William Earle Sherrod. Two of the students and two townsmen withdrew before the date of the election, leaving only six candidates in contention. The two townsmen incumbents, R. G. Muckleroy and Victor Bobo, were returned in the largest voter turnout in history. A total of 5,266 ballots were cast, estimated at approximately fifty percent of the city's qualified voters. The previous record was 1,700, but on one occasion only fifty-four votes were cast. Unusual interest in the election was generated by the new voting age requirements, now lowered from age twenty-one to age eighteen, along with the candidacy of the two students, one an African American. Lee Holbert and James D. Appling, the students, finished third and fourth in the six-person contest.

This 1972 election caused great concern among the permanent, property-owning residents of the city and precipitated the adoption of city charter amendments altering the method of selecting city commissioners. By the wide margin of almost three to one, in a 1973 mid-summer election, city voters mandated that city commissioners thereafter would be elected by a majority-place system in place of the plurality-at-large system that had long been used, and that city elections would be held the third Saturday in June instead of the first Tuesday in April.

Believing that these changes were aimed at reducing the impact of student voters on city elections and therefore were discriminatory, these amendments were challenged, resulting in a decision by the U.S. Fifth Court of Appeals in New Orleans voiding all elections conducted under the new plan. This judgment was followed by a second charter amendment election held in 1973, wherein city voters approved yet another election system for city commissioners on a majority place basis.

In keeping with the newer scheme, three places would be filled one year and two the next. In the forthcoming 1973 election, incumbent A. L Mangham was easily won election to place three, but a run-off was required for places one and five. For place one, LaDonna Simpson had outpolled incumbent Neil Todd; and Harvey Rayson, an African American college student, outpolled Ray Driver. In the run-off election, however, Simpson and Driver were elected by comfortable margins. R. G. Muckleroy, then in his tenth year on the commission, was chosen for his eighth term as commission chairman.

Two other elections held ten years apart also affected political affairs in the community. City government revenues were substantially increased as the result of August 1961 balloting which permitted the levy of a city sales tax of two percent in addition to the six-percent state sales levy. Not until 1967, however, did Nacogdoches voters by the margin of more than seven to one approve the levy of a one percent sales tax for the city. By the end of the century, voters had increased the local sales tax to 2.25 percent.

Ten years later, by the slender margin of ninety-seven votes, sale of alcoholic beverages for off-premises consumption was approved in Justice Precinct One. Eleven election precincts were included within the limits of the precinct. Only five of them voted in favor of legal sale but their voter turnout was so great that they determined the outcome of the election. That same year, voters in Justice Precinct Two by a margin of two to one rejected the legal sale of alcoholic beverages. Only one of its six voting precincts (Sacul in northwest Nacogdoches County) favored legal sale.

Although county commissioner precinct boundaries had been redrawn to comply with the one-man-one-vote formula, in 1973 a class action suit was filed in U.S. District Court in Tyler, alleging that Nacogdoches County and five other East Texas counties had created those boundary lines in such a way that they discriminated against African American residents by spreading their numbers among the four precincts and thus diluting their impact. Judge William Wayne Justice ruled in favor of the plaintiffs, and subsequently precinct lines were redrawn in such a way as to make it possible for at least one African American to serve on the county commissioners court.

In later years African American residents also challenged the results of the method by which city commissioner's districts were drawn. Contending that it too discriminated against them, the group succeeded in having the districts reapportioned to create at least one district where their numbers would virtually assure them a seat on the commission. In effect, court rulings mandated that representation on elected local boards and commissions reflect in some realistic measure the proportion of African Americans in the community.

The steadily increasing physical size and population of the city compelled city officials to make arrangements to expand the physical facilities that housed its government. In 1967, for example, the commission purchased the old Liberty Hotel near City Hall on the south side of the downtown square. The City Manager announced that the building would be used to provide additional space for city offices and meeting rooms. Then, in 1970, the city tax office, the plumbing and electrical departments, and the fire marshal's office were moved to the first floor of the hotel building. In time, other city operations were also relocated to the new site, and a new city commission meeting room and accompanying offices were provided on the first floor making it easier for interested citizens to attend commission meetings.

The combination of city offices, fire station, and police station housed in their downtown location near city hall likewise proved insufficient space for those operations. In 1970, then, the commission purchased property at the corner of West Main and Taylor Streets across Main Street from the courthouse. There a new more functional police station was constructed on approximately half of that city block.

At the beginning of the decade of the 1960s, another development made an impact on life in the Nacogdoches community. The United States was persistently becoming more and more involved in the unrest in Southeast Asia in what came to be known as the Vietnam Conflict. In time it became the longest military operation in which American military forces ever participated. Beginning in 1961, when President John F. Kennedy sent a small number of "military advisors" to assist the armed forces of South Viet Nam, by 1963, some 16,700 of those "advisors" were on duty there, 489 of whom died during the year.

Although the local newspaper and other news media devoted a great deal of space reporting the events connected with World War II and the Korean "police action," news about the Vietnam affair from 1961 through 1964 was relegated to the inner pages of *The Daily Sentinel* and to scant coverage in other media.

THE STORY OF NACOGDOCHES

Only after President Lyndon B. Johnson decided to escalate the level of American participation in 1964 and 1965 did the national and local news media begin featuring stories about "the forgotten war." At that time President Johnson told the nation that much greater American involvement was called for and that increased draft quotas would be necessary.

In December 1969 this decision led to the creation of the first draft lottery since the beginning of World War II. A new local draft board, the Texas Local Draft Board Number Ninety-four, consisting of Paul H. (Pete) Smith, Tom Maroney, and C. L. Simon representing Nacogdoches County; Miller Matthews and James Nichols representing San Augustine County; and Billy J. Nichols representing Sabine County, began the process of selecting individuals from the area to be called to active duty.

Although the Viet Nam conflict did not come to an end until 1974, its impact on the Nacogdoches community did not seriously impede progress in the old Spanish town and Indian village. It had entered the decade of the "Sixties" predominately engaged in agricultural and educational pursuits; but it had entered the "Seventies" as a growing industrial and medical-health care center. Those developments further taxed concerned city citizens to find ways to continue to stimulate economic and population growth while at the same time preserving at least some vestiges of historic past.

CHAPTER TWELVE
THE GROWTH CONTINUES

In the early years of the "Seventies" the nation experienced a series of events that threatened the "affluent society" that had emerged following the end of the Second World War and the Korean Conflict. Disillusion engendered by the nation's involvement in the Vietnam War brought on agitation in the mid-1960s in which students, minorities, women, and "hippies" among others took to the streets to demonstrate their displeasure. Young people, especially those from upper middle class homes, indulged in a form of cultural revolt. They touched off a wave of experimentation with drugs, sex, and rock music. Moreover, they maintained that the nation was not attacking the fundamental evils that confronted American society: war, racism, and poverty. In keeping with most other small towns, Nacogdoches avoided the most serious effects of those developments.

An energy crisis brought about by an Arab oil embargo in 1973 fueled rampant inflation, rising unemployment, and slowed economic growth. Those events were accompanied by some profound social changes. Among the most important of these were the shift in population concentration from the North and East to the South and West, the rapidly increasing numbers of elderly persons, the accelerating change in the role of women, the continuing failure of most African Americans to share in the general affluence, and the growing numbers of Hispanics, including native-born individuals, legal and illegal immigrants. To varying degrees, each of these social changes affected life in Nacogdoches.

How much these developments across the nation affected the local community may be gained, in part, from these statistics. The population of the county grew by more than twenty-eight percent, from 36,362 in 1970 to 46,786 in 1980; the city's from 22,544 in 1970 to 27,141 in 1980, an increase of more than twenty percent. Retail sales rose from more than $43.6 million in 1970 to $126.2 million in 1980, rising some 189 percent. The number of employed persons increased from 5,843 to 15,215, and income totals from almost $82.5 million to $315 million.

At the mid point in the decade, the *Texas Almanac* reported that ninety-five percent of all income from agriculture was derived from cattle, hogs, poultry, and timber sales with the county maintaining its rank as a major broiler producing region. The county's four principal income producing pursuits were agribusiness, manufacturing, education, and tourism. The total income of $315 million generated in the county was derived from such diverse sources as agribusiness ($70 million or twenty-two percent), manufacturing ($79.5 million or twenty-five percent), and oil and gas production ($581,000 or less than one percent).

Construction of new and renovation of existing structures continued unabated. Between 1960 and 1970, new construction totaled more than $25 million with Stephen F. Austin State University's share amounting to more than $11 million. A total of 114 new private residences valued at over $2.5 million, new apartment buildings amounting to over $4 million, and eighteen new business buildings valued at more than $6.2 million were built. This trend continued from 1970 to 1980, leading the U.S. Census Bureau to identify the county and the city as among the fastest growing counties and cities in the nation.

While the lion's share of this growth in buildings, homes, and other structures took place inside the corporate limits of the city, the surrounding rural areas registered growth as well. New rural subdivisions, increasing enrollments in the county's rural schools, and new businesses located outside the city formed the most important signs of development in the rural towns and communities in the county.

Within the city itself the rising volume of retail sales evidenced by the funds pouring into the city's treasury from its one percent sales tax, increasing occupancy of the local hotel and motel rooms reflected in the funds generated by the selective sales tax on hotel and motel room rentals, and the annual reports of the local financial institutions displaying growing deposits and assets indicated undeniable signs of economic prosperity.

All these positive statistics show that while the nation as a whole had seen a slowdown in economic growth the local community continued to experience what the local chamber of commerce, local newspaper, and civic "boosters" termed "boom times." Although there was only one civil rights demonstration during the decade, relatively few of the local college students were not caught up in drug experimentation and other aspects of the cultural revolution. However, some facets of cultural change did make themselves known locally. Interest in rock music and in at least some of its clothing styles, for example, could be easily observed.

Indicators of Prosperity

The continuing high level of prosperity in the community encouraged some of its industries to undertake major expansion programs. Among them, International Paper Company launched a $1.8 million modernization and expansion in 1974 enabling the plant to increase plywood production and at the same time comply with newly mandated environmental protection regulations. Four years later IPC undertook an additional $5 million expansion program.

In 1974 as well, Commercial National Bank finished a major expansion and renovation project in downtown Nacogdoches, while both NIBCO and Gay Products also expanded their operations. Near the end of the decade, Indian River

International undertook a major expansion of its research and production facilities located on the south loop. The firm also acquired a basic research farm, expanded facilities on its breed evaluation farm, erected a research hatchery, and increased the size of its production hatchery.

Other industries undergoing expansion included Herrider Farms which in 1977 enlarged its poultry processing plant on East Main Street, the site of the earlier Burgess Poultry operation. This expansion doubled its production capacity. The city's leading industry, Texas Farm Products, opened a new pet food plant at the Lone Star Mill complex on the city's south side. The new facility was designed to produce chunk-style dog food, "kiddle" for high protein dog food, cat food, and puppy food. In addition, in 1979, construction began on the city's first mall located on University Drive south of the East Starr intersection. Also occupied that year was the new headquarters of *The Daily Sentinel* on Colonial Drive near the intersection of University Drive and East Austin Street.

Perhaps the most important new industry to begin operations in the 1970s was McGraw-Edison. It opened a new plant on the south loop in 1974 that contained 170,000 square feet of production space and an additional 6,000 square feet of office space. Offering employment for some 200 persons, the plant was dedicated to the production of transformers and other electrical equipment.

In 1974, a third savings and loan association was granted a charter, but before it could begin operations the two existing associations--Nacogdoches Savings & Loan and First Federal Savings & Loan--instituted suit in the 53rd District Court in Austin contesting approval of the new charter by W. S. Lewis, state savings and loan commissioner. Stockholders and directors of Timberland Savings and Loan Association, the new institution, learned in early 1975 that the Austin district court had upheld the commissioner's decision and ordered him to issue the charter.

Plaintiffs appealed to the appropriate state court of appeals where the decision of the lower court was reversed; whereupon Timberland officials carried the case to the Texas Supreme Court where the district court's decision was reaffirmed allowing the charter to be granted. In July 1976, after some three years involving the application process and three court decisions, Timberland Savings and Loan Association opened its doors for business.

Large-scale discount stores also made their appearance on the Nacogdoches business scene. In 1976, Wal-Mart announced that the corporation would construct a store containing 57,000 square feet and an adjacent garden center at the intersection of North and Parmley Streets. After conducting business on this site for approximately seventeen years, construction of a new "super" store was planned. The decision concerning its location touched off a wave of near bitter contention, and after some time and negotiations Wal-Mart secured a site on the northeast loop across the highway from Medical Center Hospital and erected the larger building there. This location was also the cause of opposition by concerned residents who felt it would create a major traffic hazard and pollute the environment. Despite such determined opposition, Wal-Mart held its formal opening at the site in 1993.

In 1977, a second discount store, K-Mart, also opened its doors on University Drive south of Starr Avenue. After a number of years of only moderate success, K-Mart closed this store and ceased doing business in Nacogdoches. The building that had housed that discount operation was later remodeled and occupied by an arts and crafts business and still later by H. E. B., a Texas-based grocery chain.

In a concerted effort to attract additional industries to Nacogdoches, in 1977, the City of Nacogdoches and its local financial institutions provided the funds necessary to purchase some 446 acres of land at Redfield north of the city on Highway 59 to be developed as an industrial park. At a cost of just over $553,000 two tracts of land located between the Old North Church Road and the railroad tracks were acquired from Mrs. E. B. (Mamie Ethel) Tucker and Norman Anderson.

Two years later, a non-profit organization, the Nacogdoches Area Industrial Park, Inc., purchased 181 acres of the industrial park property. East Texas Canners, Inc. had already indicated interest in locating in the park, and the park corporation zealously courted additional industries. During that same year, Johns-Manville Corporation announced plans to construct a $15 million plant in the park that promised employment for approximately 100 persons.

A serious setback to the tourist industry and to life in Nacogdoches came during this period. Despite many years of seemingly very successful operation and the community's overall prosperity, Hotel Fredonia experienced persistent financial difficulties. As a result, Temple Industries of Diboll that had acquired the property when the original local investors were forced to sell also disposed of it. Hospitality Associates, Ltd. purchased the operation, changed its name from Sheraton Crest Inn to Fredonia Inn, and employed Dan Stansel, onetime manager of the local Holiday Inn, to oversee operations. Hospitality Associates kept the hotel running for a short time, but in the end decided to discontinue operations forcing the hotel to close and remain closed for several years.

Agricultural prosperity continued throughout the decade. Texas Power & Light Company reported that in 1976 gross farm income in the county had reached a record high of more than $62 million. Moreover, the Nacogdoches County Agent in his 1975 report noted that the county ranked among the top five counties in three of four major production areas: second in broiler production, fourth in egg production, and fifth in hen and pullet production. Three years later, he was able to record that the county was first in broiler production, sixth in egg production, and twenty-fifth among the state's 254 counties in overall agricultural income.

Stock farmers and other beef producers were not so successful. Rising food prices, limited supplies of grain and soy beans for feed, and lower prices for beef at the market forced cutbacks in production and helped precipitate the organization of a County Dairy and Beef (Producers) Association.

Although income from oil and gas production had declined to less than one percent by 1980, additional gas wells were put into production. For example, in 1975, a new gas well located in the Garrison Field began production, and in 1979 another new producing well was located in the Trawick Field. In keeping with these developments, leasing activity increased markedly. In 1975, for example, lessors paid property owners in the county about $2 million for oil and gas leases. Local observers reported that this amounted to the largest lease activity in the county's history.

Four years later, concern growing out of threatened domestic energy sources stimulated another flurry of leasing activity. Leasing at this time was concentrated in the northern part of the county. The same concerns prompted renewed "wildcat" drilling, and at least twelve new wells were begun in the county, most of which were designated as gas wells. That same year the county's wells produced more than 25,000 barrels of crude oil valued at more than $250,000 and more than 35 million MCFs of natural gas valued in excess of $36 million.

The recession of the mid 1970s caused national unemployment rates to rise to their highest levels since 1941, and those rates also rose in Nacogdoches in the wake of increased production costs and industrial cutbacks. Locally rates increased from near 2.5 percent to four percent in 1974 to five percent the next year; nevertheless, those rates were below the national rate of six percent. By 1976, the local newspaper could proclaim that the job rate for the area was high and local industries were rehiring. Local observers commented that these low unemployment figures (less than 3.5 percent) indicated that for Nacogdoches at least the recession was at an end.

Indicative of the resumption of economic development in the Nacogdoches community were the ground breaking ceremonies held in the summer of 1978 for a $2 million housing project for senior citizens located at Durst Street and Perry Drive. Completed the following year, the project consisted of 100 units in brick four-plexes, a community center earmarked for games, crafts, meetings, and meals, along with a number of small garden plots.

Education in Transition

Beginning with the presidencies of John F. Kennedy and Lyndon B. Johnson in the 1960s, the national government embarked on a series of programs designed to improve living conditions for all Americans. One of the thrusts of those efforts aimed at improving the nation's schools and providing opportunities for a better education of all the nation's youth. Those programs sought to provide aid for disadvantaged college students by channeling much of that assistance to individual students not to the colleges and universities they attended. In this way, sponsors sought to avoid the controversial issue of separation of church and state.

In addition to assistance provided for those individuals who sought to pursue further education at the college or university levels, the federal government also sought to assist those enrolled in elementary and secondary schools. The Elementary and Secondary Education Act of 1965 committed the national government to a grant program to aid school-age children living at or below the poverty level. The Education of All Handicapped Children Act of 1975 sought to provide a "free and appropriate" education for all such children with disabilities. Over several years this federal aid accounted for more than fifteen percent of the funds expended by Texas public school districts.

Moreover, the State of Texas also contributed to these efforts to provide a higher standard of education for its youth by creating a Minimum Foundation School Program that provided better funding for public schools and mandated minimum standards for many of their operations. The state also sought to assist its colleges and universities by creating a formula funding plan that based their state appropriations on numbers of students and other relevant factors and by providing more funds for construction and maintenance of buildings and other elements of their physical plants. State constitutional provisions were adopted creating dedicated funds for such purposes.

The impact of those national and state programs on Stephen F. Austin State University was dramatically illustrated in 1975 when Ralph W. Steen announced at the annual fall semester faculty meeting that he would resign its presidency at the end of the year. *The Daily Sentinel*, looking back on the years of Steen's leadership, reported that the local university had doubled its enrollment twice during Steen's first ten years as its president; the annual operating budget had increased from just over $2 million in 1958 to more than $24 million in 1975; the value of its physical plant had grown from slightly more than $6 million in 1958 to some $64 million during the same period; and numbers of faculty members from eighty to more than 500, an increase of more than 600 percent.

In the fifty-two years since the university opened its doors for its first classes, only three men: Alton W. Birdwell, Paul L.

Boynton, and Ralph W. Steen had served at its helm, an unusually small number. For its fourth president, the Board of Regents selected Dr. William R. Johnson, vice president for academic affairs and dean of faculties at Texas Tech University. Johnson, a forty-three year old native of Houston, held baccalaureate degree cum laude and master's degree awarded by the University of Houston as well as a doctorate from the University of Oklahoma. The new president in keeping with two of his predecessors had specialized in history and taught this subject at Austin Peay State College in Clarksville, Tennessee and at Texas Tech University before becoming its dean of arts and sciences and then vice president.

One indicator of the growth of SFA can be seen in its construction projects. In 1974, for example, the Board of Regents approved contracts for the construction of two four-story classroom and office buildings located facing each other across a mall just east of Raguet Street near the site of old Memorial Stadium. These structures would later be named the McKibben Education Building in honor of the first Dean of the School of Education and the R. E. McGee Building in honor of the chairman of its first Board of regents. Also contracted that year was a two-story complex to house health and physical education built around and enclosing the old Shelton Gymnasium along Raguet Street. This new physical facility was later designated the Norton HPE Complex in honor of Dr. Lucille Norton, long-time professor of women's physical education and head of that department. The same year authorization was also given for a building for an observatory for instruction in astronomy.

Finally, in 1974 a coliseum seating 8,000 spectators was begun on a site east of the main campus at the intersection of East College Street and University Drive. Near the end of President Johnson's tenure it would be designated the William R. Johnson Coliseum. At the same time the coliseum designed to be utilized by the varsity basketball program, for concerts and other types of entertainments, and for commencement ceremonies was erected, a 1,000-car all weather parking lot located across East College Street just north of the coliseum was authorized.

Both these facilities were located in the La Nana Creek flood plain and from time to time have suffered the consequences of rising flood waters. January 31, 1975, while construction was still underway on the levee surrounding the coliseum, flood waters inundated the building rising to within eighteen inches of the basketball goal at each end of the floor. From time to time in succeeding years, rising water from La Nana Creek have covered the parking lot forcing cars to be hastily removed or trapped in rising water.

In addition to this new construction, in 1974 renovation of the Boynton Building which had originally housed the library was begun. After this project was finished the building would be devoted to instruction in media communication, offices for communications personnel, and modern radio and television studios.

More renovations and other construction projects were approved three years later. They included plans for a student health facility to be located at the corner of Raguet and East College Streets. Also begun in 1979 was a two-story expansion of the Student Center (known to students as the SUB) to be erected on the south side of the existing structure designed to add 50,000 square feet of floor space, while 115,000 square feet of the existing portion of the building would undergo extensive renovation. In addition, an apartment complex for students was begun east of University Drive.

Expansion of the scope of higher education programs offered at SFA is indicated by an announcement that beginning with the spring semester 1975 the university would provide a full schedule of evening classes for undergraduate students. This would enable, university officials declared, potential students who needed to work during the regular day-time class schedule to obtain an undergraduate degree. In 1978, a nursing education program was instituted. A new Department of Nursing was authorized to offer courses leading to the B. S. degree to those already licensed as registered nurses and a limited number of additional students who had completed an approved pre-nursing program. In addition, the following year the Texas Coordinating Board approved a seventh school for the university, the School of Applied Arts and Sciences.

Meanwhile, in 1975, the university's Graduate School was notified by the Coordinating Board that its request to be permitted to award a doctoral degree in forestry was approved. This new graduate program thus became to first doctoral program every authorized for the university. That same year, radio station KSFU went on the air. An adjunct to the communications department's radio/television major, it was staffed by students in that department.

Major changes occurred in intercollegiate athletics in these same years. In February 1975, Coach John Levra, Head Football Coach and Athletic Director, resigned to accept an appointment as offensive coordinator at the University of Kansas. The following week, Assistant Football Coach Dick Munzinger was named to replace Levra as head football coach. His tenure was limited to one season, after which he was removed to make way for Charles Simmons, head football coach at Kilgore College for nine years. Simmons, a native of Nacogdoches and an SFA graduate, thus became the twelfth man to head the university's football program.

Shortly thereafter Marshall Brown, who had directed the school's basketball program for nineteen years, announced that he would retire at the end of the 1977-1978 season. In his stead the university appointed Harry Miller, a veteran of twenty-four years of coaching basketball at the university level. Miller came to SFA from Wichita State University where he had operated a successful program. Nevertheless, relatively rapid turnover in coaches became a persistent feature of athletics at SFA.

During the last years of the "Sixties" and the early years of the "Seventies," student unrest was epidemic on college campuses across the nation. On some of them students staged "sit ins" that on occasion disrupted classes and erupted into violence. On others students organized radical groups such as the Students for a Democratic Society that called into question the basic foundations of American society. Other students participated in a wide variety of protests and still others in sophomoric pranks and stunts.

Stephen F. Austin State University escaped the worst of this student unrest and those student movements. However, it did not entirely escape the advent of sophomoric pranks. A number of "panty raids" were staged during which male students attempted to gain possession of female student's undergarments; and in 1974 the phenomenon of "streaking" arrived on campus. On that first occasion, a crowd of some 1,000 provided an "enthusiastic" audience for some 100 to 120 persons who raced around the campus without clothing.

Although integration of university classes and physical facilities had been accomplished without serious incident and discrimination among students reduced drastically, the same could not be said for college employees. As a result, in 1974, the university became involved in a lengthy legal controversy. In what became known as "the Carpenter Case," an African American native of Nacogdoches, Annie M. Carpenter, filed suit in the federal district court in Tyler. She sought a permanent injunction directed to SFASU officials charging that hiring practices, promotion policies, working conditions, and job assignments discriminated against women and African Americans.

Carpenter's attorneys on her behalf filed a class action suit seeking, in addition, reinstatement and lost wages. She alleged that her discharge was based on her race and gender and that she was assigned punitive work leading to her discharge. She also alleged that the university routinely paid females and persons of her race less than other employees.

District Judge William W. Justice took the case under advisement in 1976. and in time found the university guilty of the alleged discriminations. Ultimately a settlement was reached between SFA and members of the affected classes by which the university agreed to pay all back salary and other legitimate claims to past female employees. To guard against a repetition, university administrators established a job classification system for all non-academic employees that included job descriptions, a multi-step promotion system, and advertisement of all positions to be filled. This proved to be only the first of a sizeable number of suits instituted against the university in the years to follow based on alleged discriminatory practices.

The decade of the "Seventies" was a time of significant changes in public education in the Nacogdoches community as well. Changes in leadership for the Nacogdoches Independent School District began in 1974 when Lenvill Martin, who had been Superintendent of Schools for some thirteen years, announced his retirement. As his replacement the Board of Trustees chose James G. McMath, senior educational planner for the Dallas Independent School District.

After a tenure of only five years, McMath resigned facing allegations that he had misapplied travel funds and misused a school credit card. Before he announced his resignation, the Board of Trustees had asked District Attorney Hubert Hancock to conduct an investigation and explore the possibility of prosecution for wrongdoing. McMath stoutly denied all those allegations and was never formally charged with wrongdoing. In any case, the Board accepted his resignation.

The Trustees then turned to Dr. Malcolm Rector, superintendent of schools in Beaumont, to head the local school system. Selected from a field of twenty-six applicants, Rector's experience in the Beaumont system where in nineteen years he had advanced from classroom teacher to superintendent was a determining factor. While turnover in office was a continuing hallmark of the superintendency, it also became a prominent aspect of membership on the NISD Board of Trustees. From 1974 through 1979, for example, a total of fourteen different individuals served on the board. In 1974, the board's membership consisted of Charles Wright, Branch Patton, Lee Halbert, Joe Tom Harris, J. Ed Morgan, Bailey Nations, and Joe Biggerstaff. Nations and Biggerstaff had been chosen that year in an election where an uncharacteristic number of candidates filed for the office. Incumbents Wright, Patton, and Halbert chose not to seek reelection in 1975 whereupon Dr. Thomas D. Franks, Mrs. Kathryn Robertson, and Paul Kendrick were elected to fill the vacancies. The following year, two more new members were chosen by district voters: Mrs. Dianna Walker and James Raney, bringing the number of new members to five of the board's total of seven. In 1977, a sixth new member was added when Mike Ward won a seat, signifying that six new members had been elected in three years, a rate of turnover that was probably unprecedented in the board's history. Incumbents Franks, Robertson, and Kendrick were reelected in 1978, but in 1979 a seventh new member, Jan Fuller, was chosen.

Anticipating an almost certain successful challenge of its at-large system for electing school trustees, in late 1979 the NISD board adopted a "5-2" reapportionment plan. SFA professors Leon Hallman, an urban geographer, and Ronald Claunch, an urban political scientist, were selected to map the limits of the new districts. In keeping with federal court directives, two of the five single-member districts contained population distributions of more than fifty percent minority individuals. Officers and other members of the local branch of the National Association for the Advancement of Colored People (NAACP), dissatisfied with the allotment of seats on the board, challenged the new arrangement, but it remained in place. Along with more rapid turnover, this new selection plan would guarantee noteworthy changes in board composition and philosophy.

During this time, the district's physical facilities were also being modified. In 1975, for example, the existing Brooks-Quinn building on Sanders Street was renovated to create classrooms and other aids for use by special education students. In 1976, district voters approved a $7.4 million bond issue to provide funds for adding air conditioning and other renovations to existing structures, to construct a new high school complex to include two gymnasiums, an auditorium, vocational education facilities, and classrooms for general instruction. Students began attending the new high school, located at the intersection of Loop 224 and the Appleby Sand Road, at the beginning of the 1980 school year.

In perhaps the most startling development in the history of education in Nacogdoches County, in 1978, the office of county superintendent of schools was eliminated. County superintendents had administered common school districts and supervised a school bus network within the county for most of the century. Chief factors in the commissioner court's decision were the consolidation of the county's common school districts into independent school districts and the decision of the Texas Legislature to discontinue funding the office. The next twenty years would bring additional changes in education within the city and the county.

Health Care Developments

As a consequence of its rapid development as a health-care center for "Deep East Texas," modifications in this phase of its growth occurred in Nacogdoches. In 1974, for example, construction got underway on the new Medical Center Hospital on the North Loop. When completed this new medical facility contained 130 general patient private and semi-private rooms, eight intensive care beds, delivery and labor rooms, emergency treatment facilities, operating rooms, and a large nursery. Scott D. Evans, then assistant administrator of Medical Center Hospital in Tyler, was named local administrator, and Dr. Charles Morgan was chosen to serve as chief of staff for the hospital.

In the next five years, a Medical Center Clinic Building adjacent to the hospital and an extension to the original structure would be added. In 1978, Scott Evans was promoted to regional manager for Medinco, Inc. hospitals, and Bryant Krenek, himself a former assistant administrator of Tyler Medical Center Hospital, was named to replace Evans.

Memorial Hospital also underwent expansion following 1974 decision by its board that authorized a fifty-two room addition. This three-level, $2.3 million project was completed in 1976, adding twenty-two private rooms and eight suites on two of its floors. Administrators for Memorial also changed relatively rapidly. In 1974, Glen Heifner resigned the position, and George Culbertson, a Nacogdoches native and administrator of Woodland Heights General Hospital in Lufkin replaced him. After approximately one year, Culbertson also resigned to be replaced by James A. Molsbee, the hospital's assistant administrator.

In 1979, both hospitals announced still other expansions: Medical Center broke ground for a 6,623 square-foot building to house offices, classrooms, a laundry, and a general storage area, and Memorial contracted for a $5.5 million remodeling and expansion project. As a result, more than sixty percent of the existing structure was completely rebuilt and 64,000 square feet were added. Memorial's expansion featured new administration areas on the ground floor facing Mound Street and a two-story complex facing Raguet Street.

Ambulance service proved a continuing problem. From 1969 through 1975 that service was provided by the City of Nacogdoches under contract with the hospital district. It was housed in the city's fire stations and manned by members of the Fire Department. In the later year, the hospital board determined not to renew its contract with the city and assume full operation for the ambulance service.

In 1977, Gloria Jean Moore and Ella A. Smith, former employees of Memorial Hospital, filed a class-action suit similar to that filed by Annie M. Carpenter against university officials alleging discrimination and seeking $500,000 in damages. The two females claimed that as African Americans and women they had been discriminated against in the areas of hiring, assignment, training, promotion, job classification, pay, scheduling, and discharge.

Construction began in 1970 on what *The Daily Sentinel* called "a medical milestone," the Nacogdoches Diagnostic Center on Mound Street near Memorial Hospital. Its 15,000 square feet of space housed nine offices and a pharmacy. Initially, six physicians and a dentist became occupants.

While turnover was a marked characteristics of other elections held in the county in the "Sixties" and "Seventies," from 1974 through 1979, only eight different individuals were elected to serve on the seven-member Board of Directors for Memorial Hospital. Incumbents easily won reelection. Charles Bright served as president and Earl Elliott as secretary for those six years. Others who served on the board included Dr. James Taylor, Mrs. Patricia Mast, William Guidry, Dr. Bobby G. Bizzell, Norman Anderson, and Dr. William C. Doyle.

Political Changes Continue

Dramatic alterations in Nacogdoches city government occurred during the latter years of the Seventies. Amendments to the city's charter adopted in 1972 and 1973 radically changing the system for electing members of the city commission. Place representation replaced the traditional at-large scheme whereby all five members were elected by plurality vote city-wide. Not satisfied with this majority-place system, in 1974, a group of African American city residents filed suit in federal district court in Tyler seeking the substitution of a ward system rather than the place system.

When informed of the impending legal action and anticipating an almost certain court order outlawing the place system, in November the commission appointed a committee to draw up a plan for redistricting the city into wards. Dr. Leon Hallman, Dr. Ronald G. Claunch, school administrator C. L. Simon, and surveyor Fred Tucker were chosen as members of this committee.

District Judge William W. Justice took the case under advisement, remarking that both the City of Lufkin and the City of Nacogdoches appeared to be "largely unresponsive to their black populations" in their schemes for electing members to their city governing boards. He ordered that single-member district plans be created and in place prior to the 1975 city elections. Two districting plans for Nacogdoches were submitted to the district court, one drawn up on behalf of the African American plaintiffs and the other by the committee appointed by the city government.

Prior to the April 1975 elections, Judge Justice ruled that the "existing at-large system for electing members of the City Commission of the City of Nacogdoches" is null and void. He also ordered the reapportionment of the City of Nacogdoches into five single-member city wards and all balloting in each ward be held in one location with one ballot box for each ward. City Commissioners appealed his decision to the Fifth Circuit Court of Appeals in New Orleans where a temporary stay of execution for the April 1975 election was forthcoming, but in all subsequent city elections, the district judge's orders were allowed to stand.

In early 1976, the City of Nacogdoches was divided into four single-member wards and one at-large district for the selection of members of the commission. Generally the four wards corresponded to north-south and east-west lines, dividing the city into northwest, southwest, southeast, and northeast wards. The commissioners elected from the southeast and southwest wards would be elected initially to serve for two years, those elected from the northeast and northwest wards would not be elected until 1977 but would also serve for two years.

In the 1974 election before the ward system was adopted, Mike Perry and Jarvis Ammons were elected with Ammons narrowly defeating C. Stanley Jones in a run-off election. The next year, the three incumbents A. L. Mangham acting as mayor, Ray Driver, and LaDonna Simpson were reelected. Following the adoption of the ward system, composition of commission membership underwent noticeable change. In the 1976 election, for example, incumbent Mike Perry representing the southwest ward and newcomer C. L. Simon representing the southeast ward won seats on the commission. Simon, the first African American to serve on the commission, defeated challenger Fred Smith, Jr.

The next year, two additional newcomers, Judy McDonald who defeated incumbent LaDonna Simpson in the northeast ward and Bob Dunn who defeated Craig Stripling in the northwest ward, gave the city commission a new look with four of its five members newcomers to Nacogdoches city government. Incumbent commissioner A. L. Mangham, who also acted as the city's mayor, won reelection as the at-large representative. All five of these commissioners were reelected in the 1978 and 1979 city elections.

At the close of 1976 J. T. Alders retired as Nacogdoches city manager after having held the position for twenty-nine years. Alders and Grady Stallings had been the only individuals to serve as city manager since the position had been created. To replace Alders the commission chose the business manager of the Nacogdoches Independent School District, Jarvis Ammons, who had also served for a time as a member of the city commission. Cleon Compton, who had been city secretary for sixteen years, was promoted to the newly-created position of Assistant City Manager.

The Nacogdoches Police Department also experienced important administrative changes beginning in 1977 after long-time Police Chief M. C. Roebuck retired and Elton A. (Stan) Stanfield was named to replace him. Stanfield was a former resident of the city but was living in Arkansas at the time of his appointment. In addition, he was a former SFA student and special agent with the Federal Bureau of Investigation. Stanfield's tenure was brief. In March 1978, City Manager Ammons announced to the press that Stanfield had been relieved of his duties as Chief because he "had not been effective in carrying out the broad scope of duties and requirements of the position." The specific reasons for his departure were never publicly disclosed and became, for a time, the object of much local speculation.

Assistant Chief Don Barlow, who had been employed by the department as a patrolman in 1967, became acting chief and within a short time was named to replace Stanfield as Chief. After a tenure of seventeen years, John Walton replaced Barlow as the department's chief administrator. Meanwhile, during Stanfield's brief stint as chief, the first female police officer for Nacogdoches was employed. In 1977, Irma Garcia, a Brownsville native who attended schools in the Nacogdoches area, joined the department as an officer.

An administrative change also occurred at the Nacogdoches Fire Department. After forty years as its chief, in 1975, Delbert Teutsch was named senior chief to act in a public relations capacity. Teutsch had joined the department in 1935 and was named its chief in 1943. In addition to I. L. Sturdevant, L. I. Muller, J. R. Horn, and E. C. Feazell had preceded Teutsch in charge of the department. Ill health had been responsible for his decision to resign from active duty. He was followed by Charles Edward Duffin who served until 1989 and who was replaced by Fred Green the next year.

The fire department faced another possible change in the spring of 1979 when forty-five of the forty-eight city firemen organized Local 2690 of the International Association Firefighters (AFL-CIO). Their announced concerns included better working conditions--particularly shorter hours--and better fire protection equipment for each firefighter. Although the local unit was chartered, the city administration stated that recognition as the bargaining agent for the firemen would depend upon the outcome of a city-wide referendum which was not immediately forthcoming.

At the same time that city government for Nacogdoches was experiencing significant changes and the domination of the old-time establishment group was being successfully challenged, county government was also being altered. Perhaps the most important driving force seeking to bring about that alteration was an ongoing lawsuit that aimed at forcing the county commissioners to redraw precinct lines. Groups determined to force the desired changes and the commission just as determined to retain the status quo each submitted plans for redrawing commissioners precinct lines in the county to the Tyler federal district court. The court ordered the reapportionment of precincts prior to the 1974 elections. Commissioners entertained the idea of appealing to the New Orleans Court of Appeals. But the projected cost of an appeal and the slight chance that their appeal being granted persuaded the commissioners to allow a redrawing of precinct lines in accordance with federal court guidelines. This action resulted in African American representation on the commission on a regular basis.

In addition, misdemeanor cases had habitually accumulated on the county court's criminal docket because a series of county judges, without legal training, were reluctant to convene court for criminal trials. When an incumbent county judge left office, he regularly left the incoming judge literally hundreds of unheard criminal cases. The newly elected usually solved this problem by dismissing most of them without bringing them to trial. In 1974, for example, Judge Carl Burrows dismissed all cases pending since May 1970, thereby allowing more than 2,400 defendants, most of whom had been convicted in a justice or municipal court and had exercised their constitutional right to appeal, to escape without final judgment.

That year the Commissioners Court initiated action to eliminate this long-standing practice when commissioners passed a resolution requesting the Texas Legislature to create a County Court-at-Law for the county. In 1975, the 64th Legislature authorized the creation of this additional county court. Commissioners then appointed Justice of the Peace J. Jack Yarbrough as the county's first judge of the Court-at-Law. Yarbrough was a 1961 graduate of Southern Methodist University's School of Law who had served for some time as a justice of the peace in the county. Upon accepting the appointment, Yarbrough resigned his justice office and his partnership in the firm of Rorie, Pederson and Yarbrough. Yarbrough would be elected to the office in 1976 and reelected every four years throughout the remainder of the century.

In 1975, the selection of members of the grand jury in Nacogdoches County was also challenged in the federal district court in Tyler. Seven county residents alleged that members of local minority groups had not been properly represented in the selection of those juries. They alleged that women over eighteen years of age constituted fifty-three percent of county population, that citizens between the ages of eighteen and thirty-five represented 47.5 percent, and that African Americans over eighteen years of age represented seventeen percent. Since 1965, they contended only forty-eight of a total of 121 jury commissioners (less than forty percent) had been between the ages of eighteen and thirty-five and the same number of African Americans had been selected. Moreover, only three African American females (about 2.5 percent) had been called. As a result, the Nacogdoches District Court agreed to bring individuals selected for grand jury service more in line with population distributions within the county.

An indicator of how far change in local political contests had gone is indicated by the fact that in 1974 four individuals sought public office through nomination in Republican Party primaries, probably the largest number in county history since 1903 when primary elections were mandated by the Terrell Election Law. None of these Republican Party nominees, including George Clark who sought to become county judge, were successful. County voters chose Steve Burgess as their county judge and Amos Henderson, Sr., as a county commissioner, both in spite of Republican challengers. Henderson was likely the first African American ever to be elected to the commissioners court in Nacogdoches County and one of only a handful of persons of his race to become a commissioner anywhere in Texas.

As late as the primary and general elections of 1976 county voters maintained their traditional practice of supporting

Democratic Party nominees, although Republican Joan Cason, wife of the County Chairman of that party, won a narrow victory over a Democratic Party candidate for the commissioners court from Precinct Three. At the national level, local voters continued their new practice of voting for Republican Party candidates, supporting Gerald Ford for the presidency by a slim margin.

In 1978, Roy Blake, a Nacogdoches native, resigned as a member of the Texas House of Representatives to seek election to the Texas Senate in a special election held that year, and Billy Haley, Center native, then sought election to Blake's vacated seat. Both won easy victories, Haley winning over five other candidates. The Nacogdoches Commissioners Court decided to try using the newly authorized punch card system for casting ballots instead of the traditional paper ballot. Favorable response from both voters and election officials caused the court to continue the practice for several forthcoming elections.

In the 1978 Democratic Party primary, Ocie Westmoreland defeated Steve Burgess for nomination as county judge, and former city commissioner Victor Bobo outpolled Mrs. Floss Todd for nomination as justice of the peace in precinct one. In the subsequent general election, voters again voted Democratic for local offices; although John Hill and Eugene (Solid) Whitaker had Republican opposition. An omen could be seen in the forty-five percent of the county's vote that the Republican gubernatorial candidate received.

Two other developments relating to county government in Nacogdoches surfaced in the "Seventies." In 1974, more than twenty-five years after its initial approval by county voters and hard on the heels of the new precincting system for electing commissioners, Commissioner Joan Cason once again moved the immediate implementation of the county unit-road system. Of the four county commissioners, Cason was the only one who voted for the motion. This ploy having failed, supporters of the unit-road plan threatened to bring suit in the appropriate court to compel compliance. In the knowledge that the suit would be successful, in March 1975, the Commissioners Court voted to obey the wishes of county voters first expressed in 1947 by implementing the Optional County Road Law.

They then chose Charles H. Walker, public works director for the City of Nacogdoches to fill the position of County Road Administrator. When Walker resigned after having served less than one year, George Lance Mettauer of Chireno accepted the position and served some three years. R. L. Baker, a Nacogdoches County native and former director of public works in Bossier City, Louisiana, then became the road administrator. This rate of turnover indicates, almost without question, that county commissioners were not cooperating nor seeking to implement total compliance with the road law.

The Texas Constitution was amended in 1979 authorizing the creation of county appraisal districts to provide uniform ad valorem property tax appraisals for all county taxing entities. By statute, participation in the appraisal district was made optional for each taxing entity. By August of 1979 all except four of the fourteen governments in the county had opted to participate. The exceptions were four school districts: Cushing, Garrison, Chireno, and Woden.

Thus, by 1980 political life in the Nacogdoches community was clearly undergoing some significant alterations. More and more voters, for example, were casting greater numbers of their ballots for Republican Party candidates, even at the local level; greater numbers of females and representatives of minority groups were being elected to local office; control of local governments was no longer the exclusive province of the old-time establishment group; and city voters were beginning to override their rural neighbors in determining policy direction for the community.

Strained Public Services

In the decade or more before 1980, residents of the local community continued to demand "bigger and better" public services. Indicative of this pressure that strained the city and county to respond were the relocation of the City Library to a bigger and better location in the old post office building on the downtown square and the city's response to the problem of animal control within the city limits.

Animal control had posed a annoying problem for most of the period following the close of the Second World War, perhaps for much longer than that. An ordinance aimed at controlling animals within the city had been in place for many years when in 1974 the city commission promised residents that "a concerted, intensive effort" would be initiated to enforce its regulations. The principal aim of the new effort was to "catch and take to the City Animal Shelter all dogs not properly tagged." That the 1974 campaign did not satisfy residents is indicated by a referendum vote taken in the spring of 1978 when a strict dog lease law for the city was approved by a margin of 3.5 to one.

Air pollution also had become a pressing problem in the mid-1970s prompting city officials to file suit against Herider Farms Processing, Inc. alleging that the company's plant was polluting the air with obnoxious odors. Roy Herider, the company's chief executive officer, asked the city to reconsider and withdraw its suit because his company was attempting to solve the problem. The city countered with a threat to shut off both water and sewer services at the Herider plant, causing the company to obtain a temporary restraining order from District Judge Jack Pierce. The city administrators had also assessed a $44,000 surcharge in the grounds that the plant was discharging high rates of solid waste into the sewer system. Among other provisions of Judge Pierce's restraining order was a fifteen-day injunction prohibiting the city from shutting off the plant's water supply.

The Herider firm then appealed its case to the Civil Court of Appeals in Tyler which issued a restraining order prohibiting the city from taking any action until the issue could be resolved in the 145th District Court in Nacogdoches. The company's attorneys challenged the constitutionality of the city's industrial waste disposal ordinance. Herider Farms ultimately sold the Nacogdoches facility to Campbell Soup and thus escaped any sort of penalty.

Flood control along the banks of Banita and La Nana Creeks was an additional ongoing problem demanding a solution. The city's officials wanted the federal government's Department of Housing and Urban Development (HUD) to assist them in funding the most pressing need, a control plan for Banita Creek. Believing that HUD was unlikely to provide that aid unless the city made a determined effort to provide subsidized housing for its disadvantaged citizens, in 1975 the commission created the Nacogdoches Housing Authority to begin planning such a project. Attorney Billy J. Early was named chairman of the authority's board, whose other members included Finis Simpson, John Sutton, Nancy Speck, and Richard Voigtel.

At last, in 1974, the need for adequate, dependable water supplies for the city's residents and businesses was addressed when final approval was granted for the construction of Lake Nacogdoches on Loco Bayou approximately ten miles west of Nacogdoches between Highway 21 and Farm Road 225. By that time delays had caused the cost of construction to escalate far beyond the original 1970 cost estimates. When finished the lake's reservoir area covered an area of 2,210 acres. The lake rapidly filled and proved able to supply the needed water, although the pumping and other distribution equipment were not able to meet the demands of a severe drouth period at the end of the century.

The projected cost of the dam and reservoir was originally fixed at some $6 million, half of which to be supplied by grants from the federal government, but by 1974 the cost estimates had risen to more than $9 million. To meet at least part of the $3 million shortfall, the City Commission called for a special bond election in August of that year. City voters by the decisive margin of more than thirteen to one approved the bond issue. When bids for the lake project were examined in early 1975, city officials learned that an additional $400,000 would be needed to finance the project. This shortfall was met by selling revenue bonds in that amount to the Texas Water Development Board.

When funding for the project was assured, the City of Nacogdoches began the process of acquiring the land need for the dam and reservoir. Some of the necessary acreage was obtained by successful negotiation with owners, but the remainder was acquired as the result of condemnation suits filed in the 145th District Court. Before construction got under way, in 1974 more than twenty-three suits were filed, at least five of which were appealed to the Texas civil appeals court in Tyler. In addition to the dam and reservoir, a thirty-inch transmission line, a three-million gallon ground storage tank, and an additional water treatment plant were placed under contract.

Lake Nacogdoches, as a water supply source for the city, was formally placed on line in September 1977, more than seven years after city officials had launched the project. City administrators were convinced that the new lake would be adequate to meet the periodic water shortage the city had experienced for more than twenty years. To provide reliable water pressure throughout the city, new storage facilities were constructed. For example, for the northeast sector, the city purchased a 1,000 square foot site for a 500,000-gallon tank on Northeast Loop 224 fronting on the Beulah Land Road also known as the Old Shady Grove Road.

A second lake for the community was projected in 1976 when county commissioners approved an issue of $525,000 in certificates of obligation to initiate the creation of Lake Naconiche in the northeast part of the county. Its principal purposes were assistance in flood control and opportunities for recreation. In an emergency, it might also be utilized for water supply. Planned as a 600-acre, multi-purpose reservoir, its construction depended upon the cost of acquiring the necessary land. Commissioner Joan Cason warned the lake's supporters that obtaining the land without undue expense would be necessary to go ahead with the project.

Seventy percent of the necessary options to purchase the land in question had been obtained by mid-1977, but considerable opposition and state legislation bearing on the project had emerged and were casting doubt on an early starting date. Construction was to be a joint operation of Attoyac Watershed Authority and the counties of Nacogdoches, Rusk, Shelby, and San Augustine. At the end of the century, nearly a quarter of a century later, Lake Naconiche had not been constructed.

Traffic control presented another pressing problem for city administration and concerned citizens. A very considerable proportion of the city's physical growth was to the north and northeast and demands for streets and other traffic facilities grew with that growth. To meet at least some of those demands, in 1974, an extension of University Drive from Main Street south to Loop 224 was approved and designated as FM 1275. It ran along the east side of La Nana Creek toward Loop 224. When completed in 1978 it provided traffic lanes from the South Loop north to East Austin Street. The following year the final segment of University Drive from East Austin Street to North Loop 224 was completed. The northeast quadrant of Loop 224 (now Stallings Drive) was opened to traffic in 1975 and in 1978 the final section, the Northwest Quadrant, was completed. A 1.5

million grant from HUD enabled the city to fund a major street project. In 1979, clearance, demolition, storm drains, relocation, paving, and other street improvements. Work was immediately begun in the Mill Pond and Eastwood Terrace areas of the city with other projects beginning thereafter.

Other noteworthy improvement activities included a $127,860 grant from the Bureau of Outdoor Recreation allowing the city to design and construct a public park on 17.5 acres of land adjacent to Maroney Drive and Dragon Stadium near the intersection of the Appleby Sand Road and Loop 224 in the northeastern part of the city. The park known as the Nacogdoches Recreation Complex ultimately contained a swimming pool, a bath house, a concessions building, picnic units, tennis courts, a jogging path, and a children's "tot lot."

Another development grew out of a Federal Aviation Administration grant of some $118,000 enabling the city to overlay a runway, a taxiway, and a parking apron at the East Texas Regional Airport west of the city. Thereafter, in 1976, Metro Airlines began regularly scheduled passenger service. This service was soon terminated, and in years to come other airlines would be enticed to offer passenger service. In every case after only a brief period they too discontinued the scheduled flights.

Although city officials and concerned city residents were aware of the danger and destruction from the periodic floods that visited the area, as late as 1975 little significant progress had been made to implement a flood control program. In February of that year, one of the worst floods in the city's history resulted in the loss of three lives--the first flood fatalities in Nacogdoches history--and damage to property estimated at more than $5.5 million. Local rain gauges recorded up to 7.5 inches of rain in a very short time.

This level of devastation caused the City Commission to enact a flood-plain management ordinance the following month to serve as a temporary expedient until the Department of Housing and Urban Development could undertake a survey and recommend permanent flood control measures. In January 1976, a $1.45 million grant from HUD enabled the city to acquire property in the Banita Creek flood plain, relocate residents living in the plain, and clear the site to make way for a public park. Land along Taylor Avenue from West Main Street northward was the target. It included eighty-five parcels of land containing seventy residences and fifteen business structures that were earmarked for relocation and removal from the flood plain.

Two years later the city obtained an additional grant of $220,000 to be used in planning for flood control construction on both La Nana and Banita Creeks. When local citizens learned that to receive the $3 million in federal funds necessary to construct such flood control projects as concrete channels, bulldoze the channels, construct the levies, and create the reservoirs, the city would be required to fund most of the cost. The city could use federal funds to help defray the costs, and the U.S. Corps of Engineers would be responsible for a portion of the work to be done. Local sentiment opposed accepting the funds on this basis, and the proposed improvements were abandoned, leaving the city without adequate flood controls as late as the end of the Twentieth Century.

Providing ample fire prevention and control service for the city also proved an urgent problem. In 1975, for example, four individuals suffered fire-related deaths, two of them dying of smoke inhalation in a tragic fire at Hillcrest Apartments, where two others were seriously injured. That year, as well, arson was identified as the cause of a blaze that destroyed offices and damaged other rooms at Emeline Carpenter Elementary School. Destroyed were the interior of the front office and school clinic, while the teacher's workroom and lounge, the cafeteria, and the library suffered extensive damage. Ultimately neighborhood fire

THE STORY OF NACOGDOCHES

stations were located about the city in an effort to provide quicker and more satisfactory service. For example, such stations were constructed on North Street, East Main, and Loop 224 near the high school campus.

The county also experienced costly fires during the same years. In 1977, grass and forest blazes swept over approximately 1,500 acres of rural land. Fanned by wind gusts up to sixty-five miles per hour, those fires created property losses over a large part of the county. Rural voluntary fire departments were severely taxed to provide the service expected of them by rural residents.

As the decade of the 1970s came to an end, the City of Nacogdoches celebrated its 200th anniversary (1779-1979), allowing its Chamber of Commerce to boast of a sound economy, growing population, and increasing educational and health-care opportunities. The mood of civic leaders and other citizens who were beneficiaries of this prosperity was one of blatant optimism. They apparently expected this progressive and prosperous trend to continue throughout the remainder of the century.

Not all of the community's residents, however, shared equally in the relative affluence of the city's civic leaders and its dominant white majority. Members of the two largest minority groups: African Americans and Hispanics, continued to lag behind national averages in wages, level of education, housing, job opportunities, and other facets of the "good life."

Moreover, a long-standing dilemma persisted. Nacogdoches and its residents were justly proud of their long and colorful history and its historic structures and other artifacts. At the same time, many, perhaps most, of the city's populace courted change and progress. Change and preserve, those are the horns of the dilemma. For some observers, the rapid rate of change threatened the survival of the town's historic sites and buildings. Could it become a modern city and at the same time retain the values and life-style of its past? In any case change continued unabated throughout the remainder of the Twentieth Century.

CHAPTER THIRTEEN
TRENDS AND DEVELOPMENTS

During the years between 1980 and 2000 Nacogdoches entered its third century as a community. In those same years, the United States underwent some fundamental changes. A declining birth rate coupled with a significant increase in life expectancy resulted in a corresponding increase in the proportion of the elderly; this in turn brought about rising health care costs and increases in the cost of Social Security. At the same time, the number of immigrants entering the country rose dramatically. Two groups, Hispanics and Asians, made up the largest proportion of those immigrating. Of those the largest percentage was composed of illegal Hispanics.

A growing sense of frustration was evident among many minority groups but especially among African-Americans and other non-Whites who continued to feel that the American scheme of things left them either far behind or totally ignored. Accompanying this development was a growing tendency toward intolerance and opposition to assimilation among persons in the dominant majority groups. Ironically, the national experience a major religious revival fueled by the resurgence of evangelical Christianity. This was a major factor in the shift of increasing numbers of Americans toward the far right in their ideological position. That shift was also reflected in the steady decline in the importance and influence of the far left in American life.

Along with other significant changes in the life style of Americans was a dramatic increase in drug use which spread from urban ghettos and far left communes to virtually all segments of society. Another serious, even alarming, development saw the gradual spread of AIDS (acquired immune deficiency syndrome) among all classes of Americans. Yet another evolving situation was a growing scarcity of housing which joined with some particular economic factors combined to produce a steadily growing number of homeless persons.

At the end of the century, the United States appeared to face a faltering industrial economy, an increasing diverse and contentious population, and growing dangers threatening its environment and the health of its people. To what extent was Nacogdoches affected by these developments on the national scene? The answer to that question perhaps can best be answered by identifying the major trends and spotlighting the most significant developments.

Trends

A survey of trends that have persisted over the two decades from 1980 to 2000 will help illustrate the course of life in Nacogdoches during those years. A look at political activity may illustrate the direction the electorate has taken. For example, women have been more often chosen for elective office that they rarely, if ever, held in the past. Judy McDonald, who had represented the Northeast Ward, in 1987 became the city's first female mayor after winning the at-large seat vacated by long-time mayor A. L. Mangham. The following year, Dorothy Tigner was appointed and later elected a county justice of the peace becoming thereby the first African American female to hold that office in county history.

A little later, Mary Cartwright, another African American woman, was elected to represent the Southeast Ward on the city commission. Still later, near the century's end, two other females were elected to local offices: Linda McKinney to represent the Northwest Ward on the city commission and Sue Kennedy to serve as county judge.

In addition to Cartwright, C. L. Simon became the first

African American male to be elected to a seat on the city commission, while Amos Henderson, Sr. and Eugene "Solid" Whitaker filled seats on the county commissioners court. These examples demonstrate that the trend toward greater and more successful participation by the community's African American voters continued.

The shift toward the political right that had been underway for some years continued as evidenced by the growing numbers of Republican Party voters and candidates. County voters have consistently supported Republican Party candidates for state senate and representative seats during the time frame. At the end of the century, three of the five members of the county commissioners court (County Judge Sue Kennedy, and commissioners Alvin Stanaland and Jimmy Daniels) had been nominated in that party's primaries. Although city commission elections are non-partisan, at least two commissioners, James Raney and Leon Hallman, were known to be members of that party when elected.

In 1997, Richard Johnson defeated James Raney and became the city's mayor, joined by two other new commissioners. The following year, Gordon Pierce was replaced by J. C. Hughes, Jr. as City Manager.

Until well into the second half of the Twentieth Century, the tenure of elected officials was lengthy with incumbents rarely unseated. Toward its end, however, more rapid turnover began to be the norm. For example, during its last two decades the average tenure for city commissioners was approximately two years. School board and hospital board positions likewise were subject to less time served by individuals elected.

The population of the city and county continued to grow in significant numbers, almost ten percent between 1990 and 2000. By the later year the number of Hispanics had grown to 2,788 or just over five percent of the total county population. The number of elderly persons grew at a rate somewhat greater than the national average. This growth was the result not only of the increase in life expectancy but also because the city and county were continuing to attract a steady number of older retired persons making this a favored retirement community.

Enrollments at Stephen F. Austin State University after more than two decades of dramatic growth tended by century's end to level off and stabilize in the 11,000 range. The university was experiencing a rapid turnover in faculty brought about by near wholesale retirements and a declining pay scale compared to institutions of higher education in other states and among the state's larger better funded institutions.

The failure of city administration after city administration to adopt a full-fledged flood control scheme meant that periodic flooding continued to occur at irregular intervals. From 1986 to 1997 three floods inundated streets, apartments, homes, and businesses. In 1986, more than 5.5 inches fell on Nacogdoches causing La Nana and Banita Creeks to damage structures on Pearl Street and on South Fredonia Street. In 1992, more than three inches of precipitation again threatened apartment complexes along Banita Creek that were within or just east of the creek's flood plain. In 1997, an estimated sixteen inches fell on the Nacogdoches area, flooding businesses along University Drive and in the flood plains of both local creeks.

Another persistent tendency involved airline service at the local airport. As had been the case in past years, two airlines, Conquest and Lone Star, were persuaded to offer regularly scheduled passenger and freight service. Conquest struggled to provide the service for almost two years before surrendering and abandoning the project., and Lone Star likewise surrendered within less than one year.

Nacogdoches continued to be a city of churches with some thirty-five buildings scattered within its territorial limits.

THE STORY OF NACOGDOCHES

For a total population of almost 33,000, this meant a church for each 950 people, an average that was almost certainly higher than the national average. In addition to most of the main-line Christian denominations, some nine or ten evangelical groups also worshiped in structures throughout the city.

As the city continued to gain population it also gained territory. Its growth was predominately in a north-northeast direction with hospitals, businesses and residences gradually appearing on the north side of Loop 224 and beyond. Growth outside the loop, however, could be seen in all directions. University Drive from its southern terminus to its north was rapidly becoming a string of businesses, shopping centers, and apartment complexes.

Successive city administrations kept on permitting, even encouraging, the destruction or removal of historical structures, especially along North Street, to make way for additional business buildings. The determined and persistent pressure brought by groups of concerned citizens did succeed in seeing that some portion of the town's historic sites were preserved. Two notable examples within the city were the Washington Square District and the downtown area including the brick streets.

Disturbed by the pace at which historic structures were disappearing from the Nacogdoches scene, Mrs. Lera Millard Thomas, a Nacogdoches native and widow of former congressman Albert Thomas of Houston, determined to salvage at least a representative sample. After her husband's death, she returned to Nacogdoches and soon began to acquire buildings and have them moved to the location of her family's homeplace five miles north of the city on Highway 59. There by 1971 she had assembled and restored four old houses and filled them with antiques she had collected over the years. By 1980 a fifth house had been added and tours regularly scheduled.

Known by the end of the century as Millard's Crossing,

the historic village had been deeded to the Communities Foundation of Texas, a Dallas non-profit foundation. At that time the complex consisted of seven houses, a one-room school house, a carriage house, a church, and a parsonage. A log house originally erected in 1830, the Millard-Lee home built in 1837, the Millard-Burrows house constructed in 1840 are the oldest buildings at the site.

Drug usage increased steadily to the point that local law enforcement officials created a Drug Task Force to combat local usage and to inhibit the passage of illicit drugs through the county. Highway 59 became a major passageway for the illegal drug trade with shipments originating in Mexico and coming through the area on their way to Chicago and beyond.

While the nation as a whole saw its economy falter, its population grow and become less homogenous, and its lifestyle plagued by environmental and health concerns, the Nacogdoches community escaped, in large measure, the worst effects of these national trends. Population growth seemed at century's end to promise further alterations in its individuality and a tendency toward becoming a mirror image of every other American city of its size.

Developments

Numerous events transpired between 1980 and the end of the century that altered the look of the old town and the lifestyle of its people. Some of them need to be included here to help round out the town's story, others will undoubtedly be dealt with in years to come as later histories are written.

The city's financial institutions were at the heart of one of the most jolting developments taking place in those years. During the decade of the Eighties a statewide banking crisis occurred in which nine of the ten largest bank holding companies in Texas failed and only some eighteen percent of its savings and loan associations survived. The five Nacogdoches banks rode out the crisis without closing their doors, but its three savings and loan institutions: First Federal, Nacogdoches Saving and Loan, and Timberland Savings, were not so fortunate.

During the decade the savings-and-loan industry was deregulated, allowing them to engage in loan activities before prohibited. Their inexperienced management overextended their loan capacities and thus could not cope with the real estate collapse of the time. Each of three became insolvent or nearly so, and those Nacogdoches residents who had invested money in their stocks suffered a total loss.

In the Nineties across the nation banks were allowed to create mergers that were designed to produce "megabanks." The city's banks were caught up in this movement. For example the two national banks that opened their doors in 1981: Security National and Southside, were acquired by other local institutions — Southside by Fredonia State Bank and Security by Stone Fort National Bank. In 1991 Commercial National Bank purchased Superior Savings Bank to prevent its closing. The bank acquired all insured deposits and some loans and eventually transferred the deposits and loans to its Main Street location. Still later, Stone Fort National merged with Regions Bank held by First Commercial Trust Company, and Fredonia State with First United Bancshares, Inc. In addition, three new banking institutions arrived in the city: Citizens First National Bank, First Bank & Trust, and Texas State Bank. Citizens First National had branches in Jacksonville and elsewhere; First Bank & Trust in Lufkin, Diboll and Cleveland; and Texas Bank in Lufkin, Huntington, and elsewhere in East Texas.

At least two substantial developments highlighted events in the community's health care area. The century's end saw Medical Center begin construction on an addition west of the original building near the corner of Highway 59 and the Northeast Loop. Near the same time Pinelands Hospital, with some regret, announced that the facility would no longer accept or care for patients.

Traditionally both the local university and public school district had experienced lengthy tenures for their top executives. SFA, for example, had only four presidents from its opening in 1923 to 1992 when William R. Johnson retired, an average of more than sixteen years each. Thereafter, Dr. Donald E. Bowen, a physicist with a doctorate from the University of Texas, served for one year before being relieved. Bowen had been vice president of Southwest Missouri State University. He was followed by Dr. Dan D. Angel, with a doctorate in communications from Perdue University, who held the position from 1992 until his resignation in 1999 to become president of Marshall University in West Virginia. Angel came to SFA from the presidency of Austin Community College.

With some deviations in the Fifties, Nacogdoches schools had known a relatively few superintendents. James G. Partin and Dr. Malcolm Rector serving from James G. McMath's resignation in 1979 until 1998 when Partin retired and Tony Riehl was named to replace him. As student numbers rapidly outgrew the "White Building" ultimately named the Chamberlain Building, a new high school complex was constructed at the corner of the Appleby Sand Road and the Northeast Loop. This complex was made up of classrooms, auditorium, cafeteria, gymnasium, athletic fields, football stadium, and parking facilities. A new middle school was also constructed on Park Street between University Drive and the Southeast Loop and Park Street was extended to accommodate persons needing to get to the new facility. Late in the Nineties, the school complex on Park Street was named the Moses Intermediate School in honor of Mike Moses, a local man who had been appointed Commissioner of

Education by Governor George W. Bush and later deputy chancellor of Texas Tech University by Chancellor John Montford.

The building erected in the center of the town square and used originally as the city's post office had subsequently housed the City Library. When the library was moved to a larger location on North Street, a debate ensued concerning future usage. Ultimately, the building was remodeled to house a tourist information center. For some years the post office was located on West Main Street near the police station and the courthouse. That location not proving satisfactory, in 1988, the postal service was moved to a larger building at the corner of University Drive and East Austin Streets.

With church memberships growing and adequate parking facilities becoming a great concern, several local congregations launched ambitious building programs. Sacred Heart Catholic Church sold its property on North Street and erected a new church, activity center, and rectory on the Appleby Sand Road between East Starr and East Austin Streets. The Redeemer Lutheran Church also constructed a new building on the Appleby Sand Road in the same general location. Calvary Baptist Church built on a new location on the north side of the Northeast Loop. After many years at their location at Mound and Starr, that Church of Christ congregation sold their property to the University and constructed a new home on the Northeast Loop.

For more than forty years residents had voiced complaints concerning lack of adequate traffic arteries on the west side of North Street. The city first responded by extending Taylor Avenue northward until it joined Pearl Street creating thus a traffic artery from West Main to West Austin Streets. Residents also voiced a need for another east-west route across Banita Creek to the Old Tyler Road and Northwest Loop. In the late Nineties, funds and right-of-way were secured and West Austin

Street was extended across the creek to cross the Old Tyler Road and intersect the Loop.

Two spectacular and costly fires visited Nacogdoches in 1984. One of them destroyed the Colony Mall location on Main Street downtown and damaged the Commercial National Bank and Stripling's Drug buildings. Arson was discovered as the cause of the blaze, and Donald and Cathy Wade, owners of Fantasies novelty shop in the mall, were charged and convicted. The second destroyed the International Paper plywood plant on the South Loop. Both structures were subsequently rebuilt.

Glen McCutchen was named editor and publisher of *The Daily Sentinel* in 1990, and Gary Borders its managing editor. Three years later McCutchen was transferred and Borders became editor and publisher. Cox Enterprises, owner of the newspaper, also acquired the local cable company in the late Nineties and began a program aimed at upgrading the city's cable service.

As the Nacogdoches community entered the new millennium, its character was slowly but inexorably changing. In some ways it was becoming more cosmopolitan, its residents no longer overwhelmingly a mixture of Anglos and African Americans with a sprinkling of Hispanics but coming to possess a greater number of ethnic backgrounds, especially Hispanic and Asian. As newcomers arrived from other states and other nations new cultural elements were being folded into the mixture. This development heralded the appearance of a growing variety of restaurants, shops, and foods appealing to those cultural backgrounds.

In other ways, its residents were beginning to display elements of diversity. In politics the candidates nominated by the Democratic Party no longer faced only token opposition if any, but Republican Party candidates were coming to dominate the local scene. They were almost evenly divided between college students, retired persons and other newcomers, and descendants students, retired persons and other newcomers, and descendants of the long-term Anglo families. As each of these sizeable groups often sought divergent goals and espoused different agenda, political conflict was on the rise.

Diversity was also evident in its economy. From the earlier years when agriculture dominated, the more recent times featured an economy made up of four elements: agriculture, education, industry, and health care.

In its physical aspect the city was being homogenized as most other communities across the nation. A growing array of fast food eating establishments — McDonalds, Burger King, Taco Bell, Arbys, Long John Silvers, Pizza Hutt, Sonic Drive-in and many others — were fast lining every major thoroughfare. In addition, "super stores" — Wal-Mart Supercenter, Staples Office Superstore, and Sutherlands, among others were appearing throughout the city. Virtually all the nationally advertised outlet stores, motels, service stations, tire services, and the like were represented.

Some observers have concluded that Nacogdoches has become a "modern town" with a sound economy, growing population, and an increasing educational, industrial and health care base. Others have concluded that it has become a genuinely progressive and prosperous community. In any event, Nacogdoches has been transformed over the course of more than 200 years from a Spanish mission to a wilderness outpost to a backwater county-seat town, to its present form as a modern American community.

ANNOTATED BIBLIOGRAPHY

Only a limited number of accounts of the history of Nacogdoches from its earliest years to the present day have been published. Nacogdoches: The History of Texas' Oldest City written by James G. Partin, Carolyn Reeves Ericson, Joe E. Ericson, and Archie P. McDonald and published in 1995 by the Best of East Texas Publishers of Lufkin, is the only cohesive narrative previously published. Earlier, in 1976, the Nacogdoches Jaycees compiled and published The Bicentennial Commemorative History of Nacogdoches which contains a number of short articles on a variety of topics written by several authors. In 1980, Archie P. McDonald compiled another group of short accounts written by a set of authors which was published by Eakin Press of Burnett with the title, Nacogdoches: Wilderness Outpost to Modern City. Much earlier, in 1935, the Nacogdoches Historical Society edited Nacogdoches, Texas Centennial, 1716-1936, which was published by the Redland Herald Printing Company. Robert B. Blake saw his short account titled, Historic Nacogdoches published by the Nacogdoches Historical Society. Another brief narrative titled Book of Nacogdoches County, Texas was written and published by the author, Nugent E. Brown in 1927. Possibly the earliest account was published in 1880, written by local newspaper editor Richard W. Haltom and titled History and Description of Nacogdoches County, Texas. Unfortunately all of these books are now out of print and some are very scarce.

For the early years, the Robert B. Blake Research Collection and Supplement composed of ninety-three volumes of transcripts and translations of materials pertaining to the history of East Texas and Nacogdoches County housed in the East Texas Research Center, Stephen F. Austin State University Library, provides valuable data, although in some cases Blake needs to be questioned. The George L. Crocket Collection composed of five thousand handwritten or typewritten items pertaining to the history of East Texas may also be found in the East Texas Research Center.

In addition to the these collections, Crocket's <u>Two Centuries in East Texas</u>, published in 1932 by the Southwest Press of Dallas, is a useful summary of the author's research in Nacogdoches area history. <u>Nacogdoches - Gateway to Texas</u>, compiled in two volumes published in 1974 and 1987, provides historical and biographical data on thousands of individuals who lived in the Nacogdoches community. <u>Migration into East Texas 1835 - 1860: A Study from the United States Census</u> written by Barnes F. Lathrop and published in 1949 by the Texas State Historical Association traces migration trails and trends and provides much valuable statistical data on those persons who immigrated to Nacogdoches in the post-revolution period.

<u>The Texas Almanac</u> published with some interruptions since 1857 also contains statistical information on the county and its residents. In recent years, it has been updated every two years. From 1857 to 1880 it was published by Richardson and Company of Galveston, thereafter the A. H. Belo Corporation of Dallas assumed publication. In addition, information concerning persons, places, and events in Nacogdoches history can be obtained by consulting <u>The Handbook of Texas</u>, a six volume set compiled by and published by the Texas State Historical Association (1996). For reports of events in the Twentieth Century, *The Daily Sentinel* in publication since 1899 is an irreplaceable source.

Information concerning specific subjects dealing with the years of the Twentieth Century can also be secured from a variety of publications. For example, an account of the Germany prisoner of war camp is Mark Choate's <u>Nazis in the Piney Woods</u> published by the Best of East Texas Press, Lufkin (1989). A useful history of Stephen F. Austin State University appeared in 1973, titled The Golden Years, written by Bettye Herrington Craddock and published by Texian Press, Waco. The lumber industry is described by Robert S. Maxwell and Robert D. Baker in Sawdust Empire, the Texas Lumber Industry, 1830 - 1940 published in 1983 by the Texas A&M University Press, College Station. Nacogdoches County Families, compiled and published by the Nacogdoches Genealogical Society (1985) contains stories of county places, institutions and persons. Martha Anne Turner wrote a history of Old Nacogdoches in the Jazz Age which was published by Madrona Press of Austin in 1976.

Other information on specific topics in Nacogdoches history is scattered among the pages of the East Texas Historical Journal and the Southwestern Historical Quarterly. The Pine Log, student publication of Stephen F. Austin State University, provides items concerning college activities written from the student point of view.

INDEX

-A-

A. W. WETTERMARK AND SON, 95
ACME BRICK COMPANY, 88
ADAMS
 George M., 66
 Moss, 188
ADOLPHUS STERNE HOUSE, 184
AGNEW
 Spiro, 234
AGREDA
 Maria de Jesus de, 4
AGUAYO
 Governor Marquis de San Miguel, 8
AHUMADA
 Lt. Colonel Mateo, 41, 42
AIKMAN
 Frank S., 97, 125
AIRLINE BUS TERMINAL, 140
AIRLINE MOTOR COACHES OF EAST Texas, 138
ALAMO, 56
ALDERS
 J. T., 189, 261
ALLEN
 Augustus C., 59
 John Kirby, 59
ALVARADO
 Luis de Moscoso de, 3
AMERICAN FEDERATION OF LABOR (AFL), 206
AMMONS
 Jarvis, 260, 261
ANAHUAC, 50
ANDERSON
 Corporal John P., 93
 M. A., 101
 Norman, 246, 259
ANDERSON COUNTY, 60
ANGEL
 Dan D., 282
ANGELINA AND NECHES RAILROAD, 96
ANGELINA COUNTY, 72, 165, 204
ANGELINA COUNTY LUMBER COMPANY, 96, 151
ANGELINA LUMBER COMPANY, 152
ANGELINA RIVER, 5, 9, 46, 48, 60, 61, 70, 87, 108, 180, 228
ANGELINA-NACOGDOCHES WATER Control and Improvement Dist., 177
ANNE BIRDWELL CLUB, 132
ANNEXATION CONVENTION, 69
APPALACHIAN STATE TEACHERS COLLEGE, 155
APPLEBY, 114, 214
APPLEBY COMMON SCHOOL DISTRICT, 223, 224
APPLING
 James Donald, 236
AQUA VITA PARK, 104, 105
ARBYS, 285
ARMY ADMINISTRATION SCHOOL
 WAC, No, 1, 157
ARNOLD
 Captain Hayden S., 55, 58, 59
 Captain James R., 74, 80
 James R., 63
ARRENDONDO
 Joaquin de, 28
ARROYO HONDO, 8, 26
ASSEMBLY OF GOD STUDENT CENTER, 195
ASSOCIATION OF BAPTIST STUDENTS, 195
ATTOYAC BAYOU, 35
ATTOYAC RIVER, 42
ATTOYAC WATERSHED AUTHORITY, 270
AUSTIN
 Stephen F., 30, 36, 37, 52
AUSTIN COMMUNITY COLLEGE, 282
AUSTIN HOUSE, 230

INDEX

AUSTIN PEAY STATE
  COLLEGE, 250(2)
AVENUE
  East Starr, 129, 232,
    244, 283
  Mimms, 128
  Starr, 112, 169, 227,
    245
  Taylor, 209, 227, 272,
    283
  Virginia, 112(2)
AYISH BAYOU, 41, 47, 48
  mission, 9, 11

-B-

BACON
  O'Neal, 235
  Reverend, 129, 130
  Reverend Samuel, 129
BAKER
  James A., 95
  Karle Wilson, 123
  R. L., 266
  Thomas, 153
  Thomas E., 98, 135
  Thomas W., 203
  W. E., 136
BALCH
  William L., 114
BANITA APARTMENT
  BUILDING, 141
BANITA CREEK, 1, 6, 10,
  65, 66, 67, 74, 83,
  99, 108, 110, 111,
  140, 179, 187, 209,
  268, 272, 278, 283
BANITA HARDWOOD
  MANUFACTURING
  Company, 94
BANITA HOTEL, 99
BAPTIST STUDENT CENTER,
  195
BAPTIST SUNDAY SCHOOL, 76
BARLOW
  Don, 261
BARR
  William, 23, 24
BARR AND DAVENPORT, 23,
  24, 25, 94
BARRET
  Lynn Taliaferro (Tol),
    87
BASKIN-ROBBINS ICE CREAM,
  209
BASSONS INDUSTRIES
  CORPORATION, 204, 205
BATES
  Colonel W. B. (Bill),
    203
  J. Harold, 218
BATTLE OF BUENA VISTA, 74
BATTLE OF HORSESHOE BEND,
  51
BATTLE OF MONTERREY, 74
BATTLE OF NACOGDOCHES,
  48, 49, 60
BATTLE OF NEW ORLEANS, 41
BATTLE OF SAN JACINTO,
  54, 55, 58, 59, 60
  First Company, 2nd
    Regiment, 55
BATTLE OF THE ALAMO, 54
BAXTER HOTEL, 99
BEALL
  Mrs. J. Frank (Ellen),
    189
BEALL BROTHERS DEPARTMENT
  Store, 209
BEAN
  Peter Ellis, 68
BEASLEY
  Gordon T., 218
BELL
  John, 79
  Kelly, 210(2)
BENNETT-CLARK COMPANY,
  138
BENNETT-CLARK PLANT, 205
BERGMAN
  Douglas, 218
BESELER
  Bieto, 188
BEVEL SETTLEMENT, 47, 48
BIBLE BELT, 160
BIBLE CHAIRS, 195
  Wesley, 134
BIDAIS CREEK
  Madison County, 14
BIDDLE
  William, 75
BIGGERSTAFF
  Joe, 255(2)
BIRD
  Charlie, 105
BIRDWELL
  Alton William, 122,
    123, 125, 126, 154,

INDEX

BIRDWELL (continued)
    167, 249(2)
  John, 84
BIZZELL
  Bobby G., 258, 259
BLAKE
  Bennett, 62, 89, 95
  Roy, 265
BLAKLEY
  William, 233
BLANCO
  Victor, 40
BLEDSOE
  Mrs. Annette Lea, 76
  Robert, 114
BLONDEL
  M., 7
BLOUNT
  E. A., 95, 101, 112, 121
  S. W., 107, 112
BLUE BONNET LITERARY
    SOCIETY, 132
BOARD OF LAND
    COMMISSIONERS
  Nacogdoches, 63
BOBO
  Victor, 236, 265
BONAPARTE
  Emperor Napoleon, 26
BOOTY
  W. N., 114
BORDERS
  Gary, 284
BOWEN
  Donald E., 282
BOX
  Eskridge, 114
BOYNTON
  Paul L., 154, 155, 156, 159, 165, 169, 170, 171, 215, 249(2), 250(2)
BRAZOS RIVER, 26
BRECKENRIDGE
  John C., 79
BREECE
  Captain Thomas H., 55
BREWER
  Albert, 135
BRIGHT
  Charles, 258
BRISCOE
  Governor Dolph, 234

BROADFOOT
  Virginia, 123
BROOKS
  Thomas D., 57
BROOKSHIRE BROTHERS
    GROCERY, 209
BROWN
  John, 70
  Lemuel B., 59
  Marshall, 252(2)
BROWN V. BOARD OF
    EDUCATION, 174, 221
BUCARELI
  settlement, 14, 15
BUFFALO BAYOU, 59
BULLOCK
  Colonel James Whitis, 48
BUNTING
  N. B., 138
BUREAU OF OUTDOOR
    RECREATION, 271
BURGER KING, 285
BURGESS
  Steve, 264, 265
BURGESS POULTRY, 244
BURK-CRAIN FURNITURE
    COMPANY, 102
BURLESON
  Colonel Edward, 52, 61
BURROWS
  Carl, 220, 263
  Cates, 142
BUSH
  Governor George W., 283
BYRD
  Corporal Louis, 93
  Jewel P., 180

-C-

CADDO INDIAN VILLAGE, 1
CADDO INDIANS, 13
  caddi, 2
  chenesi or xinesi, 2
  houses, 2
  temples, 2
CAGE
  Lee, 231
CALAHORRA Y SAENZ
  Father Jose de, 10
CALDWELL
  William, 59

INDEX

CALLIER
  Robert, 41
CAMP BOWIE, 114
CAMP CLAIBORNE
  (LOUISIANA), 167
CAMPBELL
  E. J., 172
CAMPBELL SOUP, 268
CAMPUS CRUSADE FOR
  CHRIST, 195
CARABAN HOTEL, 208
CARPENTER
  Annie M., 253(2), 258
CARPENTER CASE, 253(2)
CARTER
  Charles, 114
CARTWRIGHT
  Mary, 276
CASON
  D. K., 98
  Mrs. Joan, 234, 265,
    270
CASON, MONK & COMPANY, 98
CASTRO
  Ramon de, 20
CATE
  John H., 233
CEMETERY
  Catholic, 53
  Oak Grove, 112, 130,
    184
  Protestant, 53
  Sunset Memorial Park,
    184
CENTER HIGHWAY, 175
CENTRAL HOTEL, 102
CHAMBER OF COMMERCE, 124,
  134, 199, 208, 209,
  214, 273
CHAMBODUT
  Father L. C. M., 128
CHAPLIN
  Chichester, 39
CHAPMAN
  Lieutenant McNeil, 93
CHEROKEE COUNTY, 60, 165
CHEROKEE INDIANS, 42, 61
CHEW
  W. B., 95
CHIRENO, 79, 86, 96, 151,
  152, 229, 266
  Encarnation, 44
CHIRENO CAMP, 152
CHIRENO SCHOOL DISTRICT,
  266
CHISSUM
  William P., 59
CHORAL CLUB, 132
CHURCH
  Calvary Baptist, 129,
    194, 283
  Catholic, 99, 128
  Christ Episcopal, 92,
    112, 128
  Church of Christ, 283
  Episcopal, 99
  First Baptist, 124,
    129, 185, 186
  First Baptist
    (Southern), 128
  First C. Nazarene, 194
  First Christian, 194
  First Methodist, 195
  First Methodist
    (South), 128
  First Presbyterian
    (US), 129
  First United
    Methodist, 129
  Fredonia Hill Baptist,
    129, 194
  Grace Bible, 130, 194
  Main Street
    Presbyterian, 130
  Methodist, 92, 102
  Mound & Star Church of
    Christ, 186
  Mound and Starr C. of
    Christ, 194
  New Hope
    Congregational Meth.,
    194
  Perritte Memorial
    Methodist, 194
  Presbyterian, USA, 130
  Redeemer Lutheran, 283
  Sacred Heart Catholic,
    128, 283
  Southern Baptist, 99
  Southern Methodist, 99
  Westminster
    Presbyterian, 130
  Zion Hill Baptist, 92
  Zion Hill First
    Baptist, 112, 130
CHURCHES
  Anabaptist, 75
  Baptist, 75

INDEX

CHURCHES (continued)
  Catholic, 75
  Episcopal, 75
  Methodist, 75
  Presbyterian, 75
CITIZENS FIRST NATIONAL BANK, 281
CITY MEMORIAL HOSPITAL
  Board of Managers, 183, 184
CITY OF NACOGDOCHES
  Assistant City Manager, 261
  Board of Aldermen, 73, 108
  City Animal Shelter, 267
  City Commission, 175(2), 179, 217, 225, 226, 227, 259, 260, 269, 271
  City Council, 141
  City Hall, 189
  City Library, 231, 267, 283
  City Manager, 188, 239, 277
  City Secretary, 189
  Fire Department, 186, 258, 262
  Hospital Board, 229
  Maroney Park, 232
  Memorial Park Pool, 231
  Pecan Acres Park, 232
  Pioneer Park, 231
  Planning and Zoning Comm., 227
  Police Department, 261
  Precinct One, 180
  Temple Park, 231
CIVIL AERONAUTICS
  Administration, 210
CIVIL RIGHTS ACT, 222
CIVIL WAR, 51, 63, 69, 75, 76, 77, 85, 87, 91, 117, 171, 190
CIVILIAN PILOT TRAINING
  Program, 153
CLARK
  George, 264
  William, 63
  William, Jr., 79
CLAUNCH

  Ronald, 255(2), 259
CLEVELAND
  Ernest D., 190
CLOUDY
  Vera, 193
CO-OPERATIVE FURNITURE
  Company, 141
COAHUILA Y TEJAS, 33, 35, 39, 62
  Saltillo, 40, 43
COAST ARTILLERY COMPANY, 114
COATS
  W. M., 206
COCA-COLA BOTTLING PLANT, 204
COKE
  Governor Richard, 88
COLLEGE COFFEE SHOP, 133
COLLEGE OF NUESTRA SENORA DE
  Guadalupe de Zacatecas, 6
COLLEGE OF ZACATECAS, 8, 10
COLLINGSWORTH
  George M., 52
COLONY MALL, 284
COLVERT
  Bill, 100
COMANCHE INDIANS, 15
COMMERCIAL NATIONAL BANK, 95, 96, 98, 102, 203, 208, 243, 281, 284
COMMON SCHOOL DISTRICT
  Central Heights, 175
  Lone Pine, 175
  Union Springs, 175
COMMUNITIES FOUNDATION OF
  Texas, 280
COMPTON
  Cleon, 189, 261
CONFEDERATE ARMY, 80
CONFEDERATE CONGRESS, 89
CONFEDERATE CONSTITUTION
  1861, 82
CONGRESS OF INDUSTRIAL
  Organizations (CIO), 206
CONGRESS OF THE REPUBLIC, 55, 56, 57, 59, 62, 64, 65, 69
CONNALLY
  Tom, 159

INDEX

CONQUEST AIRLINE, 278
CONRAD
  Brevet Colonel J., 82
CONSTITUTION OF 1869, 82
CONSTITUTION OF 1876, 89
CONSULTATION OF 1835, 51
CONTINENTAL INN, 208
CONVENTION OF 1833, 51
CONVENTION OF 1836, 54
CONVENTION OF 1845, 69
CONVENTION OF 1866, 81
CONVENTION OF 1875, 88
COON
  Ephriam, 162
COPASS
  Ben A., 190, 223
CORDOVA
  Don Cristoval, 21
  Vicente, 44, 60
CORDOVAN REBELLION, 61
COS
  General Martin P., 52
COTTON BELT, 160
COUNTY CLUB, 131, 232
COUNTY DAIRY AND BEEF
  (Producers)
  Association, 247
COUNTY POLICE COURT, 82
COUNTY UNIT ROAD SYSTEM, 191
COURT OF CIVIL APPEALS
  Tyler, 108
COUSSONS
  Charles, 223
COX
  J. T., 126, 156
  Navarro
COX ENTEPRISES, 284
COX HARDWARE, 97
CRAVEN LUMBER COMPANY, 94
CRAWFORD
  Johnny, 133
CROCKETT
  Houston County, 22
CULBERTSON
  George, 247, 257
CUM CONCILIO CLUB, 101, 131
CUSHING, 180
CUSHING SCHOOL DISTRICT, 266

-D-

DALLAS COUNTY, 219
DALLAS INDEPENDENT SCHOOL
  District, 254(2)
DANIEL
  Governor Price, 217
DANIELS
  Jimmy, 277
DAVENPORT
  Peter Samuel, 23
  Samuel, 24, 29, 30
DAVIDSON
  John P., 95
  Mrs. George (Estelle
  V.), 131
  Thomas S., 207
DAVIDSON BUILDING, 102
DAVIS
  Governor E. J., 84, 88
  Mrs. C. B. (Ruth), 189
  R. F., 123
  W. S., 100
DAWSON
  Gibson, 84
DE SOTO
  Hernando, 3
DECLARATION OF
  INDEPENDENCE
  Texas, 54
DEEP EAST TEXAS, 257(2)
DEL RENTZEL FIELD, 210
DELTA DRILLING COMPANY, 206
DEMOCRATIC PARTY, 79, 190, 191, 233, 234, 265, 284
DENTON
  John B., 76
DEPARTMENT OF BEXAR, 33, 46
DEPARTMENT OF HEALTH,
  Education, and
  Welfare, 216, 221
DEPARTMENT OF HOUSING AND
  Urban Development, 268, 272
DEPARTMENT OF
  NACOGDOCHES, 46, 47, 57
DEPARTMENT OF
  TRANSPORTATION, 179
DICKENS
  Corporal George B., 93
DILETTANTE CLUB, 131
DILL

INDEX

DILL (continued)
  Alcalde James, 34
DIXIE-SUNSHINE TRAILWAYS, 139
DONEGAN
  A. Y., 107
DORR CREEK, 70
DOUGLASS, 72, 86, 172, 206, 207
  Kelsey H., 65
DOYLE
  William C., 259
DR. PEPPER BOTTLING PLANT, 202
DRAGON-NET, 185
DRIVE
  Maroney, 232, 271
  Northeast Stallings, 129
  Perry, 248(2)
  Rayburn, 227
  Stallings, 228, 270
  University, 244, 245, 250(2), 270, 278, 279, 282, 283
DRIVER
  Ray, 237, 260
DRUG TASK FORCE, 280
DUFFIN
  Charles Edward, 262
DUNN
  Bob, 260
DURST
  John, 60, 64
  Joseph, 41

-E-

E. B. HAYWARD LUMBER COMPANY, 94
EARLE
  John B., 87
EARLY
  Billy J., 268
EAST TEXAS CANNERS, INC., 246
EAST TEXAS COMMISSION COMPANY, 97
EAST TEXAS LANES, 204, 209
EDUCATION OF ALL HANDICAPPED
  Children Act (1975), 249(2)

EDWARDS
  Benjamin, 39, 40, 41, 42, 43
  Haden, 36, 38, 39, 40, 42, 43, 63(2)
  Haden H., 79
  Haden Harrison, 59
  Haden S., 70
  Peyton F., 88
EICHEL
  Julius, 185, 186
EISENHOWER
  Dwight D., 190
EL CAMINO REAL, 3, 14, 22, 65
EL LOBANILLO
  ranch, 12
EL MEXICO, 100
ELEMENTARY AND SECONDARY
  Education Act (1965), 248
ELEMENTARY AND SECONDARY ACT
  (1965), 248
ELISONDO
  Lt. Colonel Ygnacio, 28
ELKS CLUB, 132, 133
ELLIOTT
  Earl, 258
ENGLISH
  Clarence, 138
ENTRANCE CERTIFICATES, 54
EPISCOPAL STUDENT
  ASSOCIATION, 195
ETOILE, 147, 152
EVANS
  Scott D., 257(2)

-F-

FAIN
  Victor, 101
  Victor B., 100, 180
FALL
  Dr. John Newton, 79
FANTASIES SHOP, 284
FARM SECURITY
  ADMINISTRATION, 159
FARMERS AND MERCHANTS STATE
  Bank, 96
FARR
  Thomas Jefferson, 147

INDEX

FARRAR
  E. H., 88
FEAZELL
  E. C., 262
  Elmo C. (Bud), 141
FEDERAL AVIATION
  Administration, 271
FEDERAL BUREAU OF
  Investigation, 261
FEDERAL CENSUS OF 1880, 86
FEDERAL COMMUNICATIONS
  Commission, 210
FEDERAL DEPOSITORS
  INSURANCE
  Corporation, 96
FEDERAL HOUSING
  ADMINISTRATION, 209
FEDERATION OF WOMEN'S
  CLUBS, 233
FENLEY
  Rebecca Danzey, 72
FERGUSON
  C. E., 123
  Thomas E., 123, 167
FERNANDEZ
  Lieutenant Bernardo, 21
FIELDS
  Chief Richard, 42
FIFTH MILITARY DISTRICT, 82
FIRE DEPARTMENT, 141
FIRST BANK & TRUST, 281
FIRST COMMERCIAL TRUST
  CO., 281
FIRST FEDERAL SAVINGS AND
  Loan Association, 207, 244, 281
FIRST UNITED BANKSHARES, 281
FITZGERALD
  Edward, 59
FITZMAURICE
  Corporal S. W., 93
FLINN
  Reverend Glenn, 195
FLINT
  John T., 87
FLORES
  Gil, 14
  Vital, 49
FLOURNOY, 72
  Corporal Melville C., 93
FLOWERY MOUNTAIN, 80
FOOD ADMINISTRATION, 115
FORBES
  John, 61
FORD
  John, 59
FORT ST. LOUIS, 3
FOUTS
  W. Casey, 210
FOWLER
  Littleton, 76
  Reverend Littleton, 129
FRANKS
  Thomas D., 255(2)
FREDONIA INN, 246
FREDONIA STATE BANK, 207, 281
FREDONIAN REBELLION, 35, 40, 43, 45, 54
FREEDMAN'S BUREAU, 83
FRENCH AND INDIAN WAR, 11
FROST JOHNSON LUMBER
  COMPANY, 96
FROST LUMBER COMPANY, 151, 152, 182, 204
FROST LUMBER MILL, 204, 205, 206
FROST-JOHNSON MILL, 209
FUEL ADMINISTRATION, 115
FULLER
  Jan, 255(2)
  Nelson, 100

-G-

G. I. BILL OF RIGHTS, 165
GACETA DE TEXAS, 100
GARAGE COMPANY
  Ford Motor Agency, 112
GARCIA
  Irma, 261
GARFIELD
  Harry A., 115
GARNER
  W. Fletcher, 123
GARRISON, 80, 86, 88, 114, 230
GARRISON FIELD, 247
GARRISON SCHOOL DISTRICT, 266
GARRISON VITRIFIED BRICK
  CO., 88

INDEX

GARZA
  Father Jose Francisco Mariano, 15
GAY PRODUCTS, 243
GENERAL LAW CITY, 89
GENERAL OAK FLOORING COMPANY, 186
GEORGE PEABODY COLLEGE FOR TEACHERS, 122, 154, 155
GERBER
  Joseph Newton, 167, 171, 198
GERMAN PRISONER-OF-WAR-CAMP, 151
GIBBS
  Eleanor H., 128
GIBSON'S DISCOUNT CENTER, 209
GILMER-AIKEN BILL (1949), 174
GLADEWATER I. S. DISTRICT, 223
GLADEWATER SCHOOL SYSTEM, 190
GLEE CLUB, 132
GOLDBOLT
  Corporal Harry E., 93
GOLDEN
  Joe Bob, 218
GOLDSBERRY
  Joe, 136
GOLDWATER
  Barry, 233
GOLIAD, 26, 52, 56
GOLIAD MASSACRE, 54
GONZALES
  Lieutenant Jose, 12
GOSSETT
  Elijah, 57
GOYENS
  William, 49, 72
GRAEME MCDONALD COMPANY, 107
GRAHAM
  A. C., 59
  William C., 57
GRANGER
  General Gordon, 81
GRAVEL RIDGE COMMON SCHOOL District, 223

GRAY
  Clara, 184
  Roy, 136, 142, 184
GRAYSON
  William J., 84
GREAT DEPRESSION, 171
GREEN
  Fred, 262
GRIEVE
  J. J., 135
GRIGSBY
  John, 57
GUADALUPE COUNTY, 61
GUADIANA
  Don Jose Maria, 21
  Jose Maria, 23
GUIDRY
  William, 258
GUNTER
  Macon Alston, 195

-H-

H. E. B. PANTRY FOODS, 245
H. E. STONE LUMBER COMPANY, 141
H. L. HUNT PRODUCTS COMPANY, 204
HAAS
  Charles G., 218
HALBERT
  Lee, 255(2)
HALEY
  Billy, 265
HALLMAN
  Leon, 255(2), 259, 277
HALTOM
  Giles, 100
  Giles M., 114
  R. W., 100
  Robert W., 100
HAMILTON
  A. J., 81
  Charles A., 87
  E. E., 59
HAMMOND
  Raymond, 138
HANCOCK
  Hubert, 254(2)
HANSON
  Robert E., 135
HARDEMAN
  Lee, 112

INDEX

HARDEMAN (continued)
  Tolbert, 112
HARRIS
  Ed J., 134
  Joe Tom, 223, 255(2)
  June C., 105, 112
  W. H., 100
  William H., 100
HARRIS COUNTY, 219
HART
  William, 57, 66
HARVELL
  David W., 84
HASELWOOD
  R. W., 98, 99
HASINAI CADDO INDIANS, 1, 3
HASINAI INDIAN VILLAGE, 5
HASTINGS
  Thomas, 50
HATHCOCK
  Frank, 188
HAYTER
  Andrew, 80
  John J., 72, 78, 96
  Sam, 137
HAZEL FIELD COMPLEX, 232
HAZLETT
  Columbus, 84
HEIFNER
  Glenn, 257(2)
HENDERSON, 95, 98
  Amos, Sr., 264, 277
  Mrs. James Pinckney, 76
HENDERSON ROAD, 66
HENNING
  A. F., 100
HERALD PUBLISHING COMPANY, 100
HERIDER
  Roy, 267
HERIDER FARMS, 244, 268
HERIDER FARMS PROCESSING, INC., 267
HERITAGE CLUB, 131
HERNANDEZ
  Juana Luzgarda, 13
HIGH ANALYSIS PELLETED
  Fertilizer plant, 205
HILL
  John, 265
HILL TOP GROCERY AND
  Washateria, 185

HILLCREST APARTMENTS, 272
HINDS
  J. H., 132, 135
HITCH LOT, 209
HITCHCOCK
  B. F., 88
HOFFMEISTER
  W. B., 114
HOGG
  Jim, 69
  Joseph Lewis, 69, 70
HOLBERT
  Howard Lee, 236
HOLIDAY INN, 208, 246
HOLLINGSWORTH
  Benjamin P., 87
HOLMES
  Mrs. Lillie Bailey, 193
  Oscar L., 162
HOLT
  A. J., 92, 99
HOOVER
  Herbert, 115
HORN
  J. R., 262
HOSPITAL
  City Memorial, 136, 153, 183, 184, 229, 230
  Medical Center, 230, 245, 257(2), 281
  Medical Center Clinic, 257(2)
  Memorial, 131, 257(2), 258
  Pinelands, 230, 282
  Tyler Medical Center, 257
  Woodland Heights General, 247, 257
HOSPITALITY ASSOCIATES, LTD., 246
HOTCHKISS
  Archibald, 78
HOTEL FREDONIA, 203
  Oak Terrace, 204
HOUSTON
  Sam, 50, 51, 52, 56, 61, 65, 70, 79
HOUSTON COUNTY, 70, 72, 87
HOUSTON, EAST AND WEST TEXAS

INDEX

HOUSTON, EAST AND WEST
  TEXAS (continued)
  Railroad, 91, 96
HOUSTON, HUMBLE,
  LIVINGSTON
  Line, 139
HOYA
  Charles, 96
  Joseph T., 184
HOYA MEMORIAL LIBRARY AND
  Museum, 184
HUD, 271
HUGHES
  J. C., Jr., 277
HUMBLE OIL AND REFINING
  CO., 206
HUMPHREY
  Hubert H., 234
HUNT
  Andrew W., 97
  Lawrence Crawford, 136
HUNTER
  Chief John Dunn, 42
HYDE
  G. W., 138

-I-

INDIAN MOUNDS, 93
INDIAN RIVER
  INTERNATIONAL, 243,
  244
INFANTRY REGIMENT, 115
INGRAHAM
  George F., 96
INSTITUTIONS OF HIGHER
  Learning, 216
INTERNATIONAL ASSOCIATION
  Firefighters
  (AFL-CIO), 262
INTERNATIONAL PAPER
  COMPANY, 204, 243
  Long-Bell Division,
  201
INTERNATIONAL PAPER
  PLANT, 284
IRESON
  Captain James W., 93
IRION
  Robert Anderson, 59
IRVINE
  James P., 147
  Stanley, 100
IRVINE-COLBERT PUBLISHING

CO., 100

-J-

JACKSON
  General Andrew, 51
JAZZ AGE, 133
JENNINGS
  Corporal John D., 93
JESUS
  Father Jose Maria de,
  45
JOHNS-MANVILLE
  CORPORATION, 246
JOHNSON
  Andrew, 81
  Lyndon B., 190, 233,
  240, 248(2)
  Mrs. Otha (Lucille),
  193
  Richard, 277
  William R., 250(2),
  282
JONES
  Anson, 69
  C. Stanley, 260
  Roland, 112
JUSTICE
  William Wayne, 238,
  254(2), 259

-K-

K-MART, 245
KARLE WILSON BAKER
  DRAMATIC
  Club, 132
KARLE WILSON THEATRE
  GUILD, 133
KEACHI COLLEGE
  Keachi, Louisiana, 64
KEARNS
  James K., 223
KELS FM, 210
KENDRICK
  Paul, 255(2)
KENNEDY
  John F., 190, 239,
  248(2)
  Sue, 276
KENNEDY-JOHNSON TICKET,
  191
KILGORE COLLEGE, 252(2)
KING

INDEX

KING (continued)
  Sergeant George S., 93
  Sergeant William A., 93
KING COTTON, 94
KING WILLIAM'S WAR, 5
KING'S HIGHWAY
  (El Camino Real), 66
  El Camino Real, 21
KINSEY
  Joe, 188
KIRCHER
  Joseph C., 151
KNIGHT
  H. L., 124
KOINONIA CLUB, 131
KOREAN WAR, 197, 198, 239, 241
KOSF, 210
KRENEK
  Bryant, 257(2)
KSFA, 210
KSFU, 252(2)
KU KLUX KLAN, 85
KU KLUX KLAN ACT, 85

-L-

LA BAHIA, 21
LA BAHIA (GOLIAD), 28, 29
LA BAHIA ROAD, 14
LA LUCANA
  ranch, 21
LA NANA CREEK, 1, 7, 66, 67, 74, 94, 104, 130, 140, 187, 227, 232, 251(2), 268, 270, 272, 278
LA NANA LUMBER COMPANY, 102
LA SALLE
  Rene Robert Cavalier, 3
LACY H. HUNT LUMBER COMPANY, 98
LADIES HOME, 141
LAKE NACOGDOCHES, 178, 268, 269
LAKE NACONICHE, 270
LAKE PONTA, 177
LAKE STRIKER, 178
LAMAR
  Mirabeau B., 61, 63
LANG
  Sergeant Benjamin S., 93
LARA
  Bernardo Gutierrez de, 26, 28
LEAHEY
  Dan, 153
LEE
  General Robert E., 81
LEGG'S STORE, 180
LEVRA
  John, 252(2)
LEVY
  Gus, 95
LEWIS
  John T., III, 218
  W. S., 244
LIBERTY HOTEL, 153, 239
LIBERTY LOANS, 115
LIGHTFOOT
  John, 59
LINCOLN
  Abraham, 79
LINDSEY
  Robert, 105
LINN FLAT, 84
LINN FLAT RAID, 83
LITERATI CLUB, 131
LITTLE LEAGUE BASEBALL PARK, 185, 187
LOCAL DRAFT BOARD NO. 94, 240
LOCATING BOARD
  Normal College, 121
LOCO BAYOU, 226, 268
LODGE
  Henry C., 191
LONE STAR AIRLINE, 278
LONE STAR CREME MEAL, 138
LONE STAR PEARL MEAL, 138
LONE STAR PHOSPHATE COMPANY, 202
LONE STAR PHOSPHATE PLANT, 205
LONE STAR PRODUCE COMPANY, 138
LONG
  Dr. James, 30
LONG JOHN SILVERS, 285
LONGLEY
  Bill, 58
LOS ADAES, 5, 34
  capital of Texas, 8, 9, 15

INDEX

LOS ADAES (continued)
  frontier settlement, 13
  garrison, 9
  mission, 9, 11(2)
  people of, 12
  presidio, 8
LOS AIS
  mission, 12
LOUISIANA TERRITORY, 26
LOVETT
  R. S., 95
LOYALTY LEAGUE, 83
LUCAS
  Tom, 133

-M-

MADISON COUNTY
  Alabama, 72
MAGEE
  Lieutenant Augustus W., 28
MAGEE-GUTIERREZ EXPEDITION, 28, 29
MAHDEEN COMPANY, 97, 112
MAHDEEN HAIR TONIC COMPANY, 125
MANES
  Roy, 218
MANGHAM
  A. L., 237, 260, 276
MARGIL DE JESUS
  Father Antonio, 6, 7, 8
MARONEY
  Tom, 240
MARSHALL UNIVERSITY, 282
MARTIN
  Lenvill, 223, 254(2)
MARTINEZ
  Governor Antonio, 30
MARTINSVILLE, 229
MARX BROTHERS
  Zeppo, Chico, Harpo, Groucho, 104
MASONIC HALL, 210
MASONIC INSTITUTE
  Nacogdoches, 64
MASONIC LODGE, 76
  Nacogdoches, 64
MAST
  A. T., 137, 184
  Captain Milton, 58

  Corporal Eugene H., 93
  H. R., 184
  Jennie, 184
  Milton, 162
  Mrs. A. T. (Pat), 189, 230, 258
MATAMOROS EXPEDITION, 54
MATTHEWS
  Miller, 240
  Oscar, 135
MAYER
  Abraham, 98
MAYER & SCHMIDT, 98, 116
MAYFIELD
  J. E., 95
  Joseph E., 105
MAYNES
  Father Jose Francisco, 45
MAYO
  John W., 41
MAYO DAM, 140
MAYS
  Ruth, 123
MCCLAIN
  Arminda M. Jones, 58
  Walter Ernest, 58
MCCUTCHEN
  Glen, 284
MCDONALD
  Judy, 260, 276
  William H., 57
MCDONALDS, 285
MCGEE
  R. E., 218
MCGRAW-EDISON PLANT, 244
MCGUIRE
  Mickey, 219, 220
MCKEWEN
  Stanford W., 156
MCKINNEY
  Edgar P., 203
  Jack, 136, 137, 203, 217
  Katherine Monger, 203
  Linda, 276
  R. W., 136
  Susan Prentice, 203
MCKINNEY AND PARMLEY, 136
MCLAIN
  Rufus, 80
MCLEMORE
  Roy T., 114
MCMATH

INDEX

MCMATH (continued)
    James G., 254(2), 282
MCMULLEN
    Kenneth H., 192
MCMURRAY COLLEGE, 171
MEDA MOON, 136
MEDINA RIVER, 28
MEDINCO, INC., 230, 257
MELROSE, 72, 86, 113
MELROSE PETROLEUM
    COMPANY, 87
MEMORIAL HOSPITAL
    Board of Directors,
    230, 258
MENCHACA
    Antonio, 61
METRO AIRLINES, 271
METTAUER
    George Lance, 266
    Lance, 152
MEXICAN CONSTITUTION OF
    1824, 56
MEXICAN REVOLUTION, 30
MEXICAN WAR, 57, 69, 74
MEXICAN WAR OF
    INDEPENDENCE, 45
MIDDLEBOOK
    George, 220
MIDDLEBROOK
    V. E., 114
MIDLAND COUNTY, 235
MILITARY EXEMPTION BOARD,
    114
MILL CREEK, 61
MILLARD
    Mrs. Massie, 76
MILLARD'S CROSSING, 208,
    279
MILLARD-BURROWS HOUSE,
    280
MILLARD-LEE HOUSE, 280
MILLER
    Harry, 252(2), 253
MILNE
    Sergeant W. M., 93
MINIMUM FOUNDATION SCHOOL
    Program, 174, 249(2)
MISSION
    Nacogdoches, 11
MISSION GUADALUPE, 45
MISSION NUESTRA SENORA DE
    Guadalupe de los
        Nacogdoches, 6, 8
MISSION NUESTRA SENORA DE
    LA
    Purisima Concepcion, 5
MISSION SAN FRANCISCO DE
    LOS
    Tejas, 4
MISSION SAN MIGUEL DE LOS
    Adaes, 7
MITCHELL BRANCH, 231
MIZE
    B. H., 136
    W. A., 136
MIZE DEPARTMENT STORE,
    208
MIZE MODES, 136
MOLSBEE
    James A., 247, 257
MONK
    Carl, 124, 135
    Emery W., 203
    R. C., 98, 136
    Robert C., 142
MONTFORD
    John, 283
MONTGOMERY
    Roger, 217
MOORE
    Gloria Jean, 258
    Willie, 114
MOORE BUSINESS FORMS
    Southern Division, 208
MOORE CONSTRUCTION
    COMPANY, 121
MORA
    Jose Maria, 44
    Juan, 72
    Juan de la, 14
MORAL
    Don Jose Miguel de, 21
    Jose Miguel de, 22
MORAL COMMUNITY, 64
MORGAN
    Charles, 257(2)
    Ed, 223, 255(2)
MORRELL
    Z. N., 76
MOSES
    Mike, 282
MOUND STREET, 1
MUCKLEROY
    David, 57, 70, 74
    R. G., 101, 203, 236,
        237
    R. G., Sr., 100
    Wilson, 223

INDEX

MULLER
  L. I., 262
MUNICIPAL CODE
  CORPORATION, 188
MUNICIPALITY
  Jasper, 56
  Jefferson, 56
  Liberty, 56
  Sabine, 56
  San Augustine, 56
  Shelby, 56
  Spanish, 9
MUNZINGER
  Dick, 252(2)
MURPHY
  Edward, 23, 24
MUSKIE
  Edmund S., 234

-N-

NACODOCHES COUNTY
  Courthouse Box, 233
  Goyens Bill Box, 233
NACOGDOCHES
  Air port, 209
  Airport, 154
  Blount Building, 99
  Church Plaza, 22, 45
  City Commission, 183
  city government, 108
  City Hall, 103, 113
  City Library, 184
  College Heights, 182, 204
  department of, 25
  E. Tex. Regional Airport, 271
  Eastwood Terrace, 271
  Fire Department, 102, 103
  Harris Heights, 112
  Hitch Lot, 109
  Hospital, 45, 66, 73, 103
  Hoya-Driver Addition, 187
  La Calle Real del Norte, 22
  Loop 224, 214, 224, 227, 230, 232, 256(2), 269, 270, 271, 272, 279, 282, 283, 284

  Main Plaza, 44
  Memorial Park, 160, 177, 182
  Memorial Stadium, 160, 168, 182, 250
  Mill Pond, 271
  mission, 9, 10, 15
  Municipality of, 33, 34, 37
  North, 73
  North Loop 224, 257
  Opera House, 102, 103, 104
  Plaza of the Constitution, 44
  Plaza Principal, 18, 22, 42, 63, 73
  Post Office, 107, 231, 283
  Pueblo of, 17, 21, 22
  school system, 99, 113
  Spanish Bluff Road, 154
  Spanish Cemetery, 12, 22
  Spanish District of, 17
  Sunset Addition, 112
  Temperance Hall, 63
  Temple Park, 182
  Tourist Information Center, 283
  Washington Square, 63, 101, 112, 116, 123, 124, 129, 173, 186, 187, 202, 224, 232
NACOGDOCHES AND SOUTHEASTERN
  Railroad, 96
NACOGDOCHES AREA INDUSTRIAL
  Park, 246
NACOGDOCHES COMMUNITY HOTEL
  Corporation, 203
NACOGDOCHES COMPRESS &
  Warehouse Company, 94
NACOGDOCHES CONVALESCENT
  Center, 230
NACOGDOCHES COTTON SEED OIL
  Mill, 138
NACOGDOCHES COUNTY
  Aikman Gym Precinct,

INDEX

NACOGDOCHES COUNTY (continued) 233
Commissioners Court, 146, 192, 193, 228, 234, 263, 265, 266
County Agent, 198, 200, 201, 246
court houses, 74
Court-at-Law, 263
Courthouse, 111, 193, 231
District Court, 264, 269
Grand Jury, 264
High School Box, 233
Justice Precinct One, 238
Justice Precinct Two, 238
Memorial Hospital District, 229
Precinct Three, 265
Road Administrator, 266
Superintendent of Schools, 256(2)
NACOGDOCHES COUNTY INDUSTRIAL Foundation, 205, 208, 209
NACOGDOCHES COUNTY LUMBER Company, 185
NACOGDOCHES CRATE AND BOX Factory, 94
NACOGDOCHES DIAGNOSTIC CENTER, 258
NACOGDOCHES DISTRICT, 76
NACOGDOCHES FLYING SERVICE, 153
NACOGDOCHES GROCERY COMPANY, 97
NACOGDOCHES HOUSING AUTHORITY, 268
NACOGDOCHES I. S. DISTRICT
Board of Trustees, 174, 189, 221, 222, 254
Superintendent, 190
NACOGDOCHES INDEPENDENT School District, 172, 174, 175, 254
NACOGDOCHES INDEPENDENT SCHOOL District, 221, 254
NACOGDOCHES NEWS, 100
NACOGDOCHES PRINTING COMPANY, 100
NACOGDOCHES RECREATION Complex, 271
NACOGDOCHES SANITORIUM, 135
NACOGDOCHES SAVINGS AND LOAN Association, 207, 208, 244, 281
NACOGDOCHES SCHOOL DISTRICT, 64
Board of Trustees, 113
NACOGDOCHES SCHOOLS
Brook-Quinn Building, 256
Brooks-Quinn, 173, 256
Brooks-Quinn Jones School, 222
Central Elementary, 173
Chamberlain Building, 282
Dragon Stadium, 271
E. J. Campbell, 172, 173, 222
E. J. Campbell Building, 224
Emeline Carpenter, 222
Emeline Carpenter Elementary, 272
Emeline Carpenter School, 224
Fredonia Elementary, 173, 222
High School, 123, 256(2)
High School Stadium, 232
Moses Intermediate School, 282
Nacogdoches High, 172, 173
Nacogdoches High School, 222
Nettie Marshall Elementary, 173, 222
Raguet Elementary, 173, 222, 223
Red Building, 224
T. J. Rusk Junior

INDEX

NACOGDOCHES SCHOOLS (continued)
  High, 173
  Thomas J. Rusk School, 224
  W. E. Jones Elementary, 172
  West End Elementary, 172, 173(2)
  White Building, 282
NACOGDOCHES SHOW CASE AND Hardwood Manufacturing Co., 94
NACOGDOCHES UNIVERSITY, 62
  Building, 124, 232
  Female College, 75
NATCHITOCHES (LOUISIANA), 5, 8, 13, 19, 22, 24, 29, 44, 66, 77
NATCHITOCHES STATE COLLEGE, 167
NATIONAL ASSOCIATION FOR THE
  Advancement of Colored People, 256(2)
NATIONAL ASSOCIATION OF Black Students, 219
NATIONAL GUARD COMPANY, 114
NATIONAL MILITIA, 48(2)
NATIONS
  Bailey, 255(2)
NAVAL RESERVE UNIT, 198
NAVASOTA RIVER, 37
NECHES RIVER, 5
NEEDHAM
  J. L., 97
NEFF
  Governor Pat M., 121
NEIDMORE, 140
NELSON
  A. A., 73, 114, 184
  Captain A. A., 65
NERAZ
  Father J. C., 128
NEUTRAL GROUND, 25, 26, 36
NEW DEAL, 149, 150
NEW ORLEANS GRAYS, 55, 56
NEWTON COUNTY, 235
NIBCO OF TEXAS, 205, 206, 243
NICHOLS
  Billy J., 240
NISD BOARD OF TRUSTEES, 255
NIXON
  Richard, 191
  Richard M., 234
NOLAN
  Philip, 26
NORRIS
  Edmund, 29
  Nathaniel, 45
  Samuel, 34, 39, 41, 43, 44
NORTH PLACE, 230
NORTHVIEW PLAZA SHOPPING Center, 209
NORTHVIEW TERRACE, 204
NORTON
  Lucille, 250(2)
  Norton HPE Complex, 250
NUESTRA SENORA DEL PILAR DE
  Bucareli, 14

-O-

OAK HILL PLAZA, 209
OAK MANOR, 230
OCHILTREE
  William Beck, 70
ODIN
  Bishop of Texas, 128
  Rt. Rev. John Mary Odin, 128
OFFICE OF PRICE ADMINISTRATION (OPA), 145, 146
OIL SPRINGS, 85, 87, 88, 96, 113, 206
OLD NORTH CHURCH, 83
OLD SAN ANTONIO ROAD, 3 (El Camino Real), 76
OLD SOUTHWEST TERRITORY, 51
OLD STONE FORT, 73, 92, 127, 128, 131
OLD STONE FORT SALOON, 73
OLIN INDUSTRIES, 204
OPTIONAL COUNTY ROAD LAW (1947), 192
ORDINANCE OF SECESSION, 79
ORTON

INDEX

ORTON (continued)
  John, 58
  R. D., 162
  R. D. (Dick), 58
  Richard D., 84, 100
OTASCO DRUGS, 209

-P-

PANIC OF 1873, 85
PARKER
  Corporal Abe, 93
  Daniel, 51
  Isaac, 69
  J. G., 59
PARMER
  Colonel Martin, 41, 42, 43
PARTIN
  James G., 282
  Jimmy, 133
PASO TOMAS, 14
PATONIA, 70
PATTON
  Branch, 223, 255(2)
  Nat, 159
  Second Lieutenant Orland, 114
PATUXY AND GLEN ROSE SANDS, 206
PEARL HARBOR, 145, 147
PEIRCE
  Gordon, 277
PEREZ
  Lt. Colonel Ygnacio, 30
PERITTE
  H. T., 134
PERKINS
  Charles, 101
  James I., 218
  W. U., 137
  William, 101
  William Usrey, 96
PERRITTE
  Mrs. H. T., 134
PERRY
  Mike, 260
PETROLEUM PROSPECT COMPANY, 88
PIEDRAS
  Colonel Jose de las, 43, 44, 45, 46, 47, 48, 49, 68

PIEDRAS NEGRAS, 6
PIERCE
  Jack, 267
PINE LOG, 132
PIZZA HUT, 285
PLEASANT RIDGE, 122
POPULISM, 161
POTARD
  Sister Josephine, 64
POTTER
  Robert, 54
PRAIRIE VIEW STATE NORMAL College, 172
PRESBYTERIAN SUNDAY SCHOOL, 129
PRESIDIO NUESTRA SENORA DE LOS Delores de los Tejas, 6
PRITCHETT
  Ida, 123
PROCELA
  Alcalde Luis, 38
PROCELLA
  Alcalde Luis, 34
  Alcalde Pedro, 34
PROGRESSIVE ERA, 92
PROVINCE OF TEXAS, 11, 22
PUBLIC WORKS PROGRAM, 225
PURINA, 200

-R-

R. W. MCKINNEY CONSTRUCTION COMPANY, 136
RADICAL REPUBLICANS, 81, 88
RAGUET
  Henry, 65
RANEY
  James, 255(2), 277
RAYSON
  Harvey, 237
REAVLEY
  Tom, 192
RECONSTRUCTION, 77, 81, 83, 85, 91, 161, 190
RECONSTRUCTION ACTS OF 1867, 82
RECONSTRUCTION ERA, 83
RECTOR
  Malcolm, 255(2), 282
RED HOUSE, 63, 68

INDEX

RED RIVER, 5, 33, 77
REDEEMER LUTHERAN CENTER, 195
REDFIELD, 245
REDLAND HOTEL, 99
REED
  Isaac, 76
  Reverend Lawson, 130
REESE
  Elbert, 142
  J. Elbert, 100, 101
REGIONS BANK, 281
RENTZEL
  Delos W., 210
REPUBLIC NATIONAL BANK OF Dallas, 203
REPUBLIC OF FREDONIA, 42
REPUBLIC OF MEXICO, 43, 46, 69
REPUBLIC OF TEXAS, 22, 54, 60, 66, 68, 69, 139, 233
REPUBLICAN PARTY, 79, 190, 191, 233, 234, 264, 265, 266, 277
RICE
  George W., 198
RICE INSTITUTE, 155
RICHARDSON
  Charlie, 98
RIEHL
  Tony, 282
RIO BRAVO
  (Rio Grande), 19
RIO GRANDE, 52
RIPPERA
  Governor Baron de, 11
RITTERSCAMP
  Ben, 203
RIVERA
  Pedro de, 9
ROAD
  Appleby Sand, 195, 224, 227, 256(2), 271, 282, 283
  Beulah Land, 269
  Looneyville, 209
  Lower Douglas, 48
  Lufkin, 187
  Old North Church, 246
  Old Shady Grove, 269
  Press, 227
  Shawnee, 202, 206
  Spanish Bluff, 180

  Tyler, 136, 180, 185, 186, 283, 284
ROBERTS
  Harriet Fenley Callier, 72
  Major John S., 41, 42, 54, 65, 68, 72, 73
ROBERTSON
  Mrs. Kathryn, 255(2)
ROBINS
  Nathaniel, 51
ROBINSON
  James W., 51
ROCK HAVEN, 230
RODRIGUEZ
  Father Joseph, 8
ROEBUCK
  M. C., 219, 261
ROOSEVELT
  Colonel Theodore, 93
  Franklin D., 147, 148
RORIE, PEDERSON, AND Yarbrough, 263
ROUGH RIDERS, 93
ROYAL ROAD
  (El Camino Real), 11
RUBI
  Marquis de, 11
RULFS
  Diedrich A., 99, 111, 129, 130
  Sergeant C. H., 93
RUNAWAY SCRAPE, 56
RURAL HIGH SCHOOL DISTRICT, 175
RUSK
  David, 58, 162
  Thomas J., 50, 54, 55, 58, 60, 62, 65, 66, 69, 70
RUSK COUNTY, 108, 178, 180, 270
RUSSELL
  A. T., 141
  Corporal Harvey G., 93
  James R., 230

-S-

SABINE COUNTY, 240
SABINE DISTRICT, 47
SABINE RIVER, 3, 4, 5, 25, 26, 29, 33, 35, 37, 42, 43, 56, 61,

INDEX

SABINE RIVER (continued) 66
SACUL, 114, 238
SALCEDO
 Governor Manuel de, 24
SAM HOUSTON STATE TEACHERS COLLEGE, 155
SAN ANTONIO, 7, 8, 9, 11, 13, 14, 19, 21, 22, 23, 25, 26, 28, 33(2), 40, 41, 48, 53, 54, 66, 74
SAN ANTONIO DE BEXAR, 13, 29, 52
SAN ANTONIO ROAD
 (El Camino real), 61
 (El Camino Real), 70
 El Camino Real, 19
 El Camino Real), 46
SAN AUGUSTINE, 3, 12, 61, 76
SAN AUGUSTINE COUNTY, 240, 270
SAN AUGUSTINE HIGHWAY, 175
SAN FELIPE, 41, 49, 50, 51
SAN JACINTO, 56
SAN MARCOS ACADEMY, 223
SANDERS
 Mrs. Lavinia Griffith, 217
 P. L., 180
SANITARY LAUNDRY, 186
SANSON
 Reverend Henry, 76
SANTA ANNA
 Antonio Lopez, 51, 54, 56
 Antonio Lopez de, 47, 48
SANTOS COY
 Manuel de los, 44
SARAH WHITE SURVEY, 206
SCARBROUGH
 Lee, 210
SCHMIDT
 Herbert J., 98
 John, 98, 103, 111
 Philip Henry, 98
SCHOOL
 West End Elementary, 113

SCHOOLS
 Chireno, 75
 Douglass, 75
SCOTT
 Mrs. Walter (Elizabeth), 189
SCRUGGS
 Luther Rice, 129
SEALE
 A. A., 141
 Arthur A., 135
SECOND NATIONAL BANK OF Houston, 203
SECOND TEXAS INFANTRY REGIMENT
 Company B, 93
SECURITY NATIONAL BANK, 281
SEGUIN, 61
 Alcalde Juan, 34, 35
SELECTIVE SERVICE ACT (1917), 114
SELECTIVE SERVICE ACT (1940), 197
SELECTIVE TRAINING & SERVICE
 Act (1941), 147
SELLERS
 Grover, 159
SEPULVEDA
 Jose Antonio, 38, 39
SERVICEMEN'S READJUSTMENT ACT
 (GI Bill of Rights), 158
SFA STATE COLLEGE
 Agriculture Building, 215
 Agriculture Department, 167
 Aikman Gym, 125, 127, 133
 Austin Building, 126, 127, 157, 168
 Band Hall, 157
 Birdwell Annex, 168
 Birdwell Building, 168(2), 169
 Board of Regents, 216
 Boynton Building, 169
 College of Business, 218
 College of Education, 218

310

INDEX

SFA STATE COLLEGE
(continued)
  College of Fine Arts, 218
  College of Forestry, 218
  College of Liberal Arts, 218
  College of Science and Math., 218
  Commerce Department, 167
  Comptroller, 218
  Dairy Farm, 170
  Demonstration School, 126, 157, 168(2)
  Department of English, 169
  Department of Foreign Langs., 169
  Department of Forestry, 159
  Department of Geography, 169
  Department of History & Govt., 169
  Department of Home Economics, 170
  Department of Mathematics, 169
  Department of Psychology, 218
  Department of Sociology, 169
  Dormitories 10 and 13, 215
  Dormitory 14, 215
  Dormitory 16, 215
  Dormitory 18, 215
  Dormitory 19, 215, 216
  East College Cafeteria, 215
  English Department, 167
  Ferguson (Liberal Arts) Build., 215
  Fine Arts Building, 169
  Forestry Building, 215, 216
  Forestry Department, 160, 167
  Garner Apartments, 215
  Gibbs Hall, 128, 157
  Gladys E. Steen Hall, 215
  Griffith Boulevard, 216, 217
  Griffith Park, 216
  Griffiths Fine Arts Building, 169
  Guidance Division, 167
  Home Demonstration House, 170
  Home Economics Building, 215, 216
  Junior Division, 167
  Lumberjack Band, 126
  Lumberjack Luncheonette, 168
  Martha T. Griffith Hall, 215
  Memorial Stadium, 125
  Music Building, 215, 216
  Music Department, 167
  North and South Dormitories, 215
  President's Home, 170
  S. A. Kerr Hall, 215
  Science (Chemistry) Building, 127
  Science Building, 157, 215, 216
  Shelton Gym, 125, 168
  Stenographic Bureau, 168
  Student Publications, 168
  Student Union Building, 168
  Thomas J. Rusk Building, 126, 127, 168
  Units I and II, 169
  Vice Presidents, 218
  Warehouse, 215
  Wilson Hall, 215
  Wisely Hall, 127, 128, 157, 168
  Women's Recreation Center, 127, 157
SFA STATE NORMAL COLLEGE
  Austin Building, 121, 122, 123, 124
  Demonstration School, 124
  The Shack, 123, 124

INDEX

SFA STATE UNIVERSITY
  Board of Regents, 218, 250(2)
  Board of Trustees, 254
  Boynton Building, 251(2)
  Dean of Education, 250
  Department of Nursing, 252(2)
  Forestry Department, 219
  Graduate School, 252(2)
  McKibben Education Building, 250(2)
  Memorial Stadium, 250
  Norton HPE Complex, 250(2)
  R. E. McGee Building, 250(2)
  School of Applied Arts & Scs., 252
  School of Liberal Arts, 219
  Shelton Gym, 250(2)
  Student Center, 251(2)
  William R. Johnson Coliseum, 250(2)
SHARE-CROP SYSTEM, 85
SHELBY COUNTY, 165, 166, 270
SHELTON
  Robert (Bob), 123, 132, 156, 168
SHERATON CREST INN, 246
SHERROD
  William Earle, 236
SHINDLER
  Captain Charles L., 114
  Lieutenant Robert T., 93
SHIPMAN
  J. W., 95
SIEGE OF BEXAR, 54, 56, 59
SIMMONS
  Charles, 252(2)
SIMMS
  C. H., 65
  Charles H., 50
  William, 57
SIMON
  C. L., 240, 259, 260, 276
SIMPSON
  Bartlett H., 57
  Finis, 268
  LaDonna, 237, 260
SISTERS OF NOTRE DAME
  Convent of the Heart of Jesus, 63
SKILLERN TRACT, 87
SMALLWOOD
  John Clifford, 147, 148
SMITH
  Charles Thomas, 135
  Ella A., 258
  Fred, Jr., 260
  Gilbert M. L., 62
  Governor Preston, 218, 234
  Luther, 23, 24
  Mary, 62
  Paul (Pete), 223
  Paul H. (Pete), 240
  Woolam Ira M., 135
SMITH COUNTY, 61, 122
SMUGGLERS TRAIL (TRACE), 22, 46
SONIC DRIVE-IN, 285
SOUTHERN METHODIST UNIVERSITY
  School of Law, 263
SOUTHERN PACIFIC RAILROAD, 95, 140, 214
  system, 96
SOUTHLAND PAPER MILL, 151
SOUTHSIDE NATIONAL BANK, 281
SOUTHWEST MISSOURI STATE University, 282
SOUTHWEST TEXAS STATE Normal College, 122
SOUTHWESTERN UNIVERSITY, 122
SPANISH AMERICAN WAR, 93, 114
SPANISH BLUFF CROSSING, 46
SPECIAL LAW CITY, 89
SPECK
  Nancy, 268
SPINDLETOP, 88
SPIVEY
  William Frank, 236

INDEX

SPRADLEY
  A. J., 100, 162
  Andrew Jackson (John), 58
  J. M. (Matt), 58
ST. DENIS
  Louis de, 8
ST. MARY'S CATHOLIC STUDENT CENTER, 195
STALLINGS
  Grady, 188, 261
STANALAND
  Alvin, 277
STANFIELD
  Elton A. (Stan), 261
STAPLES OFFICE SUPERSTORE, 285
STARR
  Amory Reily, 88
  James H., 65
  James Harper, 62
STARR & AMORY, 94
STATE BANKING COMMISSION, 207
STATE BOARD OF CONTROL, 159
STATE GUARANTY SYSTEM, 95
STATE NORMAL COLLEGES
  Board of Regents, 121
STATE POLICE, 83, 84
STATE TEACHERS COLLEGE SYSTEM
  Board of Regents, 126
STEEN
  Ralph W., 171, 215, 249(2), 250(3)
STEINMAN
  George J., 134
STEPHEN F. AUSTIN STATE
  College, 124, 153, 154, 168, 182, 213
  Normal College, 120, 122
  Teachers College, 124, 126, 133, 134, 165
  University, 124, 147, 218, 220, 242, 249(2), 253, 278
STERNE
  Adolphus, 43, 48, 50, 55, 65, 68, 139
STEWART'S FOOD CENTER, 186

STILL
  Ma, 204
  Pete, 204
STONE
  Hilliard, 136, 142
STONE FORT LITERARY SOCIETY, 132
STONE FORT NATIONAL BANK, 96, 137, 203, 205, 208, 281
STONE FORT RIFLES, 93
STONE FORT YEARBOOK, 132
STONE HOUSE
  (Old Stone Fort), 18, 23, 42, 43, 67, 72, 73, 101
STONE LUMBER COMPANY, 186
STREET
  Bailey, 187
  Banita, 107
  Blount, 207
  Bremond, 202
  Butt, 177, 180, 200
  Church, 75, 101, 103, 110, 112, 129, 140(2)
  College, 127, 134, 168, 169, 187, 250
  Dolph, 209
  Durst, 248(2)
  East Austin, 244, 270, 283(2)
  East College, 133, 167, 195, 250, 251(3)
  East Hospital, 130
  East Main, 97, 98, 99, 116, 129, 177, 180, 182, 185, 186, 187, 219, 220, 244, 272
  Edwards, 202
  Ferguson, 230
  Fredonia, 103, 104, 108, 110, 132, 173, 189, 202, 203
  Hospital, 63, 74, 102, 104, 110, 112, 129, 140, 202, 203, 231
  Hughes, 140, 185
  La Nana, 112, 184
  Leroy, 224
  Lloyd, 207
  Logansport, 130
  Main, 74, 101(2), 103, 104, 107, 108, 110, 129, 130, 139, 140,

INDEX

STREET (continued)
141, 179, 185, 186, 208, 227, 270, 281, 284
Mound, 107, 111, 129, 130, 135, 136, 187, 189, 258
North, 45, 48, 66, 68, 74, 101, 102, 107, 108, 111, 112, 124, 128, 129, 130, 133(2), 136, 142, 168, 169, 185, 186, 189, 195, 204, 207, 209, 216, 219, 231, 245, 272, 283(2)
North Church, 112, 113, 202
North Fredonia, 98, 101, 130, 184, 186, 210
North Hospital, 208
North Main, 189
North Mound, 112, 184, 230
North Pecan, 45, 97, 128
North Raguet, 167
North-South corridor, 228
Park, 130, 180, 187, 227, 282
Parmley, 245
Pearl, 278, 283
Pecan, 66, 68, 98, 129, 208
Pilar, 65, 68, 74, 107, 141
Powers, 130, 226, 227
Raguet, 125, 127, 128, 160, 168, 169, 173, 182, 187(2), 195, 216, 231, 250(2), 251(2), 258
Richey, 226, 227
Sanders, 256
Seale, 173
Shawnee, 135, 187, 219
South, 64, 129, 140, 141, 173, 180, 189, 202, 228
South Fredonia, 140, 187, 278
South Mound, 185, 187

Starr, 170
Taylor, 239
Tejas, 229
Townsend, 177
Walker, 112
Wells, 177
West Austin, 283
West Main, 99, 202, 209, 231, 239, 272, 283(2)
STRIPLING
Craig, 260
M. M., 179, 188, 236
Sam, 137
Sam B., 98, 99
STRIPLING DRUG STORE, 185
STRIPLING'S DRUG, 284
STRIPLING, HASELWOOD & CO., 98
STUDENTS FOR A DEMOCRATIC Society, 253(2)
STURDEVANT
Captain Ira Link, 96, 103, 137, 141, 262
SUBLETT
F. B., 135
SUMMERS
Tom, 112
SUPERIOR SAVINGS BANK, 281
SUPULVEDA
Jose Antonio, 41
SUTHERLANDS, 285
SUTPHEN
James P., 95
SUTTON
John, 268
SUTTON'S GENERAL OAK FLOORING Mill, 186
SWIFT BROTHERS & SMITH DRUG Store, 132

-T-

T. J. RUSK LITERARY SOCIETY, 132
TACO BELL, 285
TALIAFERRO CIGAR COMPANY, 97
TANNER
Sam, 218
TAX APRAISAL DISTRICT,

314

INDEX

TAX APRAISAL DISTRICT (continued) 266
TAXPAYERS CONVENTION OF 1871, 88
TAYLOR
  Bennett, 62
  Charles S., 50, 54, 57, 62, 63, 69
  Corporal Robert I., 93
  First Lt. Asher C., 82
  General Zachary, 74
  James, 258
  Jim, 230
TEJAS INDIANS, 4
TEMPLE ASSOCIATES, 204
TEMPLE INDUSTRIES, 246
TENAHA, 42, 47
TENEHAW DISTRICT, 76
TENNANT FARMERS, 92
TERRELL ELECTION LAW (1903), 264
TEUTSCH
  Delbert, 262
TEXAS
  Commissioner of Education, 282, 283
  Eastern Interior Province of, 23
  Second District Court, 235
TEXAS 53RD DISTRICT COURT, 244
TEXAS A&M UNIVERSITY
  History Department, 171
TEXAS ALMANAC, 77, 85, 199, 213
TEXAS AND NEW ORLEANS RAILROAD, 96
TEXAS CHRISTIAN UNIVERSITY, 155
TEXAS COLLEGE SYSTEM, 218
  Board of Regents, 170
TEXAS CONSTITUTION
  College Building Amendment, 216
TEXAS COORDINATING BOARD, 252(2)
TEXAS COURT OF CIVIL APPEALS
  Tyler, 268, 269
TEXAS FARM PRODUCTS
  Lone Star Mill, 244

TEXAS FARM PRODUCTS COMPANY, 137, 138, 202, 205
TEXAS FERTILIZER COMPANY, 137
TEXAS HIGHWAY DEPARTMENT, 137, 179, 192, 227, 228
TEXAS LEGISLATURE, 57, 79
TEXAS NATIONAL GUARD
  Co. D, 386th Arm. Eng. Batt., 198
TEXAS NAVY, 54
TEXAS POWER & LIGHT COMPANY, 136, 153, 178, 246
TEXAS REVOLUTION, 47, 48, 53, 55, 58, 59, 162
TEXAS STATE BANK, 281
TEXAS STATE COLLEGE SYSTEM, 168
TEXAS SUPREME COURT, 54, 245
TEXAS TECH UNIVERSITY, 250, 283
  Vice President, 250
TEXAS VOLUNTEERS
  First Company, 2nd Regiment, 55
TEXAS WATER DEVELOPMENT BOARD, 269
THE ARBOR, 230
THE CLARIDGE, 208
THE CRICKET, 111
THE DAILY PHONE, 100
THE DAILY SENTINEL, 100, 101, 180, 192, 210, 239, 244, 249(2), 258, 284
THE EYES OF FATHER MARGIL, 7
THE MEXICAN ADVOCATE, 100
THE PLAINDEALER, 100
THE REDLAND HERALD, 100
THE TEXAS CHRONICLE, 100
THE TEXAS REPUBLICAN, 100
THEATRE
  Airdrome, 103
  Austin, 133
  Ideal, 103
  Lyric, 103
  Main, 182
  Pines Drive-in, 182
  Redland Drive-in, 182

315

INDEX

THEATRE (continued)
  Royal, 103
  SFA, 182
  Texan, 140
THOMAS
  Albert, 279
  C. D., Jr., 232
  C. D., Sr., 138, 232
  Dave L., 114
  Mrs. Lera Millard,
    218, 279
  Richard, 232
THOMPSON
  A. J., 100, 101, 176
  Captain Burrell J., 41
  W. A., 192
THORN
  Frost, 62, 65, 78, 129
THRASH
  Fred E., 114
TIGNER
  Dorothy, 276
TILFORD
  Gillette, 101
  Tilden, 97
TILFORD-HUNT LUMBER
  COMPANY, 97
TIMBERLAND SAVINGS AND
  LOAN
  Association, 244, 245,
    281
TN&O RAILROAD TRACKS, 200
TODD
  Mrs. Floss, 265
  Neil, 237
  Walter C., 218
TOMLINSON
  John, 72
TORRES
  Alcalde Patricio de,
    34
TOWER
  John, 233
TRANSAMERICA OIL COMPANY,
  206
TRAWICK, 206
TREBLE CLUB, 132
TRINITY RIVER, 14, 15,
  22, 33, 37, 47, 51,
  57, 60
TRUMAN
  Harry S., 190, 220
TUCKER
  Edward, 101

  Edward B., 180
  F. Hal, 95
  Francis Henry, 135
  Fred T., 135
  Hal, 136
  Mrs. E. B. (Mamie
    Ethel), 246
  Stephen B., 217
  Stephen Blount, 135
TWELFTH PERMANENT
  BATTALION, 43
TYLER
  John, 69

-U-

U. S. AIR FORCE RESERVE
  UNIT, 198
U. S. ARMY
  Battery F, 4th Field
    Artillery, 114
  Battery F, 64th Field
    Artil., 114
U. S. CENSUS (1940), 175
U. S. CENSUS BUREAU, 176,
  242
U. S. CONSTITUTION
  Fourteenth Amendment,
    82, 174
  Nineteenth Amendment,
    116
  Twenty-fourth
    Amendment, 235
U. S. CORPS OF ENGINEERS,
  272
U. S. COURT OF APPEALS
  New Orleans, 263
U. S. DEPARTMENT OF
  JUSTICE, 222
U. S. DISTRICT COURT
  Tyler, 238
U. S. FIFTH COURT OF
  APPEALS, 237
U. S. FOREST SERVICE, 151
U. S. FORESTRY
  EXPERIMENTAL
  Station, 159
U. S. STATE DEPARTMENT,
  223
U.S. CENSUS BUREAU, 163
UNION BAPTIST CHURCH
  (Old North church), 76
UNION CHURCH
  African American, 130

INDEX

UNION DEPOT, 111
UNIVERISITY OF HOUSTON, 250
UNIVERSITY OF CHICAGO, 122
UNIVERSITY OF HOUSTON, 250
UNIVERSITY OF KANSAS, 252(2)
UNIVERSITY OF KENTUCKY Department of Psychology, 155
UNIVERSITY OF MISSOURI, 122
UNIVERSITY OF OKLAHOMA, 250(2)
UNIVERSITY OF TEXAS, 282
UNIVERSITY OF TEXAS AT AUSTIN, 122, 132, 171

-V-

VALDEZ
  Father Jose Antonio, 45
VANDERBILT UNIVERSITY, 122
VANNOY
  Roland, 207, 223
VEGA
  Jose de la, 23
VERAZADI
  Don Manuel Gaspar de, 20
VET VILLAGE, 169, 173
VETERANS' VILLAGES (Vet Villages), 166
VIET NAM CONFLICT, 239
VIET NAM CONFLICT, 240
VIET NAM CONFLICT, 241
VOIGTEL
  Richard, 268

-W-

W. T. WILSON GRAIN COMPANY, 112
W. T. WILSON WHOLESALE GRAIN, Hay, and Flour Company, 97
WAC SCHOOL, 153
WADE
  Cathy, 284
  Donald, 284
WAL-MART, 245
WAL-MART SUPERCENTER, 285
WALDEN'S BUSINESS COLLEGE, 113
WALKER
  Charles H., 266
  Mrs. Dianna, 255(2)
  Richard S., 70
WALLACE HOTEL, 102
WALTHALL
  Captain Richard B., 115
WALTON
  Ellen, 130
  Frank, 130
  John, 261
WANAMAKER
  George, 153
WAR DEPARTMENT, 154, 156
WAR FINANCE CORPORATION, 115
WAR LABOR BOARD, 115
WAR MANPOWER COMMISSION, 152
WAR OF 1812, 41, 48
WAR RATION CARD 1, 146
WARD
  Mike, 255(2)
WASHINGTON-ON-THE-BRAZOS, 49, 52, 77
WATERS
  A., 59
  Matthew, 114
WATKINS
  Reverend Richard O., 129
WATTS
  W. W., 99
WEAVER
  Glenn, 202
WECHES (HOUSTON COUNTY TEXAS), 4
WESTERN AUTO STORE, 186
WESTFALL
  Fred G., 114
WESTMORELAND
  Ocie, 265
WESTWARD TRAILS, 230
WETTERMARK
  Colonel Benjamin S., 95
WETTERMARK BANK, 91, 95
WHEELER

INDEX

WHEELER (continued)
  Jesse G., 114
WHITAKER
  Corporal Guess, 93
  Corporal Harry E., 93
  Eugene (Solid), 265, 277
  William, 51
WHITE
  Mary, 62
  Mary Jane, 133
  Meade, 188
WHITE PRIMARY, 163
WHITTEN
  H. W., 220
WHITTON
  Florence, 141
  Kate, 141
WICHITA STATE UNIVERSITY, 253(2)
WILKINS
  Edna, 123
WILKINSON
  General James, 26
WILLIAMS
  Reverend Samuel A., 129
  T. J., 95
WILSON
  Herbert, 203
  Reggie, 153
WILSON HOTEL, 99
WINGFIELD
  William Wilson, 57
WINN-DIXIE GROCERY BUILDING, 231
WISELEY
  J. H., 127
WODEN, 96
WODEN SCHOOL DISTRICT, 266
WOMAN IN BLUE, 4
WOMEN'S ARMY AUXILIARY CORPS, 156
WOMEN'S ARMY CORPS, 156
WOODLAND HILLS DEVELOPMENT
  Corporation, 232
WOODSON
  J. M., 135
WORKS PROGRESS ADMINISTRATION, 142, 154
WORLD WAR I, 105, 111, 134, 162
WORLD WAR II, 120, 125, 126, 139, 143, 154, 160, 163, 165, 167, 171(2), 175, 179, 182, 194, 197, 208, 220, 223, 239, 240, 241
WRIGHT
  Charles, 223, 255(2)
  Joe, 202
  M. S., Sr., 137
  Steele, 137, 202
  Tom, 202

-Y-

Y'BARBO
  Antonio Gil, 9, 12, 13, 14, 15, 17, 19, 20, 67
  Jose Ignacio, 44, 49, 50
  Maria Carmel, 72
  Matheo Antonio, 13
YARBOROUGH
  Ralph W., 190
YARBROUGH
  J. Jack, 263
YELLOW HOUSE, 195
YOUREE
  H. H., 95
  Pete, 95
YSLETTA CREEK, 49

www.ingramcontent.com/pod-product-compliance
Lightning Source LLC
Chambersburg PA
CBHW071956220426
43662CB00009B/1152